Peking's UN Policy

Byron S. J. Weng
foreword by
Jerome Alan Cohen

The Praeger Special Studies program—
utilizing the most modern and efficient book
production techniques and a selective
worldwide distribution network—makes
available to the academic, government, and
business communities significant, timely
research in U.S. and international economic, social, and political development.

Peking's UN Policy
Continuity and Change

PRAEGER SPECIAL STUDIES IN INTERNATIONAL POLITICS AND PUBLIC AFFAIRS

Praeger Publishers   New York   Washington   London

PRAEGER PUBLISHERS
111 Fourth Avenue, New York, N.Y. 10003, U.S.A.
5, Cromwell Place, London S.W.7, England

Published in the United States of America in 1972
by Praeger Publishers, Inc.

Library of Congress Catalog Card Number: 74-176400

Printed in the United States of America

IN MEMORY OF MY PARENTS

By the time this volume appears, the People's Republic of China (PRC) finally may have taken its place in the United Nations. This momentous event, which should have occured 22 years ago, will have a profound impact upon the international system. Diplomats, politicians and commentators are currently seeking to assess the precise implications of Peking's belated participation in the Security Council, General Assembly and other organs of the principal world institution. Extrapolation from the past is their principal aid in forecasting the future. To be sure, since the theory and practice regarding the UN of a national elite that has been excluded from its deliberations for over two decades are likely to change significantly once it has been allowed to participate. Nevertheless, there is much to be learned from its experience as an outsider, which may leave enduring marks upon its subsequent attitude.

Yet political scientists have not done all that one might expect to facilitate analysis of Peking's record regarding the UN. Byron Weng's comprehensive study fills a basic need, comes at the right time and should prove a valuable aid to those who seek a sophisticated understanding of the prospects for Chinese cooperation with the world community. This work reflects a variety of scholarly approaches, a great deal of painstaking research and an objective, detached outlook.

Professor Weng carefully distinguishes between stable and dynamic aspects of Peking's UN policy. For example, he notes that Peking has never wavered in its refusal to enter the UN so long as there is any form of representation for Taiwan other than through the People's Republic. But he emphasizes that the intensity of Peking's interest in entry has changed markedly through a number of distinct stages that began with an optimistic and direct attempt to replace the rival government on Taiwan. Disappointment evolved into frustrated antagonism and then a noisy search for a substitute organization. Recently the wheel has come almost full circle with a less direct, but better orchestrated effort to achieve the long-awaited multilateral recognition as the sole legitimate government of China and as a great power.

Another contribution of this volume is its success in relating Peking's UN policy not only to the Maoist world outlook and the PRC's overall foreign policy but also to both China's domestic situation and the international environment. Professor Weng is especially alert to

the extent to which Peking's attitude toward the UN has been shaped by
the UN's often far more unfriendly attitude toward Peking. He provides a timely reminder of the basic, but often overlooked, truth that
many of the PRC's actions have been reactions rather than initiatives.

The most important proposition set forth in this study is about
to be tested: that contrary to the fears and predictions of some observers, there is no fundamental incompatibility between the UN and
the PRC. New China's presence will surely complicate UN politics
and decision-making, but it will also endow them with greater significance. Like other major powers, China will strive to make the UN
serve its needs and policies. Its representatives can be expected to
act in an independent, yet correct, manner. Should Chou En-lai come
to New York, he is unlikely to pound his shoe on the table à la Khrushchev.
The PRC will undoubtedly insist on certain changes in UN practice and
personnel and will probably add its support to the movement for institutional reforms within the UN. Once Peking has a prominent role in
the organization, however, it can be expected to develop an increasing
stake in it, and we should witness the growth of PRC cooperation with
many of the diverse UN activities that are gradually bringing the
members of the world community closer together.

Jerome Alan Cohen

In November 1970, for the first time since the establishment of the People's Republic of China (PRC), the Albanian Resolution on the Question of Chinese Representation received a majority vote in the General Assembly of the United Nations. Although another Assembly decision stipulating that a change in the representation of China will require an affirmative vote of a two-thirds majority still barred Peking's entry into the UN, a commentator speculated that 1970 might be considered as the year 1 B.C. (Before China).

As of June 30, 1971, the whole affair does look very much alive. No less than ten nations, including nine UN members, have concluded agreements with the PRC to establish diplomatic relations since November 1969, and indications are that more will follow. A pleasant round in the international love-hate match between the US and the PRC has been touched off by a very original move made by Peking across ping pong tables. Political flirtations taking various forms have been exchanged across the Pacific, and in mid July the world was startled by a communique issued simultaneously in Washington and Peking that President Nixon would visit Peking before May 1972.

The time, indeed, is opportune for a careful examination and interpretation of Peking's UN policy now that the family of nations may soon welcome the PRC into its meeting halls.

There are two other even more compelling reasons for writing this book. One is that Peking's policy regarding the UN represents a deviant case that deserves an explanation. The PRC is the sole nuclear power that has not been a direct participant in the activities of the UN. Furthermore, the views expressed by Peking's leaders on the UN have at times been diametrically opposed to the favorable opinions of most of the other nations. Some opponents of the PRC argue that Peking's hostility toward the UN is a manifestation of the fact that the UN and the PRC are two incompatible systems, that is, the principles and purposes of the UN contradict those of the foreign policy of the PRC.* It follows that the PRC, if incorporated into the UN, will either weaken

---

*Dr. Wei Tao-ming, Foreign Minister of the Republic of China, stated before the Twenty-fifth session of the General Assembly on November 12, 1970:

the UN or endanger her own identity in the short run and eventually either destroy the UN or meet her own dissolution and downfall. Such being the case, the argument goes, Peking cannot find the UN useful for its foreign policy purposes unless it is confident that it is capable of overwhelming the UN. With that confidence absent, Peking's negative attitude toward the UN is understandable.

This line of reasoning sounds plausible. But it is also over-simplified. What is important here is not whether, in the observation of a third party (who might have extraneous purpose in mind), the two systems--the PRC and the UN--are objectively incompatible, but whether Peking subjectively believes so. Only if Peking recognizes a fundamental incompatibility and makes decisions on that basis, can one say that Peking's attitudes are correctly explained by the above reasoning. Otherwise, other interpretations will have to be found.

It is a curious fact, however, that there have been no careful and systematic studies concerning Peking's attitudes and approaches toward the UN. This is the other reason for the present work.

There is no denying that the subject "China and the UN" has been a favorite for students of both Chinese foreign policy and UN affairs ever since it was first raised in 1949. It is so extensively studied that one finds many recent writings on the subject to be little more than repetition of platitudes uttered many years ago. Yet, one aspect of that subject seems to have received very little attention: namely, the PRC's views on the UN.

Most writers have been studying the subject from the standpoint of either the UN or the US and not of China. Students of the UN exchange views freely on the merits and shortcomings of the principles of universality and of restricted membership that involve the China question. Many of them argue at length on the proper procedures for

---

Over the years, my delegation has time and again called attention to the fact that to seat the Chinese Communist Regime in the UN is to negate the basic principles and purposes of the Charter. . . . It has not been sufficiently appreciated that the Charter and the so-called 'Mao Tse Tung Thought' are diametrically opposed to each other both in purpose and in spirit.

This same theme has been often repeated by pamphlets issued by the Committee of One Million.

solving the question of Chinese participation--whether by admission, or by accreditation or by special ad hoc measures. Voices are heard from all quarters either supporting or opposing the seating of the PRC in the UN, usually in the interest of the UN. Students of American foreign policy likewise debate, often emotionally, whether the United States should or should not support Peking's entry into the UN on moral, legal or political grounds. Even the probable effects of Peking's presence at the UN have not escaped continuous hedging and speculation by politicians, scholars and laymen. But a student of Chinese foreign policy can hardly find a serious investigation specifically on the positions and arguments of the Peking government, even though that government has perhaps the greatest stake in the matter.

To explain Peking's UN policy is of course not an easy task. This study actually represents a product of many years' continuous observation and research. It is the author's hope that the publication of the study will fill a small part of a very large and obvious gap and that the part it fills will become a solid basis upon which related works can be built.

In the course of the preparation of this book, a number of individuals rendered indispensable assistance to the author. Among them are Professors Bernard C. Cohen and Llewellyn E. Pfankuschen, both of the Department of Political Science, University of Wisconsin, Madison, who not only read the whole original manuscript and offered many helpful suggestions but gave me the encouragement of concerned teachers and friends; Professors Edward Friedman and David A. Kay, also of the University of Wisconsin, who read earlier versions of the manuscript and generously offered their critical comments. I am particularly indebted to Dr. Robert G. Thobaben, my colleague at Wright State University, Dayton, Ohio, who spent innumerable hours and days on my behalf when I most needed intellectual stimulation and friendly guidance. My thanks go also to another colleague, Dr. Reed M. Smith, who made it easier for me to write while carrying a full teaching load; to Mr. John Mashburn who helped prepare the index; to Miss Linda Geitman who typed parts of the manuscript; to Mrs. Jane Hill of Wright State University Publications; and to the editors at Praeger Publishers, Mrs. Mary-Stuart Garden, Miss Mervyn Adams, and Mr. William D. Drennan, whose professional expertise helped make this book more presentable. To Professor Jerome Alan Cohen of Harvard Law School, I wish to express my sincere appreciation for writing the Foreword, knowing that he has specially taken time from his extremly busy schedule to do so. Last but not least, I am deeply grateful to my wife, Carolyn, for her patience, understanding and love, in addition to editing and typing.

Needless to say, I alone am responsible for what the book is or is not.

CONTENTS

LIST OF TABLES

LIST OF ABBREVIATIONS

CPPCC	Chinese People's Political Consultative Conference
CPSU	Communist Party of the Soviet Union
GPCR	Great Proletarian Cultural Revolution
KMT	Kuomintang
NPC	National Peoples' Congress
PLA	People's Liberation Army
PRC	People's Republic of China
ROC	Republic of China (Taiwan)
SEATO	Southeast Asia Treaty Organization
UN	United Nations
US	United States
USSR	Union of Soviet Socialist Republics

Peking's UN Policy

The central proposition of this study is that, despite its exclusion from the UN, Peking has always had a UN policy that involves aspects of both continuity and change. More specifically, this is to say (1) that despite popular assumption to the contrary, there is no fundamental incompatibility between the UN and the PRC as systems; (2) that the UN has been a constant factor in Peking's foreign policy deliberations; (3) that Peking's perspectives on "the UN factor" and, collaterally, its attitudes and approaches toward the UN have changed from time to time; but (4) that Peking's UN policy has been continually characterized by certain legal, political and psychological traits.

This proposition must be understood in the context of the following explanations.

First, Foreign policy, for this study, is defined as the system of activities evolved by a nation to induce, or to adapt to, changes in its international environment.[1] Foreign policy problems, in this sense, are problems of internal and external adjustment over periods of time. By the same token, international relations are exchanges, or more pointedly, challenges and responses, among international actors. From a particular nation's point of view, all other international actors are present or potential foreign policy systems that it may choose to encounter or be induced or forced to encounter. In some cases, the very existence of an international actor is sufficient reason for most other international actors to feel the challenge it creates for them. The United Nations is one such international actor.[2]

It is the author's premise that both the PRC and the UN are major actors in contemporary international politics and that the decision-makers of the PRC, like those of the UN, are fully aware of this fact. It is assumed that Peking's leaders are aware of the difficulties that the UN and the PRC have created for each other and that Peking's leaders have at some point considered the merits of adjusting toward the political reality of the UN.

There can be little doubt that the PRC, as an international actor, has established itself as a major power. In fact, some are not hesitant to cast the PRC as another potential superpower, the third in George Orwell's perpetual triangle. Supporters of Peking are fond of pointing out that the UN--a quasi-universal international organization aimed

3

at maintaining international peace and security and contributing to the
betterment of the future life of mankind--is entirely unrealistic in
excluding the PRC--one of the most ancient continuing civilizations and
the most populous nation in the world--from its chambers. Peking's
opponents are quick to mention the PRC as a threat to the international
status quo and thus implicitly affirm the importance of that power in the
workings of the UN. Peking's own official and semi-official pronouncements are widely circulated in all parts of the world and actually command some, if limited, respect for their claim to speak for mankind's
future on the basis of the Thoughts of Mao Tse-tung. Certainly one
cannot expect to postpone indefinitely the participation of the PRC in
UN decisions affecting the world's present and future course of development. The interdependence of nations and the common fate of mankind
is not mere fiction. Particularly on questions that require direct cooperation from Peking--e.g., disarmament and arms control, world
health, population control--operating without the PRC in its assembly,
councils and committees, the UN is limited in its capacities.

On the other hand, the UN also has a unique place in present-day
world affairs. It can be said that one of the twentieth century's most
important developments is the creation of a quasi-universal, general
international organization such as the League of Nations or the United
Nations. With the advent of the League of Nations and succeeding it--
the United Nations--the European-oriented notion of a world characterized by the classic concept of balance of power gradually lost some
of its validity as a theory for explaining contemporary politics among
nations. In the present context, the very existence of the United Nations
signifies a fundamental change in the international system. With every
passing year, the UN grows in both its membership and recognition by
its members as a going concern. To the degree that this going concern
is recognized by a nation, whether a member or not, there is a United
Nations angle, both in perspectives and in pragmatic consideration, to
every major subject of that nation's foreign policy. This UN angle is
significant not because the UN has the power of world government, or
even international government. It is significant because nations run
certain political risks when they defy the moral authority of the world
organization. Moreover, the UN also serves its members, large and
small, in many positive ways for which no satisfactory substitute can
be found. In some ways, the UN is indispensable. This is the meaning
of the transformation of the international society from a balance of
power system to a loose (rather than tight) bipolar system, of which
Morton Kaplan speaks.[3] Indeed, it is hard to imagine Kaplan's loose
bipolar world without this quasi-universal organization that gives the
small non-aligned nations both the mechanism and symbol of their
collective strength. No nation that fails to realize this fundamental

change in the international system can successfully cope with the
reality of world politics. Seen in this light, a study of Peking's attitudes toward the UN is a necessary step in understanding that government's international behavior and, perhaps, its intentions.

In short, it is our assumption that Peking's leaders do, of necessity, consider their foreign policy decisions against the policies of the
United Nations and the ramifications that the very existence of the UN
entails. Put differently, this means Peking behaves just like most
other nations of the world in acknowledging the UN as an international
actor as well as an arena, despite the severe treatment it has received
from the UN. There is perhaps a parallel between Peking's attitude
toward the UN and its attitude toward the United States. Although the
United States and the PRC have not established diplomatic relations
through mutual recognition, both have found it expedient to conduct the
Warsaw ambassadorial talks. Peking has not approached the UN in
order to hold direct talks, but it has not written off the UN either. In
actuality, there is evidence that the UN occupies a constant position in
the thinking of Peking's foreign policy-makers.

Second, the discussions shall focus on the aspects of continuity
and change in Peking's UN policy. The rationale is that Peking's UN
policy cannot be explained satisfactorily in the simple terms of acceptance or rejection. On the one hand, the aspects of continuity explain
Peking's views on the fundamental nature of the UN system and the
expectations Peking might harbor regarding that system. They explain
the ways in which Peking's leaders think about and try to deal with the
UN and its officials. And they also reveal Peking's objectives and
strategies over a long time span.

Simultaneously, the aspects of change explain Peking's estima-
tion of the net worth of the UN for safeguarding and promoting the more
specific interests of the PRC during a shorter time span. They help
to explain Peking's assessment of its own short-term capabilities,
priorities or goals. And they indicate the trends in Peking's thinking
regarding Peking's own role in the advancement of the international
communist movement and the utility of the UN system. Thus, only when
the aspects of continuity and change have been clearly spelled out can
one hope to explain Peking's UN policy realistically.

In considering the aspects of continuity, this study will proceed
with the hypotheses (1) that "the UN factor" in Peking's foreign policy
deliberations has been necessitated by the very existence of the UN in
general and by the nature of the relationship between the UN and the
PRC in particular and (2) that Peking's fundamental position on the UN

has been substantially affected by doctrinal elements. Discussions on
such aspects of continuity will involve a theoretical comparison of the
two systems, the purpose of which is to discover whether there is a
fundamental incompatibility between them. Concurrently, the legal,
political and psychological traits that have characterized Peking's UN
policy in actuality will be investigated.

In considering the aspects of change, the hypotheses are (1) that
pragmatic rather than doctrinaire elements determine Peking's short-
term positions, and (2) that Peking's attitides and approaches toward
the UN during any given period are affected by changing developments
in the internal conditions of the PRC, in the UN itself, and in the PRC's
relevant international environment. Discussions on such aspects of
change will take into consideration all these changing developments
and their impact upon the approach or the attitude of Peking.

Third, the question of Chinese participation in contemporary
international politics almost invariably involves the question of Taiwan's
international status. One might say that all problems relating to the
solution of the China puzzle in the UN ultimately lead to the question
of Taiwan. The China puzzle is impregnated with the Taiwan dilemma.
From Peking's vantage point, the whole question of Chinese participation in the UN and other international organizations is insoluble so
long as a counterclaim to China's seat exists, no matter in what form.
For this reason, as the UN is studied in Peking's foreign policy, an
investigation of the Taiwan question in some detail cannot be avoided.
However, the Taiwan question is a complicated subject that requires
a separate analysis.[4] The investigation will be limited to those facets
of that question with a direct bearing on the UN question.

The methodology of this study varies from part to part. Part I
deals with the fundamentals of possible interactions between the UN
and the PRC as an international actor. The basic method of analysis
is systemic: that is, Peking's foreign policy complex is considered as
a system. Part I is not a complete treatise on the Chinese foreign
policy system, but merely a brief theoretical outline of it, specifically
geared to our inquiry about the place of the UN in that system. The
UN factor is identified and interpreted in light of what function it performs for the system, or what need the system might have for it.
This systemic perspective provides a frame of reference for a researcher to gather, analyze, evaluate and organize his data. It enables
him to ask meaningful questions that may otherwise escape him, since
a social system usually incorporates such concepts as inertia toward
equilibrium, integration, adaptation and so forth. To a certain extent,
it also frees the researcher from possible personal prejudices and

sensitizes him to the need to be empathic. However, treating an ongoing concern such as the foreign policy complex as a system also has serious drawbacks. As Franz Schurmann has pointed out, social systems are formulated in a more or less static manner.[5] To call China a system is to abstract it from time. What structural and functional analyses resulted from such an approach would serve little purpose over time. In this study, therefore, the systemic scheme is applied only insofar as it helps to sharpen one's thinking and to formulate the key questions involved. Efforts are made to prevent this application from blurring our views regarding the dynamic nature of the topic under scrutiny.

Parts II and III are empirical policy analyses dealing respectively with aspects of change and aspects of continuity. In Part II, historical method is used to delineate and describe changes that have taken place in Peking's adjustment to the UN. From period to period, as various elements--compostion of UN membership, relative position of the PRC in the international political arena, Sino-Soviet relations, Peking's own capabilities and domestic priorities, etc.--are perceived to have changed, Peking's attitudes and approaches also changed accordingly. These changes are best analyzed by historical phases.

To establish meaningful contrasts of Peking's UN policy from period to period, four pairs of adjectives are used as a sort of conceptual framework. This framework, defined at the beginning of Part II, turned out to be instrumental in describing the seven distinctive periods dealt with in Chapters 5 through 11.

Part III summarizes the continuing characteristics and patterns of Peking's words and deeds vis-à-vis the UN. The main method of analysis here is legal, supplemented by some political and psychological observations. Legal analysis is helpful in uncovering the fundamental position that Peking's statements reflect. Generally, Peking's most basic positions are couched in fairly clear legal terms. This is so because law, including international law, usually serves to bolster the status quo. Nations who invoke legal principles usually do so in order to take advantage of the protection of established rules. Even nations interested in promoting change have to rely on certain principles of international law, either established ones or new "revolutionary" ones, to protect their basic rights and to legitimatize their new claims.

Throughout the chapters, the comparative approach is also employed to indicate similarities and differences in the positions and attitudes of the PRC and other nations, particularly the Soviet Union and the United States. This approach is most educational. As it turned out,

Peking's responses toward the challenge of the UN are not particularly difficult to explain when juxtaposed with those of the other two major powers in similar situations.

Although the nature of this inquiry does not lend itself to highly sophisticated quantitative techniques, efforts have been made to check and recheck the empirical evidence adduced to support the propositions. For instance, simple content analysis is made of Peking's direct and formal communications to the UN's several main organs and other related international agencies from period to period. Some basic quantitative analysis is made of membership change and of voting records on the Chinese question in the UN to indicate change in the international political climate. The appendixes at the end serve similar purposes.

PART

I

**THEORETICAL ANALYSIS:
THE PLACE
OF THE UN
IN PEKING'S
FOREIGN POLICY SYSTEM**

In systemic terms, a foreign policy system is a process of input-conversion-output, which operates by certain precepts and principles prescribed by a given political culture.[1] Structurally, it is composed of four main parts: the political culture, the decision-makers, the input-structure and the output-structure. The political culture of a foreign policy system denotes the Weltanschauung or world view of a nation that is either deeply rooted in that nation's historical traditions or superimposed on that nation by its totalitarian authority. It overshadows the organization and the functions of all other structures within the foreign policy system. The decision-makers constitute the core authority that performs the function of conversion, i.e., converting input into output. Such decision-makers are usually conditioned by their role expectations as stipulated by law and customs and by their own idiosyncracies. The input-structure and the output-structure each contain an aims-aspect and a means-aspect. On the input side, demands are made upon and support is given to the decision-makers by competing groups (substructures of the system). Demands are aims conveyed to the decision-makers, commonly called foreign policy interests. Support designates the means of policy implementation in the forms of both materials and services made available to the decision-makers, usually referred to as foreign policy power. On the output side, there are the aims that the decision-makers choose as the aims of all groups. These are foreign policy objectives. There are also the means that the decision-makers employ in order to fulfill the objectives. These means constitute a nation's foreign policy strategy and tactics. The dynamism of a foreign policy system is propelled by the endless interactions in the process of input-conversion-output. Input-structures are stimulated by the feedback from output-structures. The output of a system, conversely, generates a new series of inputs and the process continues.

This very brief sketch of a foreign policy system is not readily applicable by statesmen confronted with policy-making or administration, nor by scholars attempting to describe and explain certain policy or policies. Nevertheless, it does provide a framework for limited analytical purposes.

In the following chapters, the place of the UN in Peking's foreign policy culture (world outlook), its decision-making structure (role expectations and idiosyncracies), its aims (interests and objectives) and its means (power and strategy and tactics) will be considered.

1

**PEKING'S
WORLD
OUTLOOK**

If one were to put on Peking's brand of tinted glasses, what would the world, and in it the UN, look like?

The most authoritative statement on Peking's world outlook is found in the preamble to the Constitution of the Communist Party of China. Examining the three texts[1] of the Constitutions of the Communist Party of China (CPC) adopted since Mao assumed undisputed power, we find the following passages:

> The CPC takes the theories of Marxism-Leninism and the combined principles derived from the practical experience of the Chinese revolution--the ideas of Mao Tse-tung--as the guiding principles of all its work; it denounces any one-sided tendencies toward dogmatism and impiricism. The CPC is based on the dialectical and historical materialism of Marxism, accepting with critical attitude its historical heritage both in China and in other countries, and denouncing any idealistic or mechanistic-materialistic conception of the world. (Seventh National Party Congress (NPC), June 11, 1945)

> The CPC takes Marxism-Leninism as its guide to action. Only Marxism-Leninism correctly sets forth the laws of development of society and correctly charts the path leading to the achievement of socialism and communism. The Party adheres to the Marxist-Leninist world outlook of dialectical and historical materialism and opposes the world outlook of idealism and metaphysics.

> Marxism-Leninism is not a dogma, but a guide to
> action. It demands that in striving to build socialism and
> communism we should proceed from reality, apply the
> principles of Marxism-Leninism in a flexible and creative
> way for the solution of various problems arising out of the
> actual struggle, and thus continuously develop the theory
> of Marxism-Leninism. Consequently, the Party in its ac-
> tivities upholds the principle of integrating the universal
> truths of Marxism-Leninism with the actual practice of
> China's revolutionary struggle, and combats all doctri-
> naire or empiricist deviations. (Eighth National Party
> Congress, September 26, 1956)

> The CPC takes Marxism-Leninism-Mao Tse-tung Thought
> as the theoretical basis guiding its thinking. Mao Tse-tung
> Thought is Marxism-Leninism of the era in which imperi-
> alism is heading for total collapse and socialism is advanc-
> ing to world-wide victory. (Ninth National Party Congress,
> April 14, 1969)

These passages indicate that Peking's formulation of its ideological
guidelines has undergone significant modifications. The 1928 version
of the CPC's Constitution mentioned only Marxism-Leninism as the
Party's guiding ideology. In 1945, on the eve of victory over the
Kuomintang (KMT), "the combined principles derived from the practical experience of the Chinese revolution--the ideas of Mao Tse-tung"
were added. And the Party, in anticipation of power, also announced
its preparedness to accept "its historical heritage both in China and
in other countries," albeit "with critical attitude." In 1956, at the
height of its successful first Five-Year Plan, references to "the ideas
of Mao Tse-tung" were omitted, which suggests the possibility that
Mao might have suffered a demotion on the ideological ladder between
1945 and 1956. At the same time, a clearer distinction was made
between the "universal truths" of Marxism-Leninism and the "actual
practice of China's revolutionary struggle," giving the latter its independent place. The 1969 version, for some reason not yet clear to us,
not only reverted to Mao's personal contribution, but put "Mao Tse-
tung Thought" forth as the "continuator" to Marxism-Leninism. The
document went so far as to claim that

> Comrade Mao Tse-tung has integrated the universal truth
> of Marxism-Leninism with the concrete practice of revolu-
> tion, inherited, defended and developed Marxism-Leninism
> and has brought it to a higher and completely new stage.[2]

These modifications in Peking's ideological formulation reflect the flexibility in the thinking of Chinese Communists. Peking's world outlook is not to be a dogmatic one, or at least it has been so stated. As a guide to action, the teachings of Mao say that all should follow the paradoxically changing universal truth of Marxism-Leninism-Mao Tse-tung Thought.

THE LAW OF CONTRADICTION

Despite the modifications, the basic ideas of "dialectical and historical materialism" remain in each of the three versions. This is the core of the total ideology. If we understand this, we may have a key to the inner mind of the Chinese Communists. For this "dialectical and historical materialism" as interpreted by Mao constitutes the basic world outlook (Shih-chieh kuan) as well as the cosmology (Yu-chou kuan) and the life philosophy (Jen-sheng kuan) of both Mao and his followers. Its roots are found in Hegelian dialectics, in Marxian economic determinism and, beyond, in the ancient Chinese Taoist concepts of Yin and Yang. In his own way, Mao conceptualized it as the law of contradiction.

In an essay, "On Contradiction," Mao wrote in August, 1937:

Throughout the history of human knowledge, there have been two conceptions concerning the law of development of the universe, the metaphysical conception and the dialectical conception, which form two opposing world outlooks.[3]

The metaphysical world outlook, Mao said, sees things as isolated, static and one-sided. It regards all things as eternally isolated from one another; the world changes only because of an increase or decrease in quantity or a change in place. Such an outlook is a trap. It inevitably leads to the conclusion that "capitalist exploitation, capitalist competition, the individual ideology of capitalist society, and so on, can all be found in ancient slave society, or even in primitive society, and will exist forever unchanged."[4] In opposition, the world outlook of materialist dialectics holds that "the development of things should be seen as their internal and necessary self-movement, while each thing in its movement is interrelated with and interacts on the things around it." The internal and necessary self-movement of things is an absolute, universal process. It is explained by the law of the unity of opposites, i.e., "the division of a unity into mutually exclusive opposites and their reciprocal relation." Hence, "the fundamental cause of the development of a thing is not external but internal;

it lies in the contradictoriness within the thing."[5] The Chinese revolution, for instance, is a matter of domestic development; external causes are the condition rather than the basis of change.

The law of contradiction, according to Mao, is both universal and particular in nature. The universality of contradiction means that contradiction exists in objective reality and in subjective thought, i.e., in the process of development of all things. It also means that in the process of development of each thing, a movement or struggle of two opposites exists from beginning to end. It manifests the unity of opposites; it is positive and negative; it is male and female; it is action and reaction; it is war and peace; it is victory and defeat; it is Yin and Yang. In natural science, it is motion; in social science, it is (class) struggle.

The particularity of contradiction means that each contradiction has its own peculiar characteristics and requires differentiated means of handling. In Mao's own words:

> the contradiction between the proletariat and the burgeoisie
> is resolved by the method of socialist revolution; the con-
> tradiction between the great masses of the people and the
> fuedal system is resolved by the method of democratic
> revolution; the contradiction between the colonies and im-
> perialism is resolved by the method of national revolution-
> ary war; . . .[6]

In connection with the particularity of contradiction, Mao points out that many contradictions coexist in the developmental process of a complex thing. It is necessary in such cases to identify the principal contradiction, whose existence and development determine or influence the existence and development of the secondary contradictions. Even within a contradiction, there is also a principal aspect that dominates the secondary aspect. The ability to separate the principal contradiction or the principal aspect of a contradiction from the secondary ones bespeaks the ability to identify the main target of one's action.

The universality and particularity of contradictions together support the rule that everything must be studied from two angles: the general and the special. Failure to do so will result in either superficiality or onesidedness.

Mao also explained the identity and struggle of the aspects of a contradiction. A contradictory aspect cannot exist all by itself; it presupposes the existence of the other aspect. Simultaneously, each of the contradictory aspects are identical and may transform themselves

into each other. This is the meaning of the identity of the aspects of
contradiction. War and peace, for instance, are two aspects of a contradiction. One cannot think of one without presupposing the other, and
each transforms itself into the other under given conditions.

In identity there is struggle; for the opposites are also mutually
exclusive, and are in constant motion. They are not dead and rigid
but living and conditional, transitory and relative. All things, i.e., all
unity of opposites, are in either of two states of motion: that of relative
rest or that of conspicuous change. Both are caused by the struggle
between the two contradictory aspects within. This is the meaning of
the struggle of the aspects of contradiction. The contradiction between
the ruler and the ruled, for instance, is characterized by struggle.

Finally, Mao cautioned against viewing antagonism as the only
form of struggle. The importance of this point is underlined by a
separate essay, "On the Correct Handling of Contradictions among the
People," which Mao wrote in 1957: "We are confronted by two types
of social contradictions--those between ourselves and the enemy and
those among the people themselves. The two are totally different in
their nature."[7] The former are antagonistic, but the latter are non-
antagonistic or only partially antagonistic and must be resolved by
different methods. The guiding principle for handling contradictions
between "the people" and the enemy is to draw a distinction between
"the people" and the enemy. For handling contradictions among "the
people" it is a matter of transforming the antagonistic aspects into
non-antagonistic aspects and of distinguishing between right and
wrong. Mao advocated that the people support and rely upon the "people's democratic dictatorship" to suppress internal "enemies of the
people" and to protect the country from subversive activities and
aggression by external enemies. As to contradictions among the
people, the correct way to handle them is through democratic centralism, i.e., a policy of criticizing, discussing, persuading, educating
and uniting. It is a pathological approach, with a "unity-criticism-
unity" formula, i.e., "to start from a desire for unity, and thrash out
the question of right and wrong through criticism or argument, and
so achieve a new unity on a new basis."[8]

WORLD VIEW

The practical implications of the law of contradiction and the
theories derived from it for world politics in general and for Peking's
foreign policy in particular are far reaching.[9]

The law of contradiction reduces the complexity of international relations to a set of relatively simple phenomena which explain reality for the Communist Chinese elite and imbue them with the conviction of their righteousness.

At the time the PRC was established, a simplistic view of the world based on the law of contradiction guided Peking's thinking. Peking's leaders saw a world of continuous struggle between two camps: the capitalists, representing the world bourgeoisie and led by the United States, and the socialists, representing the world revolutionary forces and led by the Soviet Union. The contradiction between these two camps was the principal contradiction in the world. Within it were a number of subordinate but equally fundamental contradictions, namely, those between the imperialists and the oppressed nations, among the imperialists themselves, and between the bourgeoisie and the proletariat in capitalist countries. In each case, the former was the exploitative, oppressive and aggressive, while the latter was the exploited, oppressed and victimized. The former was static, the latter progressive. In each case, the coexistence of the opposites was temporary, but the struggle between the two was continuous. In the struggle between the two opposite camps, class wars and wars of national liberation were inevitable because the contradictions were antagonistic.[10] Such wars were necessary and justified, since they were fought in behalf of "human progress."

This world image has since been modified as the Sino-Soviet schism widened and the Communist Chinese elite acquired a higher degree of sophistication in world affairs. The world as a whole is still a unity of opposites. But the two camps are no longer as clearly drawn. On the one hand, the oppressive, exploitative, and aggressive forces now include both the "imperialist" US and the "revisionist" USSR who collaborate with each other. On the other hand, the revolutionary forces are now led by the PRC and include the oppressed peoples and nations of the three continents. For a time, the contradiction between the PRC and the USSR was considered as non-antagonistic, but that too seems to have changed during the late 1960's. The contradiction between the US and the USSR has now become a secondary contradiction.

China, in other words, is now a leader of the revolutionary aspect of the two opposites in her current world image. The struggle ahead is to be long and tortuous.

PRECEPTS OF FOREIGN POLICY

Foreign policy is a matter of extreme complexity that involves a multiplicity of problems and requires consideration and evaluation from both the perspectives of the whole and the parts, the general and the specific. The law of contradiction has a built-in code that stipulates precisely that.

The concept of the universality of contradiction enables the leaders of Peking to handle foreign challenges with greater equanimity. Foreign challenges are in this sense more or less expected developments of known contradictions about which resolute struggles are to be waged. For instance, Sino-Soviet difficulties are a manifestation of such contradictions. In the developmental process, one must anticipate and accept both progress and setbacks before the end is reached. It is the ultimate contradiction that matters. As long as one sets his eyes on the final triumph and resolutely engages in the necessary struggle to achieve that end, frustrations are calculated obstacles that can be and must be overcome.

Concurrently, the concept of particularity of contradiction demands that in facing a contradiction, one be cognizant of the particular features involved and avoid being misled by generality. It calls for careful studies and discriminating applications of diplomatic and military strategical and tactical concepts and techniques. These are guiding concepts that prescribe for Peking's leaders the course of action to be taken under a given situation. If the theory of universality of contradiction guards against shortsightedness, the theory of particularity of contradiction warns against lightheartedness. The former emphasizes stability and the latter flexibility. Thus the law of contradiction is no less than a broadly conceived operational code of conduct.

Closely related to this, the theory that the opposites of a contradiction may be identical and may transform themselves into each other under certain conditions suggests that it is sometimes possible and desirable to develop peaceful measures of resolving contradictions, or to pursue a course of detente and peaceful coexistence. This concept, as Franklin W. Houn observes, "injects an element of flexibility and pragmatism into an ideology that tends to be rigid and dogmatic."[11]

The distinction between principal and secondary contradictions or aspects of contradiction has an even more direct bearing in Peking's formulation of foreign policy. It spells out the necessity and means for Peking to identify its principal and secondary allies and enemies

at any given time. At the same time, the theoretical possibility that
a principal contradiction may become a secondary contradiction
sensitizes Peking's leaders to beware of drastic developments in the
world--yesterday's enemies, today's friends and vice versa--and be
prepared to cope with it. This is a point of paramount importance in
the acutal formulation of foreign policy in Communist China as the
statements below attest:

> Since the founding of the PRC, the basic policy of our inter-
> national relations has been to develop relations of friend-
> ship, mutual assistance and cooperation with the Soviet
> Union and the other fraternal socialist countries; to strive
> for coexistence with countries of different social systems
> on the basis of the Five Principles and to oppose the im-
> perialist policies of aggression and war; to support the
> revolutionary struggles of all oppressed peoples and na-
> tions against imperialism and colonialism. This is the
> general line of our policy. (Speech by Liu Shao-ch'i, July
> 1961) (Emphasis added)[12]

> The foreign policy of our Party and government is consis-
> tent. It is: to develop relations of friendship, mutual assist-
> ance and co-operation with socialist countries on the prin-
> ciple of proletarian internationalism; to support and assist
> the revolutionary struggles of all the oppressed people and
> nations; and to strive for peaceful coexistence with coun-
> tries having different social systems on the basis of the
> Five Principles. . . .and to oppose the imperialist policies
> of aggression and war. Our proletarian foreign policy is
> not based on temporary expediency; it is a policy in which
> we have long persisted. (Lin Piao's Report to the Ninth
> NPC of the CPC, April 1969) (Emphasis added.)[13]

The general line of Peking's foreign policy is to divide the world into
categories and formulate appropriate policy principles in regard to
each. The compositon of each of the categories may change in the
short run but the categories themselves are likely to change only in
the long run. In Lin Piao's statement quoted above, the Soviet Union,
now a "modern revisionist," has been dropped from the prominent
position that Liu Shao-ch'i accorded it. At the same time, omission
of "colonialism" might be a subtle preparation for possible improvement of relations with the former European "colonial" powers.

THE PLACE OF THE UN

What does the UN look like through the tinted spectacles of Peking? To answer that question, one must look further into the fundamental nature of the UN itself.

The UN, as a general, universal international organization, possesses a dual personality: It is at once both an arena and an actor in the global international make-up. As an arena, the UN is a field in which the actors, i.e., the different foreign policy systems, interact with each other. Looked at from this angle, the UN is a "contradiction" in itself. It is, to the extent that it functions effectively, a battleground where the struggle between the opposites takes place. In this sense, there is no question as to which camp the UN belongs; the question simply does not apply. For Peking, as with all other actors in international politics, the UN is to be evaluated in terms of whether it is a useful field, i.e., a field that will facilitate the resolution of the contradictions in Peking's favor. The relevant questions are: What facilities are available through the UN? What rules of the game are applied there? Who runs the arena? and so forth.

As an actor, the UN is unique. It differs from the national political systems in that it does not have territorial boundaries within which it can exercise sovereign authority, nor does it have its own individual citizens to whom it grants protection and from whom it collects revenues. Nevertheless, it acquires its own independent personality and status as it becomes a going concern representing the collective will of its members. To the extent that it is supported by its members and deferred to by other actors, it is capable of role performance in its own right. Seen from this perspective, the UN may become an element in opposition to the PRC system under certain circumstances. It is here that the question of contradiction between the UN and the PRC arises. But the answer here is not a simple one either. While a more detailed comparison and contrast of the two actors will be made in Chapter 13, a brief theoretical analysis here will spell out two levels of answer.

First, by an abstract systemic comparison, based on the constitutional features in each, one might conclude that the PRC and the UN are basically discordant with each other, if not incompatible. One way of doing this is to borrow David Apter's models of political systems.[14] In a recent publication, Ernst Haas has quite convincingly established that the systemic characteristics of the UN meet all of the requisites of Apter's reconciliation model.[15] Its values are preponderantly instrumental and its authority structure pyramidal. Its decision-making organs possess considerable information regarding the member nations and use little coercion against them. Norms are sanctioned by its Charter and accepted international custom. The mechanism of integration is provided by a bureaucracy (the Secretariat), working closely with the national delegations and the representatives of relative international agencies. Loyalty to, and identification with, the system rests primarily upon satisfaction with its performance. The authority is highly accountable, and the recruitment of elites is largely based on skill and merit and national access. And the enforcement of norms is selective and flexible, resources are allocated through bargaining, and consent groups are co-opted into the governing structure.

In contrast, the PRC appears to resemble a prototype of Apter's mobilization model, which Apter described as follows:

> Behaviorally, it is made up of units whose singular characteristic is potentiality. Individuals, for example are perceived as nothing more than potentials. Structurally, the political community is the means of translating potentiality into some sort of reality. Hence, the society is the key to social life. Moreover, as the primary instrument of socialization, the political community is essentially an educational body. It exists for the improvement of the community itself. The individual is merely a derivative personality. Normatively, the sacred collectivity is an ethical or moral unit. Thus, the morality of the individual depends on the morality of the system, which embodies those higher purposes that may be enshrined in kinship, political ideals, and so on. Included under the rubric of this essentially Aristotelian view of the political community would be most traditional societies, theocracies, and certain modernizing ones as well.[16]

It seems, by definition, the values and ways of the PRC and the UN are opposed to each other. In this sense, the place of the UN as actor in Peking's foreign policy resembles that of the United States: a target of struggle.

If one goes beyond the constitutional provisions and compares the PRC and the UN on the basis of their respective records of performance, one might find the PRC quite capable of seeing the "better side"--the compatibility--of the UN as actor. In its first quarter century of existence, the UN has experienced many a change internally. Ernst Haas, for example, has pointed out that the behavioral orientation of the UN as an actor has changed from pro-West to balancing as a result of expansion in membership.[17]

In the dialectics of Mao's law of contradiction, Peking's mind's eye might see as follows: (1) the UN has contradictions within itself like all other actors; (2) the UN's will and capabilities only reflect the collective will and capabilities of its members after the pluses and minuses have cancelled each other; (3) the UN as an actor may be either a partner or a foe in the higher-level struggle between the oppressing forces led by the US (and the USSR) and the revolutionary forces led by (the USSR or) the PRC, depending upon which of the two opposites of the UN's principal contradiction comes out on top in their struggle against each other; (4) Marxist-Leninist teachings indicate the ultimate victory of the socialist forces over the capitalist forces in the next historical stage; hence, (5) there is a definite possibility that the UN as an actor will become a neutral and eventually even a member in the PRC-led camp.

In short, the place of the UN, either as an arena or an actor, in Peking's world outlook, is not necessarily a negative one. Rather the reverse is probable. As an arena, the UN possesses a neutral character. As an actor, it may become Peking's friend or foe, depending on how its internal contradiction is shaped, its seeming constitutional discordance with the PRC notwithstanding. Fundamentally, therefore, the place of the UN in Peking's foreign policy is a matter for decision by the PRC's leaders.

2

DECISION-MAKING
STRUCTURE

Do the government apparatus of the PRC and the inclinations of the elite occupying key roles in such apparatus favor or shun Peking's adaptation to the UN?

FOREIGN POLICY APPARATUS

About the workings of the PRC's foreign policy apparatus, the outside world has only some sketchy knowledge. In general, the most outstanding known feature of such apparatus is the overshadowing of the State machinery by the Party machinery at the decision-making level and the Party's infiltration into the State machinery at the implementation level.

For our purpose, the question is whether Peking's Party-controlled foreign policy apparatus is an element that might have some impact upon Pekings's deliberations regarding its own participation in the UN. Is there any built-in feature that might function as either a sanction or an obstacle for Peking's adaptation toward the UN?

The answer is negative. In a recent publication, J. D. Simmonds traced and analyzed the principal responsibilities of Vice Ministers in Peking's Foreign Ministry between 1949 and 1968.[1] He found that the assignment of duties for the Vice Ministers was concerned largely with geographic rather than functional affairs. Simmonds paid no special attention to international organizations in his study. However, his findings seem to suggest that participation in international organizations receives no special attention above and beyond what is normally the case.

It is known that within the Ministry of Foreign Affairs, a Bureau
of International Affairs routinely handles matters relating to international conferences and organizations. According to available information, this Bureau has been under the direction of Tung Yueh-ch'ien
from 1951-58 and Kung P'u-sheng since 1965.[2] Neither Tung nor Kung
is a ranking member of the Party. Tung assumed the post in 1951
while serving concurrently as Deputy-Director of the Foreign Ministry's
General Office. Since then, he has served as the Director of the General
Office from 1955-58, Ambassador to Sweden from 1958-64, Assistant
Minister since 1964 and concurrently the Director of the General Office
again since 1965. It seems clear that he is a career diplomat although
we have no further information on his personal background. Kung
P'u-sheng, wife of Vice Minister Chang Han-fu and older sister of
Assistant Minister Kung P'eng (wife of another Vice-Minister Chiao
Kuan-hua) was trained in the US and worked in the Human Rights Commission of the UN Economic and Social Council. In 1949, she was
appointed a Deputy-Director of the International Affairs Bureau. She
served in that capacity until 1965 when she was promoted to the position
of Director. Between 1949 and 1965, she also participated in many
important international conferences as a delegate. In December 1950,
she was one of eight delegates who accompanied Ambassador Wu Hsiu-
ch'uan to the UN debate on Korea in New York. She was also a Deputy-
General Secretary of the Executive Committee of the PRC's delegation
to the Inter-Parliamentary Union in 1955, a representative to the Afro-
Asian Women's Conference in Colombo in 1958, a member of the PRC's
delegation to the 50th Anniversary of the International Women's Conference in Copenhagen in 1969, and an advisor in Ch'en Yi's delegation
to the Geneva Conference on Loas in 1961, among other appointments.
It does seem that Kung is forever in the list of Peking's delegates to
major international conferences that have something to do with international organization. But, in the final analysis, both Tung and Kung
are life-time professional technocrats, not potential power wielders
in any sense. This is not to say that the State machinery neglects or
obstructs Peking's participation in international organizations such as
the UN. What it does say is that no evidence exists that an inertia
favoring Peking's adaptation to the UN might be a built-in feature of
the existing State foreign policy apparatus.

Party control of State machinery raises another consideration.
It is evident that the Party operates by the principle of democratic
centralism, which is legitimized by both Party and State Constitutions.
Although there are two parts to this principle--centralism on the basis
of democracy and democracy under central guidance--the tendency is
that centralism will manufacture rather than follow the democratic

basis. The leadership that allows the Party organization to become routinized, specialized and bureaucratized does so at the risk of losing its own power of control. What is likely to prevail, therefore, is the following stipulation of that principle:

> Party decisions must be carried out unconditionally. Individual Party members shall obey the Party organization, the minority shall obey the majority, the lower Party organizations shall obey the higher Party organizations, and all constituent Party Organizations throughout the country shall obey the National Party Congress and the Central Committee. (Art. 19, para. 6 of the Constitution of the CPC, 1956)

The logical outcome is that major decisions, especially foreign policy decisions, are made by a handful of Party leaders at the summit--the Politburo, and specially its Standing Committee, of the Central Committee. Who (what kind of individuals) occupy the select seats at the summit, therefore, becomes a matter of grave importance in determining the direction the PRC takes, particularly in foreign policy-making.

LEADERSHIP CHARACTERISTICS

The leadership to be considered here include two important groups: At the decision-making level, it is the Politburo of the CPC, headed by Mao Tse-tung. At the implementation level, there is the Foreign Ministry personnel under the direction of Chou En-lai and his protege, Ch'en Yi.

The Politburo

Prior to the Ninth Party Congress, the Politburo seats of the CPC generally belonged to first generation leaders. The 19 full and six alternate members of the Politburo elected by the eighth Central Committee, including the six men mentioned above, averaged almost 60 years of age at the time of their election. About this group of first generation top leaders, A. Doak Barnett found these characteristics: (1) Most of them came from middle class families and were well educated. (2) All shared an overriding sense of ethnic-cultural unity and were generally agreed on what China's goals should be. (3) All believed in Marxism-Leninism as the right ideology for extricating

China from her semi-colonial and semi-feudal status. (4) All were self-made men who had proven themselves to be the fittest during the revolution. (5) Their main channels of career had been "Party organizational work and service in the Party's revolutionary army." Consequently, (6) their skills were largely limited to those of military combat, political organization and ideological mobilization, rather than technical or professional skills of other sorts; and (7) their working style had been typically "the mass line."[3] Foreign observers have been impressed with the unity and cohesion of this group, despite the recent Cultural Revolution which seems to have made a shambles of the lives of many Long March heroes.

But this same group was also easily the most isolated among the leaders of nations. Donald W. Klein's quantitative analysis of foreign travels of the Politburo members in 1961 yielded the figures presented in Table 1.[4] The most striking thing about this Table is that only seven members had visited "advanced" nations in post-World War II days. Klein pointed out that the "advanced" nations actually included only four--the United States, Switzerland, Italy and France. The visit to the US consisted of Tung Pi-wu's 1945 trip to the San Francisco Conference that established the United Nations.

It is important to point out that these characteristics of the Politburo members do not necessarily suggest that Peking's top echelon leaders are dogmatic revolutionaries blinded by their own belief and experiences and incapable of flexible adaptation toward the outside world. Isolated and limited in their knowledge about the outside world, yes; but inflexible and incapable of adjusting, they are not. This becomes clear if we examine briefly the idiosyncrasies of the leading men.

Individually, the man most influential in Peking's foreign policy-making, aside from Mao Tse-tung, undoubtedly has been Premier Chou En-lai. Next to these two men, at least four other figures also have played major roles. Up until their removal from offices, Liu Shao-ch'i and Teng Hsiao-p'ing were in a position to implement their ideas regarding both internal and external policies. Lin Piao, the Defense Minister, remained in the background before 1965 as far as foreign policy was concerned. But his recent ascendance to the number two position suggests that his probable influence must be considered. Ch'en Yi was the Foreign Minister between 1958 and 1968, though not a member of the Standing Committee of the Politburo. He too must have been in the inner circle on foreign policy-making.

TABLE 1

Foreign Travels of Politburo Members (25)

Never Abroad	2
Abroad (Pre- or post-1949, to bloc or non-bloc)	23
Bloc Travel	
Pre-1949 (usually as students)	12
Post-1949, to bloc only	14
Korean War participants	2
Non-bloc Travel	
Pre-1949	9
Post-1949, to non-bloc only	0
Post-1949, to "advanced" nation	7
Post-1949, to Southeast Asia	5
Post-1949, to "other areas"	0
Pre- or post-1949, to any non-bloc nation	12
Combined Bloc and Non-bloc Travel	
Pre-1949	16
Post-1949, to bloc or non-bloc	22
Post-1949, to bloc and non-bloc	8

Source: Derived from Donald W. Klein, "Peking's Leaders: A Study in Isolation," China Quarterly, July-September 1961 (No. 7), pp. 40-41.

Mao Tse-tung

Mao's biographers have used such words as liberator, populist, egotist, revolutionary, nationalist and Marxist-Leninist to describe him. He is all of these. There are also popular images of Mao the blood-thirsty executioner or Mao the frantic war-monger. Such images are product of highly exaggerated anti-Mao propaganda.

To many who observed or studied him, Mao's ways are not as tyrannical and dogmatic as they are often made out to be. When Edgar Snow went back to China in the early 1960's, he found Mao a popular leader among China's masses:

> Today's image of Mao among the masses is hardly that of an executioner. What makes him formidable is that he is not just a party boss but by many millions of Chinese is quite genuinely regarded as a teacher, statesman, strategist, philosopher, poet laureate, national head of the family, greatest liberator in history. He is to them Confucius plus Lao-tse plus Rousseau plus Marx plus Buddha. . . .[5]

Mao seems much more tolerant and reasonable than many dynasty-founders in China's past history. He is not as bloody as Stalin was in the treatment of purged comrades. For Mao is an egotist, but not an egoist; he is romantic as well as altruistic. His thinking process is dialectical. Perhaps that is why he prefers "persuasions" and "education" as means of correcting comradely mistakes; for a dialectic thinker is prone to think of two sides to one issue and does not lose sight of the higher unity for the two opposites.

Still, Mao the egotist and the revolutionary is now being deified in mainland China and even in some other parts of the world. Mao himself lectured in 1956 on the need for China and Chinese people to "learn from other countries";[6] but most observers found Mao inclined to see the whole world through the prism of China's own revolutionary experiences. China's anti-imperialist, anti-feudalist struggles have been won with the Yenan spirit--the reliance upon self-sacrifice, egal-itarianism, moral incentives, mass organization, ideological indoctri-nation and a series of strategic and tactical concepts to fight a pro-tracted war. Mao's heir-apparent, Lin Piao, now wants the world to learn from Mao Tse-tung Thought, which propagates this Yenan spirit.[7] As Mao is deified, so is his unreal world view. This is probably one of the worries that Liu Shao-ch'i and Teng Hsiao-p'ing might have tried to do something about. Their failure will undoubtedly prolong the PRC's wedlock to Mao Tse-tung Thought for many years to come.

This unreal world view was undoubtedly nurtured by the fact that Mao is quite isolated from the world outside of China. Throughout his life of over seven decades, he has so far made only two short trips abroad, both to the Soviet Union, in 1954 and 1957.[8] He has never set foot in an "advanced nation" such as the US, France or Japan. He has never seen in person the affluence of a capitalist country or the faces of the men in the streets in an advanced Western society. His world view is derived solely from the law of contradiction and his own readings and experiences. There is every indication that he sincerely believes in the accuracy of such a world view. Even though he seems flexible in interpreting and applying his own theory of the ultimate unity of the opposites, Mao believes that the masses in the US and other "capitalist countries" are suffering miserably from the oppressive exploitation of the bourgeoisie and are, therefore, ready to rise in revolt like the Chinese peasants did in the 1920's, if only the necessary organization can be established to lead them. If the McCarthyistic image of an enslaved China in the 1950's was any guide, it is quite probable that there also existed, and maybe still exist, Mao's own distorted image of an exploited US.

At the risk of being too hasty and speculative, it might be suggested that as long as Mao remains the helmsman in Peking, the PRC's international posture will be somewhat more adamant than otherwise. The times made Mao a revolutionary; and Mao in turn seems bent on making the times revolutionary. He thrives on revolutionary struggle. Herein, one suspects, lies the central element of his charisma. At every occasion when he was pressured, by his father, by the KMT during the Long March and Yenan period, by the US in relation to the American Consulate compound in Peking in 1949, by the UN forces in Korea, by the Russians in the summer of 1960 and by his own associate (the Liu-Teng forces), he has never failed to hit back, if sometimes a little later. If this is a correct assertion, Mao has to be considered as the single leader most responsible for the PRC's intransigent appearance on the world stage during some periods of the last 22 years. It was Mao who announced Peking's policy of "lean to one side" in 1957, and repeatedly called for "the peoples of Asia, Africa and Latin America" to wage a resolute struggle against world imperialists and colonialists.

Lin Piao

Mao's "close comrade-in-arms and successor," as the 1969 Party Constitution now formally refers to him, Lin Piao, emerged as a Party and government spokesman only in recent years.[9] Since he was a career soldier, Mao's principle that "the Party controls the gun" demanded that he stay behind the scenes. However, since his essay, "Long Live the Victory of People's War!" appeared in September 1965, he has come to world attention.

Like Mao, Lin Piao has never travelled outside of China except for two trips to Russia for medical treatment in 1937 and during the Korean War. He shares much of Mao's nationalist sentiments, his belief in the importance of man over machine, the mass line, as well as the cause of Marxism-Leninism. His views on world affairs resemble those of Mao. His report to the Ninth Party Congress carried with it the authority of Mao's own proclamations. In retrospect, it was probable that, in 1959, Lin was instrumental in the decision to dismiss P'eng Teh-huai, his predecessor, as Peking's Defense Minister. P'eng was accused of favoring military professionalism and capitulation to Soviet chauvinism; both were mistakes that Lin would not have tolerated.[10]

One analyst had this to say about Lin's style of operation:

Lin's strategy can be described as agressive, imaginative and dramatic, but with much thought and preparation taken ahead of time and alternate courses of action thought out in case of failure. From Lin we should expect long periods of deceptive inactivity; followed by lightning moves in specific directions using all the force at his disposal; followed either by consolidation or quick retreat, and then finally, by a further period of waiting and planning.[11]

Liu Shao-ch'i and Teng Hsiao-p'ing

Both Liu and Teng were organization men and communist theoreticians.[12] For 17 years before Lin Piao, it was Liu Shao-ch'i who occupied the number two position in Peking. Liu and Teng, also a member of the seven-man Standing Committee and the Party's Secretary-General until 1968, were both pushed aside during the Cultural Revolution. These two leaders are both devoted nationalists like Mao and Lin. But their ways differ.

In the analysis of Tang Tsou, there are four significant differences in the perspectives and approaches of Moa Tse-tung, the supreme ideological leader, and Liu and Teng, the leaders of "the Party organization" between 1958 and 1968.[13] First, on the basic issue on overall direction, Mao favored rapid and continous implementations of the revolutionary programs, while the Party organization gave priority to the consolidation of revolutionary gains and new institutions. Second,

Mao, as the charismatic leader, relied on personal, ideological and nationalistic appeals to mobilize the masses, while Liu and Teng worked with and through "the establishment" and the more privileged groups and individuals in various social sectors and relied more on material interests. Third, the Party organization emphasized functional special-ization and creativity, but Mao tenaciously held on to his almost mystical faith in the simple Yenan model and demanded that ideological and political criteria override professional and technical ones in making decisions and judging work performances. Fourth, Mao sought con-sensus at philosophical and political levels through indoctrination, study sessions, and the system of criticism and self-criticism as means of controlling men, but the Party organization tended to resort to rules and regulations.

These differences, Tsou noted, produced few difficulties until the failure of the Great Leap policy led to a national crisis. Between 1959 and 1962, Mao's control over Party affairs diminished as the Liu-Teng Party organization practiced the "tricks" of "waving the red flag to oppose the red flag" in order to gain time to extricate China from the national crisis with a series of pragmatic policies.

During the Cultural Revolution, Liu was labeled by the Mao-Lin group as "the No. 1 Party person in authority taking the capitalist road in advocating the system of capitalist exploitation" and as "China's Khrushchev."[14] Teng was denounced as an accomplice of Liu and of being against Mao Tse-tung Thought and the Cultural Revolution.[15] For these and similar circumstantial reasons, some observers allege that the Liu-Teng Party organization, which held the upper hand for the period from 1959 to 1965, was responsible for the relatively mod-erate and conciliatory tones in Peking's dealings with some Western nations.[16] This might be. They both have first-hand knowledge about the outside world than either Mao or Lin, having personally visited non-Communist countries at some time in their adult lives. Personally, Liu has been described as "thorough and intellectually able but lacking Mao's warmth and flair"[17] and Teng is known as "adroit, argumentative, articulate and ambitious."[18] But we have no direct evidence indicating the Liu-Teng Party organization was at liberty to make Peking's for-eign policy in that period.

Chou En-lai

Two men, Chou En-lai and his protege Ch'en Yi, have been most directly involved in Peking's foreign affairs throughout the last two decades.[19] It is Chou who must have provided the subtle guidelines for Peking's foreign policy whether Mao or Liu controlled the Party

organization. Among the top leaders in Peking, Chou En-lai is the one
truly sophisticated and widely travelled intellectual. In fact, one might
say that he has had a hand in making the world what it is today. Undisputed and unchallenged chief administrator and master diplomat of
the PRC as well as of the CPC for 35 consecutive years, Chou nego-
tiated with the KMT following the Sian incident in 1936 and signed the
cease-fire between the CPC and the KMT in 1946 which General
Marshall mediated. After 1949, it was Chou who issued policy statements on behalf of the new regime and brought Peking's case to Moscow,
East European capitals, Geneva, Bandung and other parts of Asia and
Africa. And it has been Chou who has directed the off and on Sino-
American talks since 1953.

Chou En-lai's biographer, Kai-yu Hsu, describes him as "the
unique revolutionary in whom the past meets the future, the politico-
military strategist who is most likely to salvage Chinese communism."[20] He has been "always the indispensable number two who came
just in time to save the Party from disintegration and defeat."[21] Chinese observers say that "something of the traditional Chinese Philosophy of yielding, of recognizing ebb and flow as an organic part of any
life" is reflected in him.[22] Foreign visitors shake their heads when
they comment on the cool temperament of Chou and his masterful
art of dealing with other diplomats in the most trying circumstances.
According to Joseph P. Lash, the late Secretary-General of the UN
Dag Hammarskjold supposedly marveled at Chou's subtlety with an
air of disbelief after his visit to Peking in 1955.[23]

To see China regain her status as a first-rate power in the
world, Chou has devoted his life as a planner and a practioner. Personal ambition in Chou's case seems to be equated with the resurgence
of China. It is not wealth or fame. It is remarkable, for instance,
that Chou never has pronounced or written a theory or a doctrine that
bears his name. He is his own man as a pragmatic nationalist. When-
ever Chou is relatively free to steer the course in China's foreign
policy, the outside world probably has a greater chance to expect more
pragmatic and flexible behavior from Peking.

Ch'en Yi

Chou's protege, Ch'en Yi, is also an intellectual with experience
abroad.[24] He first became involved in the Communist revolution
while in Paris with Chou, Teng and others. But his reputation was
made first in the military. Until the ranks were abolished in 1965, he
was a marshall of the Peoples Liberation Army (PLA). Before 1958,
his political post was in the city of Shanghai. In 1955, he went to

Bundung with Chou, but it was only in 1958 that he became Chou's chosen helper in foreign affairs.

Like Chou, Ch'en Yi is a pragmatic nationalist. He is also considered a gradualist who sees real merit in the rules and regulations of an organization. But he does not belong to the Liu-Teng group. Ch'en Yi's talents are many-sided. He is an excellent guerrilla tactician and a poet in addition to being a diplomat. But he too has no personal political theory or doctrine to offer, his strength lies in his strong personal character and the military following he seems to have maintained in his old command units. His style, unlike that of Chou, is relatively brisk and unrestrained.

During the Cultural Revolution, Ch'en Yi came under Red Guard attack on a number of occasions.[25] He sternly criticized the Red Guards and made sarcastic remarks about their sponsors but still escaped public humiliation, thanks to Chou's protection. Whether he retained his position as Foreign Minister after the Ninth Party Congress of 1969 is not clear as yet. His name no longer appears in the roster of the Politburo, although it is still among those of the Central Committee. In May 1969, he was appointed a Vice Chairman of the Military Affairs Committee of the Central Committee.[26] Hong Kong sources indicate that, since late 1968, the responsibilities of the Minsitry of Foreign Affairs have been in the hands of Li Hsien-nien, Vice Premier and Minister of Finance prior to the Cultural Revolution, and Vice Ministers of Foreign Affairs Ch'iao Kuan-hua, Chi P'eng-fei, Han Nien-lung, and Hsu Yi-hsin and several new figures that emerged only after the Cultural Revolution.[27]

Foreign Ministry Personnel

As a group, the Foreign Ministry Personnel, including administrators within the Ministry and field envoys, possessed quite different kinds of talent and experience from the Politburo members. In his analysis of the Ministry in 1960 Klein discovered that this group was significantly lacking in prominent CPC members.[28] Aside from Ch'en Yi, who was a member of the Politburo, only one full and three alternate members of the Eight Central Committee were represented. On the other hand, almost all Vice Ministers, Assistant Ministers, and the division heads had received higher education, many in Western universities, and had extensive experiences abroad as ambassadors. This, Klein suggested, was one of numerous indicators that foreign service personnel were being increasingly drawn from more qualified young echelons. It is known that thorough and systematic inservice training of young foreign service personnel at specialized institutions

such as the Chinese Institute for International Relations has been a
high priority in Peking's educational programs.[29] As a rule, the
Foreign Ministry has the first call on university graduates in the social
sciences, in foreign languages and in area studies. Those employed
by the Foreign Ministry also enjoy a relatively high standard of living
compared to other government functionaries.

Better education and better professional qualifications compete
poorly with the more politically aware and the more loyal for power,
however. Even during the period in which the Liu-Teng Party organization was in charge, the rule of thumb for high level cadre recruitment in the PRC was "red and expert," with "red" coming first. One
of the by-products of such a rule is the relative isolation of Peking's
diplomats stationed in non-Communist countries. Reports from West
European capitals note that Peking's ambassadors have been the most
ostracized among the chiefs of missions. These seasoned diplomats
who possess the necessary training and skill but lack the Party's confidence allegedly have often been dispatched to the field while their
family members remained back home as hostages.[30] In the field, they
are constantly under the watchful eyes of their deputies who are Party
functionaries in charge of intelligence. Frequently, and particularly
during the Cultural Revolution, they were instructed to appear with
their staffs on ceremonial occassions in those pretentiously drab
khakis, with quotations from Chairman Mao in hand. Peking's diplomatic practice also generally forbids extravagant social activities.[31]
Thus, the ambassadors from Peking might be left out by other members
of the diplomatic corps because they are too boring. Conversely, the
ambassadors themselves may impose their self-isolation for reasons
of tight security or a personal desire to avoid embarrassment.

In sum, it seems clear that, in Peking, the individuals and the
group actually holding power tended to be Party-oriented and isolated
from the reality of the outside world while the individuals and the group
that had factual knowledge and understanding of world reality tended
to be mistrusted and without real power. This is a somewhat simplified
yet essentially correct description of the dominant characteristic of
Peking's foreign policy leadership up to 1969. True, Chou En-lai had
been instumental in providing the continuity and perhaps the guidelines
of Peking's conduct of foreign relations. Still, he had never been the
most powerful man in Peking. With all his charm and skills and power,
Chou had always been an advisor to someone in a superior position.
Further, Chou's past behavior suggests that he is not likely to insist
on his own judgment when it is contested no matter how correct it seems
to him. If Chou were given a free hand, he would perhaps stick to the
orthodox Party line instead of letting his personal leanings prevail as

official policy. In all likelihood, the idiosyncratic traits of Mao, the
supreme leader, or those of Liu and Teng when Mao was functionally
absent, would have the greater impact upon the direction and contents
of Peking's foreign policy, despite Chou's prominence in that realm.
Under Chou and Ch'en's administration, implementation of Peking's
foreign policy was in capable hands. However, the inclinations of the
"experts" probably had only limited impact at the foreign policy-making
level throughout the last 20 years.

THE PLACE OF THE UN

Are there signs that idiosyncratic inclinations of Peking's top
leaders lean one way or the other on the question of participation in
the UN? Do the most influential individuals in foreign policy-making
have any strong belief or feelings that tend to favor or shun an international organization like the UN?

In answer, there are pointers to opposite directions. First, the
isolation of the Politburo members, particularly Mao and Lin Piao,
from the outside world tend to point to a negative direction. Prolonged
isolation from the reality of the world outside creates definite possibilities of their misunderstanding and miscalculation about international
politics. These first generation top leaders of Peking, a group of proud,
stubborn and nationalistic individuals, know one way of political suc-
cess--the revolutionary way, the Yenan way. In decision-making, they
tend to look first to this experience for inspiration. They are also
Communist, and so they turn next to Marxism-Leninism. Only last
do they "learn from other countries," i.e., non-Communist countries.
Seasoned China watchers have probably noticed that Peking's propaganda machine--the Peking Review, for example--occasionally printed
an article or an analytical map of world politics under the heading
"The International Conditions Are Excellent," Or "China Has Friends
All Over the World."[32] Such propaganda represents more than just
Peking's realization that proper lies must be issued for domestic
consumption periodically. Nor does it reflect merely the wishful
thinking of Peking's leaders. To this reader, it suggests Peking's
awareness of its own difficulties and its determination to persist in
its own ways. This means, for the question of Peking's adaptation to
the UN, an inclination on the part of Peking's leaders to insist on their
own terms rather than to compromise in favor of terms stipulated by
the UN. Since Mao and his colleagues in the Politburo tend to be isolated from the outside world, their terms might be inaccurate. Hence,
the net outcome may be a tendency toward further isolation and non-
adaptation toward the UN.

On the other hand, if we consider the possible motivations on the part of Peking's decision-makers, the picture becomes blurred again. Before the Cultural Revolution, cohesion among the first generation leaders was an outstanding characteristic. Brought together in the past by a sense of national purpose, they endured together through the hardships of revolutionary struggles. Their cohesion continued after the victory in 1949 and enabled them to function as a united leadership group. Motivated less by personal ambitions or gains than by Marxist-Leninist convictions and, above all, by nationalistic purposes, the foremost consideration of this group of remarkable men is to revive China's splendor and power. This is also their common vulnerable characteristic. Vulnerable, because such a motivation has sometimes blinded them and led them to mistakes, such as the Great Leap Forward. For such a group of intensely nationalistic men, the lure of the permanent seat in the UN Security Council must be a tempting one. Where else can Peking find a readily available, popular world arena to stage international dramas with itself as one of five permanent stars?

These two conflicting inclinations might have made the Politburo members of the CPC a frustrated group, tempted but unable to gain entry for lack of a workable formula. Under such circumstances, the dominant personalities might be expected to exert even greater influence. Mao's defiant instinct might surface, urging a hard line of struggle. Chou might see things differently, but he would probably defer to Mao. The net inclination then would be an adamant if not negative policy toward the UN. If the frustration of the top leaders in Peking is multiplied by the indignation incited by the non-recognition policy of the US and its Western allies, such a hard line might be expected as a natural tendency on the part of the PRC's decision-makers.

What is the place of the UN in Peking's own hierarchy of interests and objectives?

When a nation engages in certain activities to induce, or to adapt to, change in her external enviroment, it does so in order to protect or advance its interests. There are, generally speaking, two kinds of foreign policy interests. National interests are those that will contribute to the survival and betterment of a nation; international interests, those that will enhance the development and improvement of the international community. National interests are rooted in both rational and irrational factors. The rational factors are measured by the physical properties (assets and burdens) of a nation's ecological elements such as geography, demography, technology and economy. The irrational factors embrace a nation's emotional experiences and tendencies such as historical heritage and national temperament. International interests also have two components: those complementing the national interests of a national actor (e.g., interests conveyed by one's own bloc or caucusing group) and those competing against the national interests of a national actor (e.g., interests of universal or regional international organizations that require total or partial self-abnegation on the part of a sovereign member).

These varied interests are not all of the same importance to a nation. Some are vital and must be protected at all costs; others may be guarded only under special conditions and with calculated risks; and still others may require no defense or may even be sacrificed when circumstances so demand.

The decision-makers of a foreign policy system are responsible for making the authoritative determination as to which interest belongs to which category. Such decisions are the objectives that determine the order of priorities in commiting a nation's limited resources. The word "objectives" implies that there is a hierarchy of interests. Conversely, the word "interests" implies the necessity of authoritative decision-making.

While definitive discussion on a nation's foreign policy objectives is beyond the scholar's realistic purview, a general, theoretical speculation is not necessarily a vain effort. If our knowledge about international politics in a nation-state system is an acceptable guide, it seems safe to postulate the following as the normal order of priorities in respect to a given nation's foreign policy interests:

1. rational national interests: those relating to national survival;

2. rational national interests: those contributing to national betterment;

3. irrational national interest: those bringing emotional satisfaction;

4. international interests: those complementing national interest;

5. international interests: those competing against national interests.

This brief analytical framework will serve as a guide for discussing the PRC's foreign policy interests and objectives.

INTERESTS

The rational national interest of the PRC, articulated by many writers, need be summarized only briefly.

Geographically, China has a large territory, conditioned by a wide-ranging climate, a checkerboard-like topography and an uneven endowment of natural resources. She shares a long border line with the USSR, a powerful neighbor who is more often a foe than a friend. Demographically, China has the largest population in the world (four times that of the US), with a fairly homogeneous ethnic or racial composition. Its quality--age distribution, health, education and skills-- however, has not been very satisfactory. The level of development in modern technology is low in China, even though in the last century some

large strides have been made in transportation, communication, and
weapon systems improvement. Economically, the Chinese are predom-
inantly agricultural and still at the subsistence level by comparison
with the advanced economies of the world. These elements indicate
that China is (1) large in size, both in population and territory, and by
any definition, a major actor; (2) agrarian and generally "have-not"
as well as underdeveloped; and (3) Asian-oriented, but having to contend with a very strong neighbour to the north. The PRC's rational
foreign policy interests normally should be those of a nation with these
characteristics.

There is, however, an intervening irrational national interest
dictated by China's historical traditions.[1] The history of China is
both a chronicle of grandeur and a memory of humiliation for its people.
The grandeur of China is recorded in more than 20 centuries of her
primacy over her vassal neighbors. With her ancient culture so
superior to the "barbarian," the Chinese ruling elite became convinced
early in its history that China was the "Middle Kingdom." Their ruler
was the "Son of Heaven" who ruled by the "Mandate of Heaven" all
that was under Heaven's jurisdiction. Such was China's splendor that
many "barbarians," including the few who conquered the territory of
China, took to the Chinese way, boosting the Chinese "superiority complex." But, when faced with the new technological culture of the West
in the nineteenth century, the snobbish Chinese gentry suddenly found
themselves at wits' end. For 100 years, the Chinese people suffered
humiliating experiences at the hands of the Western colonialist powers.
In order to revive their dignity and splendor, the Chinese turned to
emulating the West. Yet their pride as a people of past grandeur also
made them deny their own inferiority. The psychological expression
of this dilemma is a mixture of "foreign worship" and xenophobia.
This traumatic experience of the Chinese people no doubt lives with
all patriotic Chinese. For decades, the heated debate among Chinese
intellectuals was whether China should or should not "Westernize"
herself in order to modernize.

These are the psychological needs China's rulers must try to
satisfy.[2] Whoever fails to answer this deep yearning of the Chinese to
right past wrongs and revive China's national dignity cannot hope to
remain in the position of leadership for long. This emotional interest
is so strong that the possiblity of its occupying a position prior to the
rational interests cannot be ruled out. One might say that, looked at
strictly from the decision-makers' point of view, bringing emotional
satisfaction to the people in this case weighs equally heavily as China's
rational national interest.

As to the international interests of the PRC, proletarian internationalism of the Chinese version entails Peking's support of the
international communist movement. Beyond this, Peking also has a
deep interest in national liberation movements. In its early years,
the international communist movement was the main concern of Peking's leader; in this, they differed to the Soviet Union and performed
the role of a lieutenant within the Communist bloc. During the 1960's,
Peking's main international interest seemed to move to championing
revolutionary activities in the "intermediate zone" of Africa, Asia and
Latin America. It is entirely possible that Peking is now more interested in overthrowing the "establishment" at the world level, which
included the US as well as the USSR, than in promoting the realization
of the othodox communist utopia. If the other Communist countries
are not ready to go along, Peking seems ready to bend Marxism-
Leninism to suit Mao's way, instead of the other way around.

Since China's international interests are revolutionary in nature,
it would seem logical to speculate that sacrificing her sovereign rights
and prerogatives for the sake of comradely international organizations
would be acceptable; supporting status-quo-oriented international
organizations created or operated by the word "establishment" would
have to be ruled out. This has not been a clear-cut rule unequivocally
followed, however. Scanning Peking's action records show that Peking
has been comradely mostly in words and nationalistic in deeds. In this
regard, Peking's behavior seems not strikingly different from others
in similar situations.

OBJECTIVES

Based on these foreign policy interests, what objectives have
the leaders of the PRC decided upon? The following passages suggest
an answer.

> The foreign policy of the PRC is based on the principle of
> protection of the independence, freedom, integrity of ter-
> ritory and sovereignty of the country, upholding lasting
> international peace and friendly cooperation between the
> peoples of all countries, and opposing the imperialist
> policy of aggression and war. (Art. 54, Common Pro-
> gram of the CPPCC (Chinese People's Political Con-
> sultative Conference), September 29, 1949)

> China has already built an indestructible friendship with
> the great USSR and the People's Democracies, and the

friendship between our people and peace-loving people
in all other countries is growing day by day. Such
friendship will be constantly strengthened and broadened.
China's policy of establishing and extending diplomatic
relations with all countries on the principles of equality,
mutual benefit, and mutual respect for each other's
sovereignty and territorial integrity, which has already
yielded success, will continue to be carried out. In international affairs our firm and consistent policy is to strive
for the noble cause of world peace and progress of human-
ity. (Preamble to the Constitution of the PRC, September
20, 1954)

The CPC advocates a foreign policy directed toward the
safeguarding of word peace and the achievement of peaceful coexistence between countries with different systems.
The Party stands for the establishment and development
of diplomatic, economic, and cultural relations between
China and other countries of the world, and for the broadening and strengthening of friendly relations between the
Chinese people and the peoples of all other countries of
the world. The Party is resolutely opposed to any act of
aggression against China by imperialist countries and to
any imperialist plans for a new war. It supports all
efforts made by the peoples and governments of other
countries to uphold peace and promote friendly relations
between nations, and expresses its sympathy for all
struggles in the world against imperialism and colonialism. The Party endeavors to develop and strengthen
China's friendship with all other countries in the camp
of peace, democracy, and socialism, headed by the Soviet
Union; to strengthen the internationalist solidarity of the
proletariat; and to learn from the experiences of the world
communist movement. It supports the struggle of the
Communists, progressives, and the working people of
the whole world for the progress of mankind, and educates
its members and the Chinese people in the spirit of internationalism, as expressed in the slogan "Proletarians of
all lands, unite!" (Preamble to the Constitution of the CPC,
September 26, 1956)

The CPC upholds proletarian internationalism; it firmly
unites with the genuine Marxist-Leninist parties and
groups the world over; unites with the proletariat, the
oppressed people and nations to overthrow imperialism

headed by the United States, modern revisionism with
the Soviet revisionist renegade clique as its center
and the reactionaries of all countries, and to obolish
the system of exploitation of man by man on the globe, so
that all mankind will be emancipated. (Constitution of the
CPC, April 14, 1969, Chapter I, General Program)

These passages, in general, tend to uphold the ranking of interest
stipulated above, although in the last document there is a drastic
deviation in appearance.

Table 2 is an attempt to postulate Peking's foreign policy objectives in order of their importance. In order to ascertain the meaning
of each objective, three examples of concrete goals or programs are
provided in each case.

It is of interest to note that in the Common Program of 1949,
objectives 1, 2, 3 and 7 in Table 2 were separately enumerated and
4, 5 and 6 were not mentioned. This was perhaps an indication of the
weakness and uncertainty on the part of Peking's leadership at that
time. As the regime gained in confidence, it began to stress objectives
4 and 5 (the principles of equality, mutual benefit and mutual respect,
etc.) as the 1954 state Constitution attests. The same trend continued,
and by 1956, the Constitution of the Party was clearly emphasizing
objective 6.

The passage cited from the 1969 Party Constitution deserves
special analysis because it appears to deviate from our general scheme
in two respects: (1) there is no direct reference to objectives 1
through 5 at all; and (2) objective 6 seems to have been equated with
objective 7. One explanation for this curious change is that it was a
tactical maneuver by the Mao-Lin forces. Richard Solomon, for instance, argues that Peking's continuing support to wars of national
liberation in Vietnam and elsewhere, its calculated hostility toward
the USSR and its verbal offensive that seems to take on the entire world,
are all "the embodiment of the Lin-Mao approach to placing foreign
relations in the service of China's domestic political process."[3] At
the time the 1969 Party Constitution was adopted, the internal leadership crisis was so serious that this explanation seems plausible. As
Solomon puts it, "as the stability of Mao's domestic political position
has decreased, the claims made for the universal acceptance and
validity of his doctrines have concurrently increased."[4] In other words,
the international interests were played up, and the national interest
played down, as a deliberate measure to boost the position of the

TABLE 2

The PRC's Foreign Policy Interests,
Objectives and Goals
(in probable order of importance)

INTERESTS	OBJECTIVES (Abstract Priorities)	GOALS (Concrete Programs)
A. Rational National Interests: Survival (Geographical, demographical, technological, economic)	1. National freedom (independence and sovereignty)	1. a) Abolition of all unequal treaties b) Diplomatic recognition by other nations c) Membership in the ICO's
	2. National unification (territorial integrity)	2. a) Liberation of Taiwan b) Delineation of boundaries c) Protection from foreign encroachment
	3. National security (freedom from aggression)	3. a) Mutual defense pact (with USSR, 1950) b) Removal of American military presence from Asia c) Creation of a buffer zone along the orbit of China
B. Rational National Interests: Betterment (geographical, demographical, technological, economic)	4. National power (modernization and development)	4. a) Trade expansion b) Cultural exchange with as many countries as feasible c) Import of technical know-how
C. Irrational National Interests: Emotional Needs (historical traditions and experiences)	5. National prestige (foreign respect)	5. a) Eradication of all strains of humiliation b) Acceptance as an equal by international community c) Deference by others as a major power
D. International Interests: Complementary (fraternal socialists, fellow "have-not")	6. Revolutionary change in international system	6. a) Better relations with other members of Communist bloc b) Propagation of the Chinese model c) Spreading national liberation movements
E. International Interests: Competitive (universal community)	7. World peace and human progress	7. a) Socialist international law b) Socialist international organizations c) General and complete disarmament

Mao-Lin faction in the domestic power struggle. That is why objectives
1 through 5 have been left out even though the related goals have not
been achieved. The passage quoted, therefore, cannot be considered
as the accurate description of the PRC's foreign policy objectives even
as of 1969. This conclusion is confirmed when Lin Piao's report, which
was adopted by the Ninth National Party Congress the same day as was
the new Party Constitution, is read with care. In it, Lin still adheres
to "the Five Principles of mutual respect for territorial integrity and
sovereignty, mutual non- aggression, non-interference in each other's
internal affairs, equality and mutual benefit, and peaceful coexistence"
as the basis of China's policy toward "countries having different social
systems." [5]

This same explanation also sheds light on the other deviant
aspect--the equation of international revolutionary movements with
world peace and human progress. Mao's doctrines are primarily
formulae for national anti-feudal, anti-imperialist struggles. To
claim universal validity of Mao's doctrines is the same as propagating
world-wide national liberation movements. Mao also justifies his doctrines as "progressive." The universal validity of Mao's doctrines,
therefore, will necessarily have to be justified on the same grounds,
i.e., toward the abolition of the system of exploitation of man by man
on the globe. The sequential relationship between revolutionary change
and human progress is thus projected onto the world picture by logical
necessity. That is why Lin Piao's aforementioned verbiage painstakingly repeated the importance of vigilance in Peking's effort to
champion the revolutionary struggle against the US and the USSR.

THE PLACE OF THE UN

The UN, as an objective in itself, belongs to the seventh, i.e.,
the last of Peking's priorities. What the UN aspires to achieve, Peking has repeatedly echoed in words. If Peking were genuinely interested in working toward world peace and human progress, and if the
UN and what it represents were judged worthy of its loyalty and support,
then Peking would do its share in strengthening the UN.

However, it must be remembered that the UN is essentially a
competing, not complementary international interest. This is true
for Peking as it is for most other nations of the world. Peking's
world view and its value system dictate that the ideals of the UN
should not be downtrodden or discarded. But Peking's priorities put
the ideals of UN at the bottom, i.e., there should be general verbal
support but minimum materials commitment for it.

This is not to say that the UN would receive little material support from Peking under all circumstances. If the UN per se as an objective belongs to the last of Peking's priorities, the UN as a policy instrument is an entirely different story. As a policy instrument, the UN may serve the PRC in relation to the first five, and perhaps even the sixth, of Peking's objectives. Whether this is so depends upon Peking's foreign policy means--capabilities, will and strategical conceptions.

Like aims, means of foreign policy also have input and output aspects. Means-input is power, which has two components: objective capabilities and subjective will. Means-output includes strategy and tactics. Power is the substance of means; strategy and tactics are the procedures of means. The test for the former is its feasibility; the test for the latter is its efficiency. These are the two sides of the "means" of policy implementation.

CAPABILITIES AND WILL

Were the PRC to adapt to the UN, would that add to or subtract from (strengthen or weaken) her foreign policy capabilities and will?

The capabilities of a nation denote the military, economic and political means that her government can mobilize in order to induce changes in, or to adapt to challenges from, her external environment. These means are derived from that nation's geo-demographic resource base, the political and socio-psychological capacity of her population for collective action and her ability to contract foreign alliances.[1]

The will of a nation is the conscious, self-directed and persisting determination of her people and government to obtain her goals in the face of resistance. Such a determination is usually expressed in the autonomous, self-conscious nature of a nation's pronouncements in the clarity, lucidity and directness of her demands upon others, in the frequency, saliency, and continuity of her action, and in the risks taken and costs incurred in the process of trying to obtain her goals.[2]

49

Capabilities and will thus constitute the objective and subjective components of what have conventionally been referred to as "national power" in international politics.

Available data on the capabilities and will of the PRC reveal (1) that there has been a substantial discrepancy between Peking's objectives and its capabilities, and (2) that, in the short run, Peking's leaders seem to be trying to substitute the subjective will of the Chinese people for what China lacks in objective capabilities. The PRC is, as Robert North puts it, "the only underdeveloped totalitarian major power."3

Without making an extensive analysis, which is beyond the purview of this study, the PRC's strengths and weaknesses can be summarized briefly to prove the point. Table 3 lists some of the most important quantitative aspects of capabilities of select countries, as of 1966. A study of the table indicates the following:

1. The PRC had "man power" estimated at 772,000,000, which is over three times that of the USSR and nearly four times that of the US. Except for this, in all other columns, the PRC lags behind the other major powers.

2. In absolute figures, the PRC's GNP is barely 10.8 percent that of the US and 22.4 percent that of the USSR. It trails behind four other countries: West Germany, UK, France, and Japan.

3. In per capita terms, the PRC's GNP estimated at $104 is one of the lowest in the world, falling even behind South Vietnam and the two Koreas. The distance between the PRC's standard of living and those of the US and the USSR is such that it is practically impossible to imagine China ever catching up with her two arch-rivals.

4. In military expenditures, the PRC spent over 8 percent of her total GNP, about the same percentage as the US, but the absolute value came to just 10.2 percent that of the US and 13.9 percent that of the USSR.

5. Despite her large population, her regular military personnel of 2.5 million was substantially less than the Russian 3.165 million and American 3.094 million.

6. The PRC's foreign aid was a mere token sum, compared to that of every other major nation. This clearly indicates her capability limitation.

TABLE 3

Capabilities Data of Selected Countries, 1966

COUNTRY	POPULATION (1,000's)	GNP Total (Mil. $)	GNP $ per capita	MILITARY EXPENDITURES Total (Mil. $)	MILITARY EXPENDITURES percent of GNP	ARMED FORCES (1,000's)	ARMED FORCES percent of Pop.	FOREIGN AID (Mil. $ given)
1. US	196,920	747,600	3,796	63,283	8.5	3,094	1.6	4,011
2. USSR	233,105	357,000	1,531	47,000	NA	3,165	1.4	300E
3. UK	54,744	105,310	1,924	6,150	5.8	424	.8	610
4. France	49,400	101,380	2,052	5,300	5.2	523	1.1	823
5. Japan	98,865	97,480	986	933	1.0	246	.2	310
6. Germany, W.	60,076	119,580	1,990	4,950	4.1	450	.7	595
7. Germany, E.	17,067	28,300	1,658	1,100	3.9	122	.7	NA
8. PRC	772,000E	80,000E	104E	6,500E	8.1	2,500	.3	80E
9. ROC	13,326	3,138	235	350	11.2	544	4.1	-65
10. Korea, N.	12,400	2,900E	234E	225E	7.8	368	3.0	NA
11. Korea, S.	29,086	3,822	131	150	3.9	572	2.0	-215
12. Vietnam, N.	19,500	1,500E	77E	300E	20.0	350	1.8	NA
13. Vietnam, S.	16,543	2,086E	126E	302	14.5	565	3.4	-510
14. Albania	1,914	700E	366E	70E	10.0	38	2.0	NA

NA = Not Available

E = Estimate

Source: US Arms Control and Disarmament Agency, Economic Bureau, World Military Expenditures and Related Data, Calendar Year 1966 and Summary Trends, 1962–67. Research Report 68-2, December 1968, 9–13.

7. Finally, even if all that her allies--Albania, North Vietnam, North Korea--could muster were put under Peking's command, the PRC's total capabilities would still be relatively limited.

Compared with the objectives and goals outlined in the previous section, these figures leave little doubt that Peking's capabilities are inadequate. Further investigations on qualitative aspects of the indexes do not alter this basic picture significantly. Militarily, it is true that the PRC also has a tremendous number of militia. But it is also true that her men and arms are primarily land-oriented; her air and naval forces are rather negligible and antiquated compared to those of the two superpowers.[4]

It might be argued that Peking's military strength dwells in the combination of the deterrent capability of its small but growing strategic (i.e., nuclear) wing and the protracted systems of combat for which its conventional forces have been trained. As of this writing, it is unrealistic to speak of Peking's strategic deterrence against the two superpowers. Nor can the PRC boast any real offensive capability against either the US or the USSR in the forseeable future.[5]

Economically, the picture is gloomy, partially because of the population pressure. In per capita terms, the country has little chance of quick and substantial improvement. The problems of illiteracy, poor health and low productivity must be solved. Multiply all that with the dimension of size, and the job ahead becomes almost beyond solution. The efforts of the Peking regime in the last two decades to overcome such difficulties and to push for a "great leap forward" have been extraordinary and the means employed have been drastic as well as innovative. But economists generally agree that, after initial success, the PRC suffered serious setbacks in the late 1950's and early 1960's so that the peak of production figures in both agriculture and industry achieved in 1958 has not been surpassed as late as 1966. Almost all commentators who have researched the PRC's material sources conclude that Peking's capabilities in the international scene have been, are and will be limited relative to its ambitions.[6]

When faced with an imbalance between objectives and capabilities, a nation's leadership has three alternatives: adjust its objectives, or its capabilities, or both. Peking's leaders seem to have opted to increase the PRC's capabilities rather than to scale down her objectives. Since capabilities cannot be increased at the desired speed, Peking's remedy in the meantime is to find a substitute in "will." Put differently, this means Peking is to avoid economic-military confrontation with any enemy who is more powerful than the PRC and to resort to political-psychological struggle instead.

Since Peking's experiences in the past had time and again proven
that a revolutionary force that was weak in material strength but believed in its own righteousness and had the will to fight could achieve
final victory over an apparently stronger enemy, it would seem the
application of this formula in foreign policy is a natural step for Peking.
Witness this quotation of the "paper tiger" thesis from Mao Tse-tung:

> The atom bomb is a paper tiger that the US reactionaries
> use to scare people. It looks terrible, but in fact it isn't.
> Of course, the atom bomb is a weapon of mass slaughter,
> but the outcome of a war is decided by the people, not by
> one or two new types of weapon.
>
> All reactionaries are paper tigers. . . . From a long-term
> point of view, it is not the reactionaries but the people who
> are really powerful. In Russia, before the February Revo-
> lution in 1917, which side was really strong? On the sur-
> face the tsar was but he was swept away by a single gust
> of wind in the February Revolution. . . . Wasn't Hitler
> once considered very strong? But history proved that
> he was a paper tiger. So was Mussolini, so was Japanese
> imperialism. . . .
>
> Take the case of China. We have only millet plus rifles to
> rely on, but history will finally prove that our millet plus
> rifles is more powerful than Chiang Kai-shek's aeroplanes
> plus tanks. Although the Chinese people still face many
> difficulties and will long suffer hardships from the joint
> attacks of US imperialism and the Chinese reactionaries,
> the day will come when these reactionaries are defeated
> and we are victorious. The reason is simply this: the
> reactionaries represent reaction, we represent progress.[7]

This "paper tiger" thesis is a good example of Peking's maneuver
to substitute political-psychological struggle for military-economic
confrontation in the international scene. It also spells out the formula
for making one's "will" work in place of capabilities to win the final
victory. This formula seems to have four conditions: (1) a just (progressive) cause; (2) the support of the people (the minds of men); (3)
the determination to wage a protracted struggle; and (4) correct
application of strategic principles and tactical techniques. In short,
history favors he who possesses these four conditions, even if his
initial capabilities are meager.

As far as Peking's leaders are concerned, there is no question that the PRC represents a progressive force in the revolutionary struggle against the imperialists of the world. Confident that their cause is supported by the Chinese masses (under their leadership, the Chinese have again become a proud nation after a century of humiliation), they seem to believe that the people of the world will also side with them in due course. The problem then is one of leadership; leadership that will see to it that the determination to wage a protracted struggle is a persistent one, and that no mistakes are made in the application of strategies and tactics. For a time, the Kremlin was expected to provide that leadership. Now, Peking sees itself as the real candidate-- the Soviets having turned "modern revisionist." This is another explanation for the intensification of Peking's verbal offensive in recent years--Peking seems to be playing its self-appointed role as the new legitimate leader of the international revolutionary movement.

THE PLACE OF THE UN

Were the PRC to accommodate itself to the UN, would that add to or subtract from her foreign policy capabilities? Also would that strengthen or weaken her will? In what ways?

Militarily, in all likelihood, accommodating to the UN would have no direct impact upon Peking's capabilities. Presumably, Peking would be asked to support the UN system of collective security. Legally, should the PRC happen to become a victim of armed aggression, Peking might resort to the UN and ask for the latter's intervention on its behalf. In that case, Peking's capabilities would have been extended through the UN. The sort of speculation, however, stretches one's imagination beyond reason in the present context. In any case, the UN would be utterly helpless when faced with a delinquent powerful enough to take on the PRC. The UN forces as an extension of Peking's military capabilities, therefore, are only a mirage.

On the other hand, as an active member, the PRC might be subject to UN members' inquiry because it refused to sign the agreements of nuclear test ban and nuclear non-proliferation. That is to say, Peking might be put on the defensive in the world arena. Judging from the French experiences, however, that would be no more than added inconveniences with which Peking might have to deal. It is certainly conceivable that Peking could continue its nuclear development as long as no preventive attack against it became a real threat. UN inquiries would not actually lead to the curtailment of Peking's own nuclear policy.

Undoubtedly there would also be greater pressure to draw Peking into negotiations on disarmament and arms control once Peking entered the UN, and Peking might have to oblige.[8] This might be both a relief and a burden. It would be a relief for Peking to know that such important decisions were not being made without its participation. It would be a burden for Peking to have to disclose information regarding its own capabilities and intentions. Judging from Peking's objectives (to rival the US and the USSR, become a superpower and lead the international revolutionary movement) and its realization of the need for real military hardware, we must conclude that Peking would not accede to any international agreement that would perpetuate the nuclear monopoly or superiority of the US and the USSR and prevent its own ascendance to a superpower position. This again, is a matter whose outcome will not be affected by Peking's presence in the UN.

Economically, the PRC might have more to gain from participation in the UN. There would be some costs. As a permanent member of the Security Council, the PRC might be required to contribute a large share to the UN's regular and special operational budget. But that would be a calculable sum from year to year. There would be added diplomatic costs, but this too would not be prohibitive in any case. The benefits, on the other hand, could be both tangible and intangible and would have far-reaching repercussions. Such benefits could come either from aid received or trade expanded.

UN aid might be in the form of grants, loans or technical assistance.[9] Grants and loans might come from the United Nations Development Program (the Special United Nations Fund For Economic Development), the World Bank Group (the International Bank for Reconstruction and Development, the International Development Agency, and the International Finance Corporation), and the Asian Development Bank. Technical assistance might come from the UN's established programs such as the United Nations Development Program (the Expanded Program of Technical Assistance), the Operational, Executive and Administrative Personnel Service, the United Nations Institute for Training and Research, the United Nations Conference on the Application of Science. Technology for the Benefit of the Less Developed Areas, the Worldwide Food Program, UNICEF as well as the many specialized agencies, including the Food and Agricultural Organization, the World Health Organization, the World Meteorological Organization, the International Civil Aviation Organization, UNESCO, and so on. Just listing these possibilities is enough to suggest the magnitude of what the UN system has to offer. The sum may be small compared to China's needs, but China can use all that the UN system is able to provide.

However, there are indications that UN aid might not be very attractive to the Peking government. To begin with, Peking's attitude toward the whole question of foreign aid is somewhat unusual. Lin Piao wrote in his celebrated article on people's war:

> The Chinese people enjoyed the support of other peoples in winning both the War of Resistance against Japan and the People's Liberation War, and yet victory was mainly the result of the Chinese people's own efforts. . . .
>
> Comrade Mao Tse-tung said, . . . "We hope for foreign aid but cannot be dependent on it; we depend on our own efforts, on the creative power of the whole army and the entire people."[10]

These words were written for the benefit of the North Vietnamese after the Tonkin Gulf incident in 1965, and referred primarily to political struggles. But the theme of self-reliance is also applicable to economic development; in fact it is a doctrine repeated a hundred times since 1961.[11] As it exalts the virtue of "self-reliance," Peking is not likely to capitulate to the lure of foreign aid, even UN aid.

Next, as a giver of foreign aid, Peking has always paid meticulous attention to assuring that the give and take does not in any way violate the principles of equality and mutual benefit. This was precisely spelled out in the Eight Principles of Economic Aid that Chou En-lai presented to his hosts during his 1964 African tour.[12] But, in practice, such principles have been closely adhered to by few aid donors, if any. Should Peking become a recipient of UN aid, would that not require Peking's compliance, if only tacitly, with the wishes of the donor nations? If so, would the national pride of the Communist Chinese, still fresh from wounds inflicted by Western colonialism and imperialism, permit such disgrace, particularly if the donors were the United States or even the Soviet Union? Probably not.

Third, as mentioned already, the PRC has been an aid donor for a number of years. Accepting UN aid might not flatter the ego of the Chinese. Would that not be an admission of the PRC's underdeveloped status? Would that not tarnish the image of a regime aspiring to the leadership position in the international revolutionary movement? Mao Tse-tung and his teachings are quite tolerant and flexible; but these are real considerations that Peking would have to think hard about.

If there is doubt with respect to the attraction of UN aid, the
same is not true in the area of trade expansion. The prospects would
be mostly positive for Peking. Presumably, the UN embargo against
the PRC would be lifted, and should Peking will it, trade expansion
would be encouraged. Peking would no doubt participate in the workings
of the UN Conference on Trade and Development, the Economic Commission for Asia and the Far East, and possibly the General Agreement
on Tariffs and Trade. The International Monetary Fund might come
to Peking's aid should the need arise. Through trade expansion, both
in volume and type, and perhaps in direction also, the PRC would have
improved opportunities to accelerate as well as regulate her economic
development. True, Peking has been able to expand its foreign trade
with Japan, West Germany and other countries to some extent. That
fact would not reduce the attraction of more markets and more sup-
pliers of technological know-how for Peking.

Politically, participating in the UN activities might both facilitate
and hamper Peking's development of capabilities and will in various
ways. From the outset, the UN would probably enhance Peking's
prestige, especially if Peking were awarded the Chinese seat in the
Security Council. More importantly, there is the possibility, though
remote, that after Peking's entrance, the "third world" under a new
champion might gain substantial control over the General Assembly.
Should that happen, Peking would have organized an "international
united front" with relative ease. Such an achievement would serve
Peking well, as shall be seen in the next section.

On the other hand, the UN could become an onerous factor for
the PRC's prestige. The PRC was conspicuously stigmatized by the
official condemnation of the Security Council as an "aggressor" during
the Korean War. Whether this loss of prestige might well not have
occurred, at least not to the same extent, were the PRC present in the
UN with the opportunity to engage in diplomatic activities prior to
and during the Korean War, is a question on which one can only speculate. UN practice since tends to suggest that the use of the word
"aggression" was unusually severe, and was perhaps an exceptional
case.

Finally, participation in UN activities might also strengthen or
weaken Peking's will. In a sense, the UN as an arena is a testing
ground of national wills. Peking might be subject to hardship, or it
might be treated to sweets within the UN system. Each experience
might contribute to modification within the thinking and feelings of
Peking's decision-makers. There have been opposing opinions concerning the possible effects of participation upon Peking's behavior.[13]

Some believe that Peking's outlook, aims and strategies would not be altered, immediately or in the long run. Their arguments are familiar: that Mao and company's communist ideology would remain whether they became active in the UN or not; that Peking's external aggressiveness has been a measure to divert attention from domestic conflicts and would continue as long as it served the function of rallying the Chinese masses for Peking's masters; and that British and French recognition of the Peking government had not brought conciliatory policies from that government. There was even a claim that if the PRC were able to take the Chinese seat in the UN without first purging herself of the sins for which it had been condemned by the world organization, Peking would interpret that as a recognition of its just position and become even more intransigent.[14]

Others think the opposite would be more likely. They suggest that the outrage expressed by the Chinese government in Peking was understandable since China had been victimized by foreigners for a century; that Peking's bad manners or aggressiveness were heightened because it had been declared an outlaw and shunned by the self-appointed protectors of international virtue; and that acceptance by the family of nations as an equal and wider contact with the outside world in good faith would gradually mellow Peking's sense of indignation and help its adjustment toward the rest of the world.[15]

This debate is likely to continue indefinitely. Both points of view have strong arguments. For the present, we can only point out that the stronger root of Mao's will has been a sense of rebellion rather than a crusading spirit, even though the latter is by no means weak. One might speculate about the possible weakening of will when the second and third generation leaders succeed to power in Peking, but that would be little more than academic exercise before the dust from the Cultural Revolution settles.

STRATEGY AND TACTICS

In analyzing Peking's formula of substituting will for capabilities, Mao's emphasis on the importance of strategy and tactics has already been mentioned. The question now is: Would the UN fit into Peking's strategy and tactics? Or, more specifically: In what ways could the UN be a service or a disservice to Peking strategically and tactically?

Strategy has been defined as "the science and art of employing the political, economic, psychological and military forces of a nation or group of nations to afford the maximum support to adopted policies in peace or war." Tactics denote the science and art of "disposing and maneuvering forces in combat."[16] In contrast to strategy, tactics involve action or means of less magnitude, in more limited theaters, over shorter spans of time.

The starting point in understanding Peking's concepts of strategy and tactics is the realization that Mao Tse-tung and his pupils are all believers in "the people's war." A chapter of Quotations from Chairman Mao Tse-tung, entitled "People's War," starts with this flat statement written in 1934: The revolutionary war is a war of the masses; it can be waged only by mobilizing the masses and relying on them.[17]

This is a profound declaration. It means that a revolutionary war is not an imperial war, a colonial war, a dynastic war or any other kind of war that does not mobilize and rely on the masses; the strategy and tactics to be applied are unique. It means that a revolutionary war is necessarily a protracted one; to mobilize the suppressed and intimidated masses, organize them and directly involve them in the revolutionary struggle is a task that cannot be accomplished quickly. It also means that a revolutionary war is one to be won by more than just military means; the revolutionary forces can count on a just cause, the dedication of its cadres, and the manpower of the masses, but few military troops and little equipment until the last stage of the struggle.

The grand scheme of the people's war is "the establishment of rural revolutionary base areas and the encirclement of the cities from the countryside."[18] The rationale is that the masses scatter around the countryside while the oppressors occupy the cities, and that the oppressors do not have effective control over the countryside because they neither can nor care to. To carry out this grand scheme, Mao's revolutionaries rely on three "magic weapons"--the united front, the people's army and the party leadership--and employ the special strategy and tactics developed by Mao in line with the doctrine of protracted war.

The doctrine of protracted war stipulates that the revolutionary forces of the people, by fighting a prolonged war with political-psychological and economic-military means, can effect a gradual but decisive change in the relative power (both will and capabilities) between themselves and the oppressive forces of the status quo, and thereby achieve the final victory.[19] A protracted war is, by Maoist analysis, necessarily and "people's war." It is a lever for the people's revolution. It is the people's final recourse: "to counter war against the people by people's war."[20] Its real spirit is caught in a concise commentary by Lin Piao: You fight in your way and we fight in ours; we fight when we can win and move away when we can't.[21] Lin called this brief statement the "masterly summary of the stragegy and tactics of people's war," and attributed it to Comrade Mao.

One of the most important guiding principles of protracted war is that of "one against ten and ten against one." This principle refers to the combined application of strategy and tactics. As Mao put it,

> . . . strategically we should despise all our enemies, but tactically we should take them all seriously. This also means that we must despise the enemy with respect to the whole, but that we must take him seriously with respect to each and every concrete question. . . . Strategically, we take the eating of a meal lightly--we know we can finish it. But actually we eat it mouthful by mouthful. It is impossible to swallow an entire banquet in one gulp.[22]

The enemy can be and should be despised strategically because the law on contradiction indicates the fundamental weakness of the static, oppressive elements when faced with the dynamic, progressive forces. When a revolution spreads out, "a single spark can start a prairie fire." In other words, the enemy as a whole is politically weak, even though its military capabilities seem strong. The revolutionary should not and need not overestimate the strength of the enemy and underestimate the strength of the people. Failure to despise the enemy is "impotent thinking" and must be rooted out. This is psychological warfare; hence "to pit one against ten."

On the other hand, it is dangerous for the revolutionary to become dizzy with enthusiasm and forget to study the art of struggle. He should not pin his hopes for victory on the "sensibleness" of the dying enemy; for the nature of the enemy is "to conduct a last desperate struggle against the revolutionary forces." The revolutionary forces must not only dare to fight, but also have organization and discipline and be prepared to engage the enemy economically and militarily and win. "One mistake can lead to disaster." All efforts must be made to ensure that no mistake takes place. This "prudent thinking" requires realism, patience and restraint. Hence, "to pit ten against one."[23]

All these concepts--the people's war, the grand scheme of "surrounding cities from the countryside," the principle of "one against ten and ten against one," the strategy and tactics of protracted war-- are also valid in "the proletarian socialist world revolution." According to Lin Piao,

Wherever there is armed aggression and suppression by
imperialism and its lackeys, there are bound to be people's
wars against aggression and oppression. . . . This is an
objective law independent of the will of either the US imperialists or the Khrushchev revisionists.[24]

There is, in Peking's view, an "international people's war."
Further,

Taking the entire globe, if North America and Western
Europe can be called "the cities of the world," then Asia,
Africa and Latin America constitute "the rural areas of
the world." . . . In the final analysis, the whole cause of
world revolution hinges on the revolutionary struggles
of the Asian, African and Latin American peoples who
make up the overwhelming majority of the world's
population. . . . [25]

This is a direct implication that the grand scheme of encircling the
cities from rural bases, though tailor-made originally for the Chinese
revolution, can also be a grand scheme for the "international revolutionary movement." Once such a grand scheme is adopted, the
strategy and tactics thereof also apply. The scheme, doctrines,
principles, and precepts discussed in this section are parts of a coher-
ent whole; they can be combined differently and employed flexibly
but they relate to each other.

THE PLACE OF THE UN

The UN as an arena could be the most useful theater for Peking's
political-psychological operations, strategically and tactically.
Strategically, Peking could "despise the enemies," damage their
prestige, and undermine their will by means of propagandistic attacks
against them in the UN forum. This could be done by a member of
the minority within the UN assembly quite effectively. It has been
pointed out that, in a ten-year period between 1948-58, almost all the
debates over "threats to peace," "intervention," "imperialism" and
"rights to self-determination" in the UN dealt with problems and
tensions arising primarily within the non-Communist world and between the Western powers and the colonial areas. By comparison,
Soviet violations of the East European peoples' rights of self-determination received little attention from UN members. This is what
Strausz-Hupe and his co-authors have called "monopoly of the initiative" by the Communists.[26] Regular readers of Peking Review would
have little difficulty imagining the possible contents and styles of

speeches that Peking's delegates might deliver at the UN should they
choose this route.

In the course of the international protracted war, the UN could
be utilized to help regulate the pace of the revolution's strategic
defense during the initial stage by means of well-timed calls for UN
intervention, cease-fire, negotiations and so forth. It could also be
made to facilitate the organization and expansion of the international
united front with proper manipulation, e.g., through new caucusing
groups, or ad hoc committees organized to deal with matters of concern to the potential members of the front. During the second stage,
the UN could be the place to "tip the balance" to the revolutionary
camp's favor by political-psychological assault upon the enemies at
the pivotal time. During the last stage, the UN could become the
organ where the victorious international revolutionary movement
would acquire its legitimate status. These uses of the UN are possibilities that carry with them some values for strategical consideration.
If Peking's assumption that an anti-imperialist united front could be
organized within the Socialist bloc and in the Afro-Asian world along
the lines suggested by itself was an error, as David Mozingo has suggested, Peking would probably have discovered that error sooner
through contacts and observations in and about the UN.27

Concurrently, Peking could try to use the UN's facilities as a
market place to advertise "Mao Tse-tung Thought," etc. But this
would be more difficult. Mao Tse-tung Thought supposedly contains
a universally valid formula of national liberation. It would be a pack-
aged commodity that Peking could sell as the alternative to what its
"enemies" had been offering to the less-fortunate and unsatiated nations
of the world. Marketing such a commodity through the UN would give
that commodity a stamp of legitimacy. Whether Peking could do this,
however, would depend on how liberal the UN's rules of the game were.
Since the UN was established essentially to bolster the international
status quo, rather than to instigate radical changes, its rules might
not facilitate the marketing of a revolutionary ideology, particularly
one with the Mao Tse-tung brand.

Tactically, there could be several advantageous ways of utilizing
the arena of the UN. Peking could use the UN to engage in intelligence,
subversive and propaganda operations, broaden its contacts and support, gain diplomatic experiences and play its "mini-max" negotiating
game. The UN could be a "barometer" for measuring international
climate, for measuring Peking's world status, and for measuring the
sentiments of the members and potential members of the international
united front. Sometimes it could also be a convenient scapegoat for

Peking. These uses of the UN are possible not because the UN has goals of world peace and order, but because it is a quasi-universal international organization. There seem to be no special reasons why it could not also serve the PRC in the ways it served the Soviet Union and other nations. In other words, the instrumental value of the UN has nothing to do with constitutional compatibility or incompatibility between the UN and its members.

But, there also would be a tactical impediment for Peking. To use the UN, Peking would have to play the UN's game. This means it might have to account for its behavior in cases such as the Sino-Indian border conflicts, the Taiwan Straits crises and the suppression of Tibetan rebellions. In other words, Peking would be constantly in the limelight of world public opinion. Any blunder on its part might cause disillusionment among the developing nations of Asia, Africa and Latin America. In this sense, the UN could become a restraint on the PRC's freedom of action.

Overall, the UN as an arena would have a positive place in Peking's strategic and tactical considerations. The same would not be true with regard to the UN as an actor. The unique nature of the UN would present new problems to Peking because the proper place for such an actor would be quite ambiguous. The UN as an actor would belong to neither the cities nor the countryside. It would be hard to treat it as a part of the "international united front"; it would be just as difficult not to treat it so. Changes are that it would remain an anti-revolutionary actor until such times when the membership composition within it underwent such fundamental change that, as a result, the organization turned from an anti-revolutionary into a neutral or even a pro-revolutionary one. In essence, then, the strategical and tactical utilities of the UN would depend entirely upon the actual internal make-up of that organization. The logical step for Peking, therefore, would be to welcome UN the arena but to shun UN the actor under the existing situation.

SUMMARY OBSERVATIONS OF PART I

The last four chapters have delved into various parts of the PRC's foreign policy system--basic world outlook, decision-making structure, aims, and means--in order to discover the place of the UN in Peking's foreign policy. The findings are as follows:

1. In terms of Peking's world outlook, the UN as an arena is a "contradiction" in itself. For Peking, that arena may or may not be

preferable depending on who runs it and what rules are applied. The
UN as an actor may become a friend or a foe of Peking or remain
neutral depending on how its internal contradiction is resolved.

   2. There is no evidence suggesting that, prior to 1966, Peking's
foreign policy apparatus had an inbred bias either for or against the
UN. But Peking's decision-makers might have had some idiosyncratic
inclinations toward an adamant position regarding the UN.

   3. In Peking's foreign policy aims, the UN as an objective in
itself occupies the last place in Peking's priorities. But the UN as a
policy instrument may serve Peking in various ways for the attainment
of its foreign policy objectives, and, therefore, may be of great value.

   4. For Peking's foreign policy means, strong possibilities exist
that, were Peking an accepted active participant, the UN would be
beneficial to Peking in both tangible and intangible ways. In terms of
capabilities and will, the UN would have little impact on Peking's
development of military capabilities, although it might create some
inconveniences. Economically, the UN would contribute to the expansion of Peking's foreign trade and might provide some material and
technical aids. Politically, the UN might enhance Peking's world
prestige, strengthen its will and even facilitate its "international
united front" policy. In terms of strategy and tactics, the UN as an
arena might be the most useful theater for Peking's political-psychological operations. The UN might be all that the Soviet Union had
found it to be and more. It might be a propaganda forum, a channel
of intelligence, a market place to advertise Mao Tse-tung Thought,
a mechanism for regulating the "international protracted war," a
diplomatic center, a "barometer" for measuring the PRC's world
status, and so on. Peking might lose some of its freedom of action
were it to operate through the UN but the net advantages far outweigh
this loss. However, the UN as an actor might be strategically and
tactically something new for Peking to tackle. Its utilities for Peking
would perhaps depend upon its actual internal make-up. Peking
would, therefore, be inclined to shun UN the actor but welcome UN
the arena under conceivable situations.

   Overall, our findings lead to the conclusion that the UN's place
in the PRC's foreign policy system can be quite important and favorable. Peking's leaders may be inclined to take an intransigent position vis-a-vis the UN, if and when the UN as an actor leans toward
an anti-PRC position. But, in many ways, the PRC as a system is in
a position to benefit from the UN as an arena. In other words, the
UN could appear to Peking as it did to the Kremlin as observed by
Alexander Dallin.28 The contention that the UN and the PRC are two
incompatible systems is, therefore, too simplistic a view that should
not be accepted as a correct explanation of Peking's seemingly hostile

attitude toward the UN. Our own findings are less simplistic, although they are not more than educated guesses. They are hopefully <u>educated</u> guesses. These findings, crude and uncertain as they are, should provide a more realistic rationale for explaining Peking's words and actions regarding the UN and thus take us a step closer to an understanding of Peking's true attitudes and views.

II

EMPIRICAL ANALYSIS: PEKING'S CHANGING ATTITUDES AND APPROACHES TOWARD THE UN

In Part I, Peking's foreign policy system was analyzed in general in order to find out why Peking's attitude toward the UN deviated from the generally favorable pattern displayed by other nations. It was found that the explanation is not one of systemic incompatibility between the UN and the PRC. But the analysis in Part I has been in gross terms. It was assumed, for instance, that Peking's attitude toward the UN has always been deviant from the attitudes of other nations. That is not a correct assumption. Peking's attitude toward the UN has been deviant only for a short period of its first 22 years of existence. It seems clear that before an explanation of Peking's deviant behavior is attempted, it must be found when Peking's attitude became deviant and why.

In Part II, the actual records of Peking's international behavior will be looked into to see when, how and why changes in Peking's attitude and approach toward the UN took place. As the following discussions will soon reveal, there had been at least four changes in Peking's approach and two changes in attitude toward the UN in the course of a 22 year period--from 1949–71. These changes in Peking's behavior reflected primarily changes in the UN itself as perceived by Peking's leaders at each stage. Positively or negatively, Peking had consistently utilized the UN to advance its foreign policy objectives.

Change here means not merely minor alteration or modification of policy but an observable substitution of one policy or approach for another that differs sharply in position, direction or posture. This is to be contrasted with the word "continuity" which, in this study, shall denote not lack of interruption or modification in details, but relative persistency and constancy in position, direction or posture for the period under consideration.

Changes from period to period are designated by four pairs of adjectives: positive-negative, offensive-defensive, active-reactive, and direct-indirect. These pairs of adjectives are tantamount to the description of the major policy alternatives open to the decision-makers of a foreign policy system.

In the Introduction, foreign policy in general was defined as "the system of activities evolved by a nation to induce, or to adapt to, changes in its international environment." Put simply, a nation's foreign policy is a matter of endless adjustment. An external change is an external challenge or response. In the face of an external challenge, a given nation has the choice of adjusting to that challenge positively or negatively, offensively or defensively, actively or reactively, directly or indirectly, formally or informally, spontaneously or tardily and so on.

Fundamentally, these choices relate to either policy aims or policy means. The positive-negative aspect of adjustment is a matter of attitude, which belongs to the former, and the other aspects listed are matters of approach, which belong to the latter.

The positive-negative aspect of adjustment concerns the substance of yes or no. To make a positive adjustment means to adapt one's policy in line with the external challenge or demand. It spells "yes." Conversely, to adjust negatively means to negate or neutralize the external challenge. It spells "no." Positive adjustment implies friendship; negative adjustment implies hostility or indifference.

The offensive-defensive aspect of adjustment relates to the posture of strategy. Offensive adjustment means to stick to one's own terms without compromise. Defensive adjustment means to accept the terms stipulated by the other party without substantial alteration. The former implies determination and/or one's just position; the latter implies lack of will or acknowledgment of the opponent's just position.

The active-reactive aspect of adjustment relates to aggressiveness of strategic plays. Adjusting actively means to overtake the initiative and face the external challenger with a counterchallenge. Reactive adjustment, in contrast, involves processes acknowledging an external change or challenge and responding to it without trying to overtake the initiative. The former implies strength; the latter weakness.

The direct-indirect aspect of adjustment relates to the tactfulness in strategic maneuver. To adjust directly is to make formal or informal action in response to a challenger without employing a proxy or a third party. Conversely, to adjust indirectly is to utilize the service of a third party or a proxy rather than to approach the challenger face to face. The former implies confidence; the latter, doubt or mistrust.

At any given time, the specific foreign policy of a nation toward another international actor can be described by a combination of these four pairs of adjectives. This is true with the case of Peking's UN policy. For instance, in 1965, Peking openly called for the organization of a rival UN and encouraged others to withdraw from the UN. That is a policy of negative, offensive and active nature. If Peking were to notify U Thant through Albania that it would join the UN with the Taiwan authority still occupying the permanent seat in the Security Council at the same time, that would be a positive, defensive and indirect policy. That policy might be reactive or active depending on whether there had been an invitation conveyed to Peking with the same terms of participation.

It stands to reason that, other things being equal, the more a nation's objectives and aspirations coincide with the purposes and principles of the UN Charter (or the greater the utilitarian value of the UN to a nation), the more that nation is likely to adjust its national policy in positive support of the UN system, and vice versa. Similarly, the stronger the will (the greater the capabilities, and the firmer the confidence) of a nation the more that nation is likely to take an offensive posture (an active manner, and a direct approach) in her dealing with the UN, again assuming other things equal and unchanged. On the basis of these hypotheses, if we have a way of determining a given nation's objectives and aspirations (or her decision-makers' perception of the instrumental values of the UN), her will, capabilities and confidence (or trust in the UN), we have a way of making a tentative projection of her probable course of action with respect to the UN.

In the following chapters, each of the six major changes in Peking's attitude and approach are described and discussed.

5

INITIAL
POLICY,
1949-50

POSITIVE, ACTIVE, DIRECT
AND DEFENSIVE

Peking's earliest consideration concerning the UN was quite simplistic and friendly. It assumed that the change in China's representation was an inevitable reality that would not be prevented by either the Republic of China's (ROC) desperate effort to cling to China's seat or by any captious objections of the US.

It was mentioned in the Introduction that the very creation of the UN was an important change in China's external environment to which any one aspiring to rule China must be prepared to adapt. This was a fact acknowledged by Mao Tse-tung and his associates of the CPC. It is most interesting to note that the ideal of the UN was heralded by Mao Tse-tung in 1945. At the time of the San Francisco Conference, Mao wrote:

> The Chinese Communist Party fully agrees with the pro-
> posals of the Dumbarton Oaks conference and the deci-
> sions of the Crimea conference on the establishment of an
> organization to safeguard international peace and security
> after the war. It welcomes the United Nations Conference
> on International Organization in San Francisco. It has ap-
> pointed its own representative on China's delegation to
> this conference in order to express the will of the Chinese
> people.[1]

This is indeed a striking contrast to his earlier condemnation of the League of Nations as "a league of robbers."[2] The League of Nations

was despised by Mao because it failed to uphold China's territorial
integrity in the case of Manchuria in 1930. The UN, Mao seemed hopeful, would acknowledge China's place in the world with proper deference.

    With this background it was no surprise that Peking's initial
policy toward the UN when the PRC was first established was positive,
active, direct and relatively defensive. On October 1, 1949, the establishment of the People's Republic of China was proclaimed by its Central People's Government. It also "declared to the governments of all
other countries" that it is "the sole legal government representing all
the people" of the PRC and invited recognition and diplomatic relations
with "any foreign government that is willing to observe the principles
of equality, mutual benefit and mutual respect of territorial integrity
and sovereignty."[3] On November 15, six weeks later, Premier and
Foreign Minister Chou En-lai cabled the Secretary-General of the UN
and informed the latter that his government repudiated the legal and
factual status of the "Kuomintang reactionary government," which had
already lost the right to speak for the Chinese people.[4] A similar
cable addressed to the Secretary-General and the President of the
General Assembly was sent the same day[5] followed by another addressed
to the members of the Security Council on January 8, 1950.[6]

    Meanwhile, on November 25, 1949, the Soviet Union and members
of the Soviet bloc challenged the right of the Republic of China delegation to represent China at the meeting of the First Committee of the
Fourth General Assembly. This was the first debate on the Chinese
question in a UN organ. No action was taken. On December 29, the
Soviet delegate to the Security Council orally demanded the expulsion
of the ROC delegation. After a rebuttal by the representative from
the ROC, the matter was ruled closed by the Council President as it
was not an accepted item on the provisional agenda.[7] On January 10,
the Soviet Union submitted a formal proposal asking the Council to
disqualify and expel the delegation from the ROC.[8] On January 13,
the motion was defeated by a vote of three to six, with two abstaining.[9]
This was the first official decision by a UN organ on the question of
Chinese representation.

    This first rebuff did not discourage Peking. Peking's next move
was formal, proper and restrained. On January 19, Chou sent another
cable, this time informing the UN officials of the appointment of Chang
Wen-t'ien as the PRC's ambassador to the UN and specifically requesting a reply from the UN officials as to his demand for the immediate replacement of the ROC delegation with the new delegation
appointed by the PRC.[10] Two weeks later, another similar cable was
sent to the Economic and Social Council on the appointment of

Chi Ch'ao-ting as the PRC's representative to that body.[11] The pattern
continued with regard to other UN organs and the specialized agencies
during the following months.

GROUNDS FOR OPTIMISM

There is little doubt that Peking's ruling elite thought positively
about participating in the activities of the UN.[12] If Peking ever had a
favorable opinion of the UN, it was during this early period before its
active and direct contacts with the UN turned its high hope into frustration. There were some grounds for this relative optimism.

To begin with, the policy-makers of the PRC, as newcomers in
international diplomacy and politics, saw international problems in
rather simple, categorical terms.[13] Peking's initial UN policy reflected its policy-makers' nationalistic and revolutionary zeal rather
than their conscious and careful evaluation of policy alternatives.
Having seized power after a long and tortuous civil war, the policy-
makers were no doubt eager to secure China's "rightful place" among
the world powers. With limited experience in the conduct of foreign
relations and little opportunity to observe and evaluate the UN in
reality, both Mao and Chou maintained a positive image about the world
organization. The UN was recognized as a world organization that
was a going concern. It could become the arena where the "new China"
would play the role of a great power. There were some accusations
of US domination in the UN, but that was no reason to abandon the UN
to the "imperialistis." The UN was not the creation of the "imperialists"
alone and, therefore, not merely the instrument of the Western colonial
powers.

This positive image of the UN was not entertained by the policy-
makers alone. Mao and Chou were encouraged by the domestic political
climate as well as the external environmental developments at that
time.

Domestically, nationalistic fervor was at a peak. The ethnocentric
"Middle Kingdom" had already suffered a century of humiliation at
the hands of Western colonial powers and neighboring Japan. Many
attempts at reforms and revolutions had not been able to reunite the
country and restore its former grandeur.[14] The communist movement
came at the critical time in China's history as a favored alternative;
its austere style of operation and its doctrinal newness gained wide
support from the general populace, including many patriotic intellectuals.[15] Reporting from inside mainland China at that time,

A. Doak Branett wrote of the Communist Party leadership in these
words:

> Intellectually tough, they have purpose and determination,
> are unswerving in their devotion to their beliefs, and are
> incorruptible to a degree previously unknown in modern
> China. They are doctrinaire in their basic beliefs, but flex-
> ible in adapting means to achieve their ends, and willing
> to learn in new situations--within the limitations imposed
> by their Marxist preconceptions.[16]

To many Chinese patriots, these men might well be the only realistic
hope for China's reunification and resurgence. In short, the political
climate of China at that time seemed to favor a strong unifying force
such as the Communist Party of China led by Mao, and encouraged
Mao and Chou to pursue a course of action that would revive China's
confidence and greatness.

The external environment was not altogether unfavorable to
Peking's bid for China's seat in the UN. The UN itself was then operating on the principle of the "Big Power Concert" as planned by its
founders.[17] Even though the United States had a predominant influence
in almost all UN organs, the USSR was able to protect the Communist
bloc through the use of the veto power. There were signs that the
PRC's bid would be treated fairly as a part of a general problem of
representation. Trygve Lie, then Secretary-General of the UN, believed that the UN should seat Peking, and sought to bring this to pass.
His special memorandum on legal aspects of the problem of representation in the UN, released in March 1950, strongly supported Peking's
position.[18] The General Assembly, having rejected a Soviet proposal
to seat the PRC at its fourth session, adopted another resolution to
set up a Special Committee of seven nations to study the matter.[19]
The Ad Hoc Political Committee was then debating an item, entitled
"Recognition by the United Nations of the Representation of A Member
State."[20] In the course of that debate a Cuban (Batista's) draft resolution recommended that "subjective" criteria such as the "ability
and willingness to achieve the purpose of the Charter, to observe its
principles and to fulfill the international obligations of the State" should
be the basis for recognizing the qualification of a claimant government.[21] But a British draft, echoing the legal memorandum presented
by Secretary-General Trygve Lie, urged the adoption of "objective"
criteria. It proposed to seat, as the representative of a Member State,
the delegation of a government that "exercises effective control and
authority over all or nearly all the national territory, and has the
obedience of the bulk of the population of that territory, in such a way

that this control, authority and obedience appear to be of a permanent character."[22]

Outside the UN, the United States was not uncompromisingly opposed to the seating of the Communist regime in the UN when the question was first raised. Ambassador Ernest Gross of the United States, while declaring that he would vote against the Soviet proposal, took pains to make clear that the US would accept the decision of the majority of the Security Council, for the American government considered the question procedural rather than substantive.[23] The American attitude toward the whole question of China was to "wait and see," rather than to get involved "in the civil conflict in China."[24]

There was some circumstantial evidence indicating that the Soviet Union might have actually manipulated to keep the PRC out of the UN by inciting public indignation and opposition to the PRC while pretending to sponsor Peking's cause.[25] This matter is controversial and uncertain. At any rate, this was the time when Mao had just proclaimed Peking's policy of "lean to one side" and travelled to Moscow to negotiate the Sino-Soviet Treaty of Friendship, Alliance and Mutual Assistance.[26] Peking's dependence on the "big brother," albeit only temporary, was a more significant element in Peking's policy consideration. During the period 1949-50, the PRC had a total of 25 treaty contacts with other countries, of which 22 were with the USSR, two with Poland, and one with Czechoslovakia.[27] There was little evidence that Peking believed that the Kremlin would prevent Peking's entry into the UN at that time.

It is more important to recall that, before January 13, 1950, when the Security Council first voted on the question of Chinese representation, 21 governments, including five members of the Council, had already extended recognition to Peking and many others were seriously considering the same.[28] Five more governments added their recognition by the end of June 1950. (See Appendix B.)

In terms of national objectives, Peking's priorities seemed to be political stabilization and the prevention of foreign interference in China's internal affairs. Mao and his colleagues were clearly preoccupied with the problems of consolidating their own power and with the formidable tasks of rehabilitation and reconstruction ahead of them. Next to this preoccupation with domestic programs of selfassertion, came the concern for national unification (i.e., the "liberation" of Taiwan), international recognition of the new regime's legitimacy and of China's power status and, finally, the spread of the Marxist-Leninist gospel to other corners of the world.

Thus, there were indications in October 1949, that the thinking and experiences of Peking's policy-makers, the domestic political climate, national objectives and the external environment all supported Peking's positive and active adjustment toward the UN.

Such an adjustment was made in a direct and formal manner. Between October 1, 1949, and June 30, 1950, Peking sent nine cables to the various organs of the UN and nine to the related international agencies. All of them concerned Chinese representation in the UN and the agencies. All were formal, each trying to present Peking's legal position on the question. Particularly noticeable is the case of the Universal Postal Union (UPU), where Peking had its only successful bid in May 1950. Its hopeful attitude toward the UN was clearly manifested in its persistent effort to regain a recognized position at the UPU in the years after the decision was reversed.[29] This evidence clearly indicates Peking's interest in the UN during the initial period.

Peking's posture during this initial period was also relatively defensive. The only demand that Peking made during this period was that the UN seat Peking's delegation in place of the Nationalist Chinese delegation. This was a position completely in accord with what sovereign nations were expected to do in similar situations. At that time there was as yet no serious consideration of the "two-Chinas" solution within or without the UN. Should the UN decide to grant Peking's wish, the UN's own terms would have been exactly the same.

THE PROBLEM OF TAIWAN

As it turned out, however, this single demand of Peking was to become the impossible knot in Peking's bid to enter the UN. Had the Communist Chinese been able to conquer Taiwan before June 1950, the question of China's representation would probably have been solved without further ado. But Peking failed to conquer Taiwan when the opportunity was open. The Korean War and the ensuing events made it virtually impossible for the PRC either to capture Taiwan or gain China's seat in the UN after June 1950. Since this Taiwan problem was of such fundamental importance, a closer examination of its origin, its nebulous nature and the dilemma that it created is clearly in order.[30]

The problem of Taiwan was created largely by the unsettled civil war in China and an American policy shift immediately following the outbreak of the Korean War. But once the problem came into being, its roots could be traced back to 1895. In 1895, at the end of the first Sino-Japanese War, China and Japan signed a peace treaty at

Shimonoseki.[31] China ceded to Japan "in perpetuity and full sovereignty" the Island of Formosa and the Pescadores Group.[32] From then on, Japan ruled this war prize as a colony for the next 50 years.

Before the end of World War II, China's leaders found little that was of national importance in the island of Taiwan. According to Edgar Snow, in the period before 1949 Mao Tse-tung held some very different ideas about the status of Taiwan. On July 16, 1936, Snow interviewed Mao at Yenan. Part of the converstaion went like this:

> Question: "Is it the immediate task of the Chinese people to regain all the territories lost to Japanese imperialism, or only to drive Japan from North China, and all Chinese territory above the Great Wall?"

> Answer: "It is the immediate task of China to regain all our lost territories, not merely to defend our sovereignty below the Great Wall. This means that Manchuria must be regained. We do not, however, include Korea, formerly a Chinese colony, but when we have re-established the independence of the lost territories of China, and if the Koreans wish to break away from the chains of Japanese imperialism, we will extend them our enthusiastic help in their struggle for independence. The same thing applies for Formosa. . . . ' (Emphasis added)[33]

So Taiwan was, for Mao, a former Chinese colony. Mao was prepared to help the Taiwanese people in their struggle for independence.

This was not a mere slip of the tongue. On August 15, 1937, in the document entitled "The Ten Great Policies of the CCP for Anti-Japanese Resistance and National Salvation," the Communist leader stated under item number V, "Anti-Japanese Foreign Policy": Fight against Japanese imperialism in alliance with the workers, peasants and common people of Korea, Taiwan and Japan.[34] Significantly, this same passage now appears in Mao's Selected Works with the word Taiwan deleted.[35] The reason for this Orwellian move seems rather obvious.

Along similar lines, there are indications that KMT officials also thought of Taiwan not as an integral part of China, but rather as a recovered colony. First, Ambassador John Leighton Stuart observed in 1947 that the first Chinese governor and his henchmen who took over Taiwan from the Japanese did not treat the Taiwanese inhabitants as fellow-countrymen. Instead, they "conducted themselves as

conquerors."[36] Second, even though Taiwan had just been recovered
from Japan, in April 1949, the ROC's Prime Minister, Ho Ying-ch'in,
actually "suggested a lien on the island of Taiwan, or on its products,
as security" in order to secure a silver loan from the United States.[37]
Third, a Communist source also reported that one of the prices that
Madame Chiang was prepared to pay when she pleaded for American
support in 1948 was "to give away Taiwan."[38]

Fortune turned against Chiang Kai-shek, and the KMT regime
moved to Taipei in December 1949, to escape from the pursuing forces
of the CPC. All of a sudden, Taiwan became a "bastion" for Chiang's
counterattack and an "integral part" of Chinese territory that Peking's
leaders vowed to "liberate."

It is not known for sure why Peking failed to "liberate" Taiwan
before June 1950. In retrospect, it seems Mao and his associates
ought to have known that leaving the remnant forces of the KMT in
Taiwan could mean future trouble just as allowing the CPC's retreat
into Yenan after the Long March later turned out to be an almost fatal
mistake by the KMT leaders. Limited information suggests that
Peking was not quite equipped to wage a naval and air war across the
Taiwan Strait at that time. Its leaders might have misjudged the probability of American intervention on behalf of the KMT and thought that
they had time to prepare for a sure victory.[39]

In any case, the Korean War broke out in June 1950, and President Truman ordered the Seventh Fleet to prevent any Communist attack
upon Taiwan and leashed Chiang's forces to prevent their attack upon
mainland China. The stalemate was stabilized and a dilemma created.

This inability of the Communist Chinese to capture Taiwan before
June 1950, was an even greater misfortune for Peking because of a
sudden shift in US policy toward China at that time. Prior to the Korean
War, the American position tended to be a "wait-and-see" policy. A
policy memorandum of the US State Department dated December 23,
1949, stated:

> Formosa, politically, geographically and strategically, is
> part of China. . . . Politically and militarily it is a strictly
> Chinese responsibility. It is true that the technical status
> of the island remains to be determined by the Japanese
> peace settlement, but the Cairo agreement and the Potsdam
> declaration and the surrender terms of September 2, 1945,
> looked to its return to China and the United States facil-
> itated its takeover by Chinese troops shortly after VJ-
> day.[40]

On January 5, 1959, President Truman issued a statement in which he said:

> Formosa was surrendered to Generalissimo Chiang Kai-
> shek, and for the past four years, the United States and
> the other Allied Powers have accepted the exercise of
> Chinese authority over the island. The United States has
> no predatory designs on Formosa or on any other Chinese
> territory. The United States has no desire to obtain spe-
> cial rights or privileges or to establish military bases on
> Formosa at this time. Nor does it have any intention of
> utilizing its armed forces to interfere in the present situa-
> tion. The United States government will not pursue a course
> which will lead to involvement in the civil conflict in China.
>
> Similarly, the United States government will not provide
> military aid or advice to Chinese forces in Formosa.[41]

On February 9, in replying to a series of questions contained in a House Resolution, a State Department statement said:

> For the United States government, at this date, to seek to
> establish a non-Chinese administration on Formosa, either
> through SCAP [Silent Compact Auxiliary Power] or a United
> Nations or FEC [Far Eastern Commission] -sponsored ple-
> biscite, would be almost universally interpreted in main-
> land China and widely interpreted throughout Asia as an at-
> tempt by this government to seperate Formosa from China
> in violation of its pledges and contrary to its long-standing
> policy of respecting the territorial integrity of China.. . .
>
>   . . . we do not wish to create a Formosa irredenta issue
> about which the Chinese Communists could rally support
> within China. . . . we must not place ourselves in the un-
> enviable position of the USSR with regard to the integrity
> of China and must remain free to take the position that any-
> one who violates the integrity of China is the enemy of China
> and is acting contrary to our own interest.[42]

A few months later, the Korean War erupted and the American position drastically changed. On June 27, 1950, Presedent Truman declared:

> I have ordered the Seventh Fleet to prevent any attack on
> Formosa. As a corollary of this action, I am calling upon

the Chinese government on Formosa to cease all air and
sea operations against the mainland.

. . . The determination of the future status of Formosa
must await the restoration of security in the Pacific, a
peace settlement with Japan or consideration by the United
Nations.[43]

The next day, the ROC Foreign Minister George K. C. Yeh responded
to the American change of position in a statement which stating that
although Taiwan is a part of the territory of China, "pending the conclusion of the treaty of peace on Japan, the government of the USA may
share with the government of the Republic of China the responsibility
for the defense of Taiwan," and that ROC, in accepting the American
proposal of "emergency measures," had no intention of departing from
its "dual policy of resistance against the agression of international
communism and the maintenance of the territorial integrity of China."[44]

Peking's reaction was straightforward and accusative. Chou
En-lai, the Premier and Foreign Minister of the PRC, stated on behalf of his government that "Truman's statement of June 27 and the
action of the US Navy constitute armed agression against the territory
of China and are a gross violation of the United Nations Charter."[45]
From that date on, the question of Taiwan became a major issue in
international politics. It was an item that would appear repeatedly on
the agenda of the UN and other international organizations and conferences. The ROC, with the support of the US and her allies, has
since been able to continue its participation in the UN as the government of the whole of China. The PRC, on the other hand, was to be
excluded and even became an outlaw by UN resolution.

In 1949, when Peking first requested the UN to oust the ROC
delegation from China, that request represented a reasonable position.
As the years progressed, however, the KMT regime in Taiwan gradually
gained in stature in the international community. Concurrently, as
more and more small states were admitted into the UN, the thinking
of the UN membership as a whole changed significantly. By 1961,
Peking's continued insistence on the ouster of Taiwan as a condition
of its participation in the UN was considered offensive rather than
reasonable. By that time, as we shall see, the predominant opinion
among the UN members had changed in favor of some variety of the
"two-Chinas" solution.

CHAPTER

6

**THE SHIFT
TO A
DEFIANT
OFFENSIVE,
1950-53**

FROM DEFENSIVE TO OFFENSIVE

The thesis of this chapter is that the Korean War and the sudden change in US policy toward China brought to pass a typically defiant response from Peking. When pressured for compliance, Mao's regime displayed an unquestionable determination and will to meet the challenge. However, the special place of the UN in Peking's thinking was not discarded because the PRC had to face "the UN police forces" that threatened its border. The blame was put on the US "imperialists" who were responsible for the wrongs of the UN and offensive charges were lodged against the US through the UN in accordance with the established procedures of the world organization.

During June 1950, and the following months, a series of developments took place that seemed to have led to a change in Peking's approach toward the UN. Almost all of these developments turned out perniciously for the PRC. First came the Korean War which, among other things, caused the stalemate in China's civil war between the CPC and the KMT and the resulting Taiwan problem. Then came General MacArthur's threat to the PRC's security, whereupon Peking's leaders found it necessary to send "volunteers" into Korea to fight against the UN forces. While the war went on, at the UN the General Assembly adopted the Uniting for Peace Resolution, which the Communists saw as an attempt to undermine the veto power of the Soviet Union. Following that, another resolution on the Representation of a Member State rejected the "objective criteria" thesis proposed by Secretary-General Trygve Lie's memorandum. It only vaguely stated that the question of representation "should be considered in the light of the Purposes and Principles of the Charter and the circumstances of each case," but instructed that relevant decisions by the General

Assembly should be taken into account in other organs of the UN and in the Specialized Agencies.[1] Finally a delegation that Peking sent to New York to condemn the US for "aggression against China's territory, Taiwan" met the Security Council's rebuff. Instead, the Assembly formally condemned the PRC as an "aggressor" and recommended a general trade embargo against it.

It would be an understatement to say that Peking's leaders had to rethink their whole approach toward the UN after these events; they were probably infuriated and sobered. Peking's naive and optimistic views of the UN quickly dissipated. Its behavior pattern shifted visibly toward a relatively offensive approach compared to the relatively defensive posture of the initial period.

This shift from a defensive to an offensive approach was manifested in several ways. First, soon after the UN intervened in Korea, Peking's official statements began to make a technical distinction between the UN of the Charter and the UN under US control. Peking still sought and supported the former, but the latter was denounced as an instrument of US "imperialsim" that Peking fought and opposed. Second, Peking also declared that all decisions made by the UN without its participation were "illegal, and consequently null and void," and the American "imperialists" were warned that they would bear all possible grievous results. Third, Peking further contended that without its participation, it would be impossible to settle any major international questions, above all the questions of Asia. Therefore, it was essential that the UN first "restore" the PTC's legitimate rights in the UN before it attempted to safeguard world peace and international security. Fourth, Peking lodged a formal complaint with the Security Council against US "armed invasion of Taiwan" and demanded that the Council condemn the US government and force its withdrawal from the island. It sent a delegation to the UN to make its case in November 1950. While in New York, its ambassador refused to discuss items on the agenda of which Peking did not approve.

PRECIPITATING CAUSES

This shift of approach was largely forced upon Peking by developments outside the PRC. No change inside the PRC seemed to be directly responsible for this shift. There was the possibility that military personalities such as Chu Teh, P'eng Teh-huai, and Lin Piao might have carried extra weight in Peking's foreign policy considerations during the Korean War Period. But it was highly unlikely that these men could have been especially instrumental (i.e., more instrumental

than Mao and Chou) in deciding what approach the PRC should take
regarding the UN. Aside from the Korean War, Peking was still very
much preoccupied with domestic programs. At the time the Korean
War started, the whole PRC system (including the Communist Party,
the People's Liberation Army (PLA), the democratic parties and the
semi-official mass and propaganda organizations) was geared to the
launching of the all important land reform.[2] Were there no real threat
to Peking's industrial interests along the Yalu River, it was possible
that no "volunteers" would have crossed the Yalu.[3] Besides the land
reform, there was also a host of other "democratic reforms" that required the concentrated effort of the newly established regime. The
family reform was the most far-reaching in China's history. The
Three-Anti and the Five-Anti campaigns against bureaucratic corrup-
tion and other social ills were being carried out throughout the years
1951 and 1952. All these "democratic reforms" were antifeudalist in
nature. Preparations were also underway for overall economic and
social rehabilitation and reconstruction; the first Five-Year Plan was
announced at the beginning of 1953. It is quite doubtful that any of these
policies precipitated Peking's shift to an offensive approach toward the
UN.

On the other hand, what happened beyond China's borders seemed
to convince Peking's decision-makers that such a modification in its
approach was in order. On August 17, Ambassador Austin of the US
advocated in the Security Council that the UN should attempt total
victory over North Korea and unification of the entire peninsula under
UN auspices.[4] A week later, UN Commander General MacArthur was
reported as saying that Taiwan was part of "the island chain" from
which the US could "dominate with air power every Asiatic port from
Vladivostok to Singapore."[5] Soon, American military planes were
violating China's territorial air and strafing Chinese villages border-
ing the Yalu "by mistake."[6]

On September 5, the Security Council rejected the Soviet proposal
to invite the representative of the PRC to participate in the Korean
debate.[7] On September 8, Secretary-General Lie, who had been sym-
pathetic to the Communist Chinese bid for China's seat in the UN before, reportedly echoed assertions by MacArthur saying that "the aim
of the United Nations is and must be a united and independent Korea"
and that it would "not be enough" to bring about the withdrawal of the
North Koreans to the 38th Parallel.[8] Three days later, President
Truman approved a recommendation of the National Security Council
that "General MacArthur was to extend his operations north of the
Parallel and to make plans for the occupation of North Korea, if there
was no indication or threat of entry of Soviet or Chinese Communist
elements in force."[9]

As the talk crossing the 38th Parallel became louder in the
UN, Peking issued stern warnings against "American penetration" into
North Korea. On September 30, Chou En-lai declared in a speech that:

The Chinese people absolutely will not tolerate foreign aggression, nor will they supinely tolerate seeing their neighbors being savagely invaded. Whoever attempts to exclude
the nearly 500 million people from the UN and whoever ig-
nores and violates the interests of this one-fourth of mankind and fancy (sic) vainly to solve arbitrarily any Far Eastern problem directly concerned with China, will certainly
break their skulls.[10]

On October 1, South Korean troops crossed the 38th Parallel.
Chou summoned K. M. Panikkar to a midnight conference and told
the Indian ambassador that if the "American" forces crossed the 38th
Parallel China would be forced to intervene.[11] On October 7, the General
Assembly approved the crossing of the Parallel, and the UN troops
moved onward the next day. By the end of the month, from 180,000 to
228,000 "Chinese People's Volunteers" were fighting UN forces along
the Yalu, amidst the "resist-American and aid-Korea" campaign.
Later, their strength swelled to an estimated 270,000 to 340,000 men.[12]

Then at its 1951 session, the General Assembly rejected an
Indian proposal to seat the PRC delegation in place of the ROC delegation with a vote of 11-37-4, showing a substantial increase of UN
members opposed to the PRC. (See Appendix A.) Moreover, the
General Assembly also adopted, in close succession, four resolutions
that were either generally unfavorable or especially hostile to the PRC:
the Uniting for Peace Resolution in November, the Resolution on Representation of a Member State in December 1950, the condemnation of
the PRC and North Korea in February 1951, and the trade embargo
against the same two countries three months later.

From there on, Peking's position in the UN went from bad to
worse. At the Sixth Session, the Assembly received a report of the
Special Committee stating that it was unable to make any recommendation on the Chinese Question.[13] The Soviet Union again proposed in-
clusion of the question on the Assembly agenda. The General Committee debated the matter on November 10, at which time the delegate
from Thailand orally proposed the postponement of consideration of
any further proposals to seat a PRC delegation in place of the delegation from the ROC. The proposal was adopted.[14] This was the first
of the yearly "moratorium" resolutions between 1951 and 1961.

Events outside the world organization also seemed to have contributed to making Peking take this new look at the UN. The international environment was now cold to the PRC compared with the previous period. No additional countries accorded recognition to Peking.
(See Appendix B.) Within the United States the Nationalist Chinese
lobby proved to be a smashing sucess. Washington abandoned its
"hands-off" policy regarding Taiwan. In addition to "threatening the
security" of China and leading the campaign to prevent the seating
and to outlaw Peking in the UN, America had also taken the new position that Taiwan was a part of America's "island chain" of defense,
and military aid to Chiang Kai-shek was revived. Instead of coming
to China's support, the non-Communist members of the UN had either
followed the American view that Peking was guilty of aggression in
fighting the police force of the UN, or assumed a non-committal attitude toward the whole dispute.

Indeed, Peking's struggles during the Korean War period were hard
and lonesome. As the outside challenges increased, Peking's will to
fight back seemed to have heightened (such were the idiosyncracies of
Peking's top leaders). Yet, as difficult as these events might have
been for Peking, the most frustrating experience was probably its
effort to work through the UN system to condemn the US for her alleged
"armed aggression" in Taiwan.

CHARGES OF "US AGRESSION"
IN TAIWAN

The charges of "US agression" in Taiwan were the clearest
demonstration of Peking's defiant spirit. While Peking did file numerous
charges against US forces for wrongs in connection with the Korean
War, including such alleged crimes as using prohibited bacteriological
weapons, it was the problem of Taiwan that seemed to receive the most
diplomatic effort in this period. With the assignment of the Seventh
Fleet to the Taiwan Strait, it became apparent that Peking could not
attack Taiwan without confronting American military might first. It
therefore resorted to the UN.

In a cable dated July 6, 1950, addressed to Trygve Lie, Secretary-
General of the UN, Chou En-lai said:

> . . . the statement by President Truman. . .aimed at pre-
> venting by armed force the liberation of Taiwan by the
> People's Republic of China, together with the action of the
> United States Navy in invading the Chinese territorial

waters around Taiwan, constitutes an act of open aggression which thoroughly violates the principles of the United
Nations Charter forbidding any member to use force against
the territorial integrity or political independence of any
other state. . . . In their silence in the face of this act of
open aggression by the United States government, the Security Council and the Secretary-General of the United
Nations have relinquished their functions and duties of upholding world peace, and thereby became pliant instruments
of the policy of the United States government.[15]

On August 24, 1950, another cable was sent.[16] This time, Chou demanded that the Security Council take action against the US.

On August 20, at its 492nd meeting, the Security Council placed
the item on its agenda under the title "Complaint of armed invasion of
Taiwan." On September 17, Chou cabled the Security Council that "as
the sole legal government representing the Chinese people," and being
the accuser in the case, his government has the right and necessity to
send its delegation to attend and participate in the proceedings of the
Security Council. He declared that if the Council should proceed with
this agenda item without the attendance and participation of the representative of his government, its resolutions would be illegal, null and
void.[17] The Security Council passed a resolution on September 29
inviting representatives of the PRC to attend its meetings held after
November 15, in accordance with rule 39 of the rules of procedure.[18]
On November 27, Wu Hsiu-ch'uan, representing the PRC, took his
seat at the Security Council table. This was to be the only appearance
of any official representative from the people's Republic of China at
the United Nations. In a lengthy speech delivered at the Security Council
on November 28, 1950, Wu stated, inter alia, the following:

> . . . without the participation of the lawful delegates of the
> PRC, representing 475 million people, the UN cannot in
> practice be worthy of its name. Without the participation
> of the lawful delegation of the PRC, the Chinese people have
> no reason to recognize any resolutions or decisions of the
> UN.[19]

At the end of his long speech, Wu submitted a draft resolution calling
upon the Security Council to condemn the US for committing "open
and direct aggression against Chinese territory" and to demand "the
complete withdrawal by the government of the United States of its
forces of armed aggression from Taiwan."[20] The resolution, sponsored
by the USSR, was rejected by the Council.[21]

The same charge the US sponsored by the USSR was also on the agenda of the Fifth Session of the General Assembly and was referred to the First Committee. In a cable dated October 17, 1950, Peking also claimed its right to take part in the deliberations of the First Committee, and the Committee concurred.[22] Accordingly, Wu Hsiu-ch'uan was again appointed as the representative of the PRC to the Assembly on November 26, and took part in the Committee's 407th meeting the next day. On December 7, at its 408th meeting, the First Committee gave priority to the French proposal on the "Intervention of the Central People's Government of the People's Republic of China in Korea," and delayed discussing the Russian complaint against the US. On December 16, Wu issued a statement at Lake Success,[23] saying that the Security Council's refusal of the PRC proposal was "unfortunate, though not unexpected," and that he was distributing a speech that he had prepared, but would not now be able, to deliver at the Political and Security Committee meeting.[24] That same day, the President of the General Assembly requested, through the Swiss Embassy in Peking, that General Wu be instructed to stay on in New York and meet with the UN Group on Cease-Fire in Korea. The delegation departed from New York on December 19, however. Chou En-lai replied to the Assembly President, again through the Swiss channel:

> After the Security Council unreasonably voted against the complaint against the United States armed aggression against Taiwan raised by the People's Republic of China, General Wu was instructed by the Central People's Government to continue to stay at Lake Success for participation in the discussion of the complaint of United States agression against China submitted by the USSR representative; although he has waited for a long time and until the United Nations General Assembly was declared adjourned, he was still not given the opportunity to speak. Under such circumstances, the Central People's Government deems that there is no more necessity for General Wu and his staff to remain at Lake Success and has therefore instructed him to start their homeward journey on 19 December.[25]

In February 1951, the First Committee resumed consideration of Peking's complaints and its Chairman cabled Peking and notified the latter of the date of the Committee's next meeting. Chou En-lai cabled back and requested that the lengthy speech distributed by General Wu on December 16, 1950, be read and circulated.[26] The Russian draft resolution was rejected by the Committee on February 6, 1951.

Meanwhile, the United States raised separately "The Question of Formosa" in a letter dated September 20, 1950, to the General Assembly. It suggested, inter alia, that the Assembly "should study the general situation with respect to Formosa, with a view to formulating appropriate recommendations." It was put on the agenda of the Assembly on October 5 and referred to the First Committee.[27] In a cable dated October 17, Chou En-lai protested the decision to include the item on the agenda on the ground that it would be an interference into China's internal affairs.[28] While in New York, ambassador Wu Hsiu-ch'unan also dwelt on this matter. Ceremoniously, he read Article 107 of the UN Charter and declared that the UN had absolutely no right to alter the status of Taiwan. He said:

> My government has protested in strong terms to the UN General Assembly, resolutely opposing the inclusion of the so-called "question of Formosa" concerning the status of Taiwan on the agenda of the General Assembly; whatever decision the UN General Assembly may take on the so-called question of the status of Taiwan--whether it be turning over the island to the US to administer openly under the disguise of "trusteeship" or "neutralization," or whether it be procrastinating by the way of "investigation," thereby maintaining the present state of actual US occupation--will in substance be stealing China's legitimate territory and supporting US aggression against Taiwan in opposition to the Chinese people. Any such decision will be unjustifiable and unlawful. Any such decision will in no way shake the resolve of the Chinese people to liberate Taiwan.[29]

The First Committee voted on November 12 to postpone its consideration of the item until after two other items--the Soviet complaints regarding aggression against China by the US and the ROC's complaints against the USSR--had been dealt with. In 1951, when the question was recalled, the United States supported a British move to adjourn the debate on the question "in view of the unsettled state of the situation in the Far East." The USSR voiced the opinion that the question should not be considered by the UN at any time, and, therefore, the motion of adjournment should also be opposed. The Committee, nevertheless, voted to adjourn the debate sine die on February 7, 1951.[30]

By this time, the Korean War had become the dominant issue both inside and outside the UN. The General Assembly had adopted the resolution condemning the PRC as "aggressor" in Korea. Peking had lost all its fights at the UN, and there was little left that could be done in the world organization.

Between July 1, 1950, and December 31, 1953, the government
of the PRC sent 40 communications to the various organs of the UN
and ten to the international agencies related to the UN, of which 13
were concerned primarily with the question of the representation of
China; nine concerned alleged American violations of China's territorial air, strafing of Chinese villages and illegal inspections of
Chinese merchantships by American military forces; 17 dealt with
the Korean question, including the false charges of bacteriological
warfare and the armistice negotiations; ten were related to the question of Taiwan, and one concerned China's properties and right in the
International Bank for Reconstruction and Development. In the communications addressed to subsidiary organs of the UN and to the
specialized agencies, Peking continued to demand seating of its del-
gation to replace that of the Nationalists, thus retaining its legal
position on paper. In the communications to the principal organs of the
UN, Chou En-lai presented various charges against the United States,
but also endeavored to keep the UN channel open for the PRC. Despite
its offensive posture, Peking acted essentially through the UN and
followed the established procedures of the UN with little consideration
of the outcome such action might bring. Against the UN, Peking's
verbal attacks always took the form of a warning or a regret. Formal
charges were directed against the US "imperialists" and a few of her
"lackeys" instead of the UN itself.

Considering the nature of the contacts the PRC was having with the
UN during this period, one would have to conclude that Peking's language and attitude toward the UN was still positively directed. But
the fact that its efforts to operate with and through the UN brought
little result for the PRC meant that this type of practice would have
to be re-evaluated. It was understandable, therefore, to discover
that Peking's approach toward the UN changed again after the Korean
War from active and direct to reactive and indirect. In the autumn
of 1952, Peking called a Peace Conference of the Asian and Pacific
Regions. An "Address to the United Nations" adopted on October 12
by the Conference, charged that the Organization was violating its own
Charter and called upon it to release itself from "imperialist control."[31]

As the Korean War drew to a close, Peking suffered another
humiliating experience when some 14,710 of its "volunteers" chose to
go to Taiwan rather than be repatriated to mainland China. It was
remarkable that Peking finally agreed to this innovative idea of "voluntary repatriation." Perhaps that was a sign that a new policy was
in the offing in the decision-making rooms of Peking during the latter
half of 1953.

**THE FIRST STAGE
OF A
PROTRACTED
APPROACH,
1954-57**

POSITIVE, REACTIVE, INDIRECT
AND DEFENSIVE

In this chapter, the most important proposition is that Peking came to the realization in late 1953 that, to achieve its goals of "liberating" Taiwan and obtaining China's seat in the UN, it must wage a protracted struggle rather than a quick one. Accordingly a long-term strategy was adopted. During the period 1954-57, Peking's approach toward the outside world, including the UN, was based on a clearer perception of the PRC's own weakness and, coupled with it, a sense of mistrust for the UN and of doubt about its own ability to gain an upper hand in dealing directly with the UN under the existing circumstances. Its strategical moves were characteristically those of "strategic defensive"--the first stage of the protracted war.

Two important developments in 1953 contributed to a general foreign policy re-evaluation on the part of Peking. The first of these developments was the intensification of the arms race between the US and the USSR, and the open debate on the implications of nuclear warfare in the Soviet bloc. In January 1953, President Truman confirmed in his State of the Union Message the fact that the US had developed a hydrogen bomb. A similar announcement was made by the Soviet Premier Georgi M. Malenkov in August.[1] Soviet military publications debated the implications of nuclear weapons for modern warfare. According to Alice L. Hsieh:

During the Korean War, there was some evidence of concern over the possible employment by the United States of atomic weapons against Chinese troops. Nevertheless, because of the difficulty of reconciling traditional military

doctrine and experience with modern military weapons, it
is likely that for some years the Chinese failed to come to
serious grips with the changes wrought by nuclear weapons.2

However, after the initiation of the Soviet debates, a reappraisal of
China's vulnerability to nuclear attack probably took place in Peking.3

The other important development was the death of Stalin in March
and the conclusion of the Korean War a few months later. Stalin's
death caused a succession struggle in the Kremlin and might also have
rendered possible the agreement on a Korean armistice in July 1953.
In a way, the performance of the "Chinese People's Volunteers" against
the most awesome military might of the United States and the armies
of 15 other nations that constituted the UN forces promoted the prestige
of the PRC as a world power. Peking, nevertheless, made substantial
concessions on the "voluntary repatriation" issue regarding prisoners
of war at the end of a long drawn-out negotiation.4

While the Kremlin was busily occupied with the problem of
stabilizing its new leadership, Peking was reevaluating her policies
vis-à-vis her domestic and international position. It seems a grand
strategy of "encircling the developed areas from the underdeveloped
areas"--the backbone of China's new foreign policy for many years
to come--was formulated at this point.5 The scheme was to make
the new China a champion and a leader of the new, developing forces,
and guide her "revolutionary course" more into line with her own
national interests and lessen her dependence on the Soviet Union.
The leaders of Peking were setting forth to "achieve ambitious goals
with meager means."6

To surround the cities from the countryside, one of Mao's magic
weapons was "the united front," which rallied the peasants to his cause.
To encircle the "imperialists" in the developed areas, Mao's strategy
required a similar united front to rally together the "anti-imperialist
forces" in the underdeveloped areas. Furthermore, Mao Tse-tung also
saw that the struggle in the immediate future between the "socialist"
and "imperialist" camps would take place in "the intermediate zone,"
which included some capitalist and many neutral countries, as well
as many territories in Asia and Africa still controlled by colonial
powers. The important thing then was to gain the support of these
nations and would-be nations.

Among other things, this meant the UN would become an important arena for Peking's international operations. Further, it also
meant the necessity of another modification in Peking's approach

toward the UN from active and direct to reactive and indirect. Until
the end of 1953, Peking had taken the initiative to gain her entry into
the UN. From the spring of 1954, however, its more sophisticated
way was to work on a change in the UN's membership and wait for
the UN itself to invite her in.

There were a number of indicators that such a change in approach
toward the UN took place. First, between January 1954, and December
1957, only eight communications were sent by Peking's officials to
the UN organs. None of these was primarily for the purpose of demand-
ing the restoration of its legitimate rights in the UN; all but two were
replies to cables from the UN rather than communications of Peking's
initiative. Second, outside the UN Peking supported the UN charter on
all occasions, but particularly at the Afro-Asian Bandung Conference
where China was dealing with the underdeveloped countries. So much
so that those who failed to understand Peking's technical distinction
between the UN of the Charter and the UN under American control
found such support "inconceivable after the Chinese attacks on the
United Nations during and after the Korean War."[7] Third, on the
question of the representation of China in the UN, the propaganda
machine turned to explaining the importance of, and declaring Peking's
confidence in, the restoration of the PRC's right, rather than demand-
ing or requesting it as such. Fourth, Peking's commentaries on the
UN characteristically concentrated on championing the causes of the
Afro-Asian nations.

This new approach was encouraged by favorable domestic conditions and facilitated by the timely Afro-Asian forum at Bandung. Its
offshoots reached beyond the Afro-Asian world into Washington and
Taipei--the two arch-enemies of Peking.

HOME FRONT: THE "TRANSITION TO
SOCIALISM"

For Peking, everything seemed to be falling into place in the
several years following Stalin's death and the signing of the Korean
Armistice. At home, the period of purge came to a halt, the problems
of consolidation and rehabilitation reached a conclusive stage, and the
first Five-Year Plan (1953-57) was in full swing by the end of 1953.
The stability of the regime was already beyond question.[8] The first
National People's Congress (NPC) was convened in Peking and the
Constitution of the People's Republic of China for the period of
"transition to socialism" was adopted on September 20, 1954.[9] This
new constitution designated the State Council as the new state organ

empowered to direct the conduct of external affairs, under the super-
vision of the NPC and its Standing Committee. Mao Tse-tung kept the
position of the Chairman of the PRC, and Chou En-lai remained the
Premier and Foreign Minister. The two men continued to be the most
important foreign policy-makers with the backing of the shadow Party
organs. Two years later, when the CPC adopted its Constitution at
its Eighth Party Congress on September 26, 1956, it solidified its
control over the state organs and reinforced the positions of Mao and
Chou as the leading figures in Peking's foreign policy-making.[10] If
there was a change in Peking's policy-makers at this juncture, it was
their growth in sophistication regarding international politics and
diplomacy, not component personalities.

The 1954 Constitution of the Republic reiterated "the principles
of equality, mutual benefit and mutual respect for each other's sovereignty and territorial integrity" as Peking's basis for establishing and
extending diplomatic relations with other countries. The 1956 Party
Constitution further stated that the Party "advocates a foreign policy
directed toward . . . the achievement of peaceful coexistence between
countries with different systems . . . and expresses its sympathy for
all struggles in the world against imperialism and colonialism." All
these statements seem to underscore the new "grand strategy."

All through this period, the PRC's economic, social and political
progress was of such magnitude that Mao felt confident enough to launch
the "Hundred Flowers" campaign in May 1956, and allowed it to
flourish until it became apparent nine months later that the Party
itself was the main target of criticisms by dissident intellectuals,
including those within the Party ranks. Indeed, the period between
1954 and 1957 was a success story about which the CPC and the masses
of the PRC could and did feel enthused. Such smooth sailing at home
undoubtedly facilitated Peking's "people's diplomacy" abroad.

ABROAD: THE BANDUNG SPIRIT

Abroad, Peking conducted the "people's diplomacy" geared to
the grand strategy under the banner of "the Five Principles of Peaceful Coexistence" and "the Bandung Spirit" carefully nurtured by its
master diplomat, Chou En-lai.

The Five Principles evolved from discussions between Chou and
Nehru over Tibet in April.[11] These principles were emphatically
repeated in all subsequent dealings between the PRC and other Asian
neutrals concerning border matters.[12]

At the 1955 Bandung Conference, Chou En-lai's prestige among
the Afro-Asians climbed rapidly. His conduct was marked by candor,
skill and astuteness. According to Professor George McT. Kahin,
Chou was surprised by "the extent of pro-Western sentiment and the
amount and intensity of anti-Communist feelings . . . that he encountered
at the Conference." At this, he made a "studious effort during the
Conference to declare at every possible opportunity China's support
for the principles of the United Nations Charter.[13] He told the Conference that he could have submitted "the question of recognizing and
restoring the legitimate status of the PRC in the UN," and the question
of "the tension created by the United States in the area of Taiwan,"
for deliberation by the Conference, but he did not do so "because otherwise our Conference would be dragged into disputes about all these
problems without any solution" instead of finding common ground for
establishing friendly cooperation and good neighborly relations among
each other.[14] The Foreign Minister thus tried to demonstrate to his
fellow statesmen from underdeveloped countries that the new China,
if treated with due respect, harbored no aggressive tendencies and
could even be amicable.

Following the Bandung Conference, the press in China kept urging
the General Assembly to right the wrongs committed by the UN under
United States "coercion." On September 20, 1955, Ta Kung Pao said
that the General Assembly must "stop oppression in North Africa,
see that Goa was restored to India, and put an end to colonial rule in
West Irian (west New Guinea) and Cyprus." On December 24, "Observer," whose commentary always appeared in a most conspicuous space
in Jen-min Jih-pao, welcomed the admission of 16 new members to
the United Nations as "a victory for the principles of universality"
and "a blow to America's attempt to go on dominating the United
Nations," but commented that the tenth session was "still far from
measuring up to its functions." In 1956, during the Suez Crisis,
Peking gave vocal support to Nasser, and mildly praised the UN for
resolving to call for the immediate withdrawal of British, French
and Israeli forces from Egypt. However, the credit was given to "the
Soviet Union, the People's democracies and the Asian-African countries" whose efforts caused a new trend in the tenth session of the
General Assembly that "made it not so easy for the United States to
put the UN under its thumb." On the other hand, the UN Emergency
Force was condemned as a new "plot" by the United States "imperialists," and discussion of the Hungarian question was called "illegal
interference" in Hungarian domestic affairs.[15]

There can be no mistake that all these commentaries were made
with the Afro-Asian nations and their voting strength in the General

Assembly in mind. The UN itself was still seen as incapable of carrying out any of its functions correctly and successfully as long as the
United States and other colonial powers had the control in the Security
Council and the General Assembly. But Peking saw hope in patience.
As the membership was expanded by the admission of newly independent
countries, the number and percentage of votes favoring the PRC increased after 1954 and the American controlled majority gradually
diminished in proportion. (See Appendix A.) In time, Peking must
have thought, the General Assembly would gradually be transformed
into a more balanced organ free from American domination. Then
the Communist Chinese would replace the Nationalist Chinese as a
great power in a UN where their voice would be duly respected.

Even its approach toward the question of Chinese representation
in the UN now reflected Peking's endeavor to woo the Afro-Asians.
For example, on September 24, 1955, an editorial in Jen-min Jih-pao
said,

> China's policy is one of peace. It conforms with the Charter
> of the UN. All fair-minded people acknowledge the con-
> tribution this policy makes to world peace. Public opinion
> the world over admits that without the participation of the
> People's Republic of China it is impossible to settle major
> international issues. Without her one cannot reach world-
> wide agreement on general disarmament and prohibition of
> atomic weapons, nor bring the Korean question nearer solu-
> tion. Yet these are the very questions which this session
> of the Assembly is going to discuss. Make no mistake: the
> lawful right of the People's Republic of China in the UN will
> be restored. All efforts to deny the Chinese people such
> rights will lead nowhere. She will play an increasingly
> important part in world affairs. No power on earth can
> stop her.

This quite clearly was a statement of confidence designed to convince
the Afro-Asians and any other nation that cared to listen that they
should support Peking's bid for China's seat in the UN.

PEACEFUL OVERTURES TO THE US

During this period, Peking's approach toward the US also
gradually moved from confrontation to negotiation, particularly after
the Bandung Conference. Prior to Bandung, Washington-Peking relations were a mixture of hostile exchanges and precarious talks.

With little hesititation, both Washington and Peking used the UN for their own political purposes in their exchanges and talks.

Following the Korean Armistice, Peking's representative, Ambassador Huang Hua, and the UN representative, Ambassador Arthur Dean of the United States, began a series of political talks in October 1953 at Panmunjom "to settle through negotiation the questions of the withdrawal of all foreign forces from Korea, the peaceful unification of Korea, etc."[16] The political talks led nowhere because Arthur Dean was unable to stand Huang Hua's calculated, abusive harangue against his personal authority, reliability and sincerity. Dean walked out on December 12 leaving the conference in limbo.[17] A few weeks afterward, Peking acted to resume the talks, but little that was fruitful resulted.[18]

At the Geneva Conference of 1954, Chou En-lai sat in the same conference hall in the Palais des Nations with John Foster Dulles. On April 24, at the opening of the first part of the conference, which was restricted to Korean questions, Chou demanded that the US and other Western powers be excluded from Asian affairs. Whereupon Dulles answered that the "authority of the UN" was "at stake," and if "this conference is disloyal to the UN and its decisions on how to make peace and unify Korea," then all participants "will bear a share of responsibility for destroying what protects us all." Chou, in turn, replied with an advocacy of "Asia for Asians" and a call for the removal of all foreign military personnel and bases from Asia, but did not dispute what Dulles said about the UN's authority.[19]

While at Geneva, it was reported that on one occasion Chou met Dulles alone in a lounge. Chou extended his hand but Dulles put his hands behind his back, shook his head and left the room. Years later, the Chinese premier alluded to this matter in a private conversation with Edgar Snow.[20] Despite this experience, the Communist Chinese apparently made the first overt move for talks with the Americans at Geneva, using the possible release of American prisoners in China as bait.[21] With the assistance of the British and Asian diplomats, U. Alexis Johnson and Wang Pian-nan actually had five ambassadorial-level meetings with each other in June or July of 1954.

Chou's performance at Geneva was generally considered instrumental in the Indo-China settlement and had a conciliatory hint. By contrast, the American stance at this time was overtly challenging. While Part II of the Geneva Conference was in progress, the US was busy organizing the Southeast Asian Treaty Organization (SEATO) and negotiating the mutual defense pact with the ROC. When the

Indo-China settlement was agreed upon, the US refused to sign the agreements, though promising that she would use no threat or force to undermine them.

Back in Washington, in early July, there was an anti-PRC outburst over the issue of China and the UN.[22] Senate Majority Leader William F. Knowland announced that if the PRC were admitted to the UN, he would resign as majority leader to devote his full efforts to terminating US membership in that organization. Senate Minority Leader Lyndon B. Johnson said on the Senate floor that "the American people will refuse to support" the UN if Communist China is admitted. President Eisenhower stated that he was "completely and unalterably opposed" under the existing situation to the admission of "Red China," and Vice-President Nixon not only voiced opposition to seating Peking in the UN but also bemoaned "the loss of China" to the Communist Chinese. John Foster Dulles, not to be left out, also told a press conference that he was confident of barring the PRC in the upcoming session of the UN and that he could see no reason for "American withdrawal from the UN."

Peking's reactions to such overtly hostile acts on the part of the US were intransigent but less so than in the pre-1954 period. When SEATO was being formed, Peking tried to dissuade Asian membership in the alliance but had no success. Immediately after SEATO was established, Chou reported to the NPC in Peking:

> . . . not only is the alleged 'danger of aggression' by China against Thailand, the Philippines and other countries of Southeast Asia a sheer fabrication, but the view that normal diplomatic relations cannot be established between China and Thailand and between China and the Philippines is groundless. . . . Through the military alliance formed under this treaty the colonialists are attempting to dictate the destiny of Asian countries and to trample upon the Asian peoples' right to self-determination. <u>Such a treaty runs counter to the purpose and principles of the UN charter</u>. The chief countries of Southeast Asia, such as India, Indonesia, Burma and Ceylon, treasuring their freedom and independence, all refused to take part in the Manila Conference. (Emphasis added.)[23]

It is interesting to note that Peking cited the UN purposes and principles in denouncing SEATO. In a sense, one can say that Peking had played down the significance of SEATO. But the signing of the US-ROC pact was taken more seriously. We shall have a careful analysis of that in the next section.

In January 1955, Secretary-General Dag Hammerskjold visited
Peking on a special mission to seek release of 11 US airmen and two
US civilian army employees who were sentenced to long-term imprison-
ment as spies by a PRC military tribunal on November 22, 1954.
Hammerskjold was cordially received even though Peking Radio had
previously rejected UN intervention in that matter. Upon returning
to New York, Hammarskjold told reporters on January 23 that his
talks with Chou En-lai had opened a door and that door could be kept
open, "given restraint on both sides." Soon after that, the UN publicly
declared that "Secretary-General Dag Hammarskjold has no doubt
about the safety of those members of the families wishing to visit
China to see their men." However, a State Department announcement
said that the US government could not "in good conscience encourage
those who may wish to go into an area where the normal protections
of an American passport cannot be offered." Upon learning this,
Hammarskjold commented: "One of the most curious and most upset-
ting features about the present world situation is that everybody is
afraid of everybody."24 On February 28, Chou offered to receive an
unofficial US delegation to negotiate the release of 13 Americans but
was immediately rebuffed. On June 1, four American fliers (not those
sentenced on November 22, 1954) who had been imprisoned in the PRC
for more than two years were released. The four said that Hammarskjold's January visit to Peking "had very much to do with our release."25 Then, on August 1, Peking announced that the 11 US fliers
sentenced as spies had been released. According to Joseph Lash, in
a message to Hammarskjold, Peking indicated specifically that the
airmen were released, "not because of the Assembly's decision but
in order to maintain and strengthen friendship with the Secretary-
General."26

In retrospect, there were subtle overtures from Peking in these
happenings--the offer of a hand in private, the first move for secret,
informal talks in Geneva, playing down the significance of SEATO,
the offer to receive an unofficial delegation to talk over the release
of American airmen--and the actual release of those American fliers.
But it was at Bandung that Chou made the most surprisingly conciliatory overture to the US. On April 23, Chou issued the following statement:

> The Chinese people are friendly to the American people.
> The Chinese people do not want to have a war with the
> United States of America. The Chinese government is
> willing to sit down and discuss the question of relaxing
> tension in the Far East, and especially the question of
> relaxing tension in the Taiwan area.27

This was an offer to abandon the direct battle with the US in the UN
and elsewhere and to regularize face-to-face communication and
discussion. On July 25, agreement on ambassadorial talks was reached
between Washington and Peking and the actual talks began August 1,
1955. Although the talks were to prove not very fruitful, largely owing
to the Taiwan problem, they have become institutionalized since that
time.28 At any rate, in 1955, the overture that Peking extended to
Washington was, along with its offer to negotiate with the Indonesians
on the question of overseas Chinese and its offer of negotiations with
the ROC authority, a new "peaceful offensive" policy. Even if such
offers did not lead to any actual agreements, Peking would still have
scored a psychological point with the Afro-Asian nations.

FORCEFUL OR PEACEFUL "LIBERATION" OF TAIWAN?

In September 1954, while the National People's Congress was in
session in Peking and Chou En-lai was waving the banner of "the Five
Principles of Peaceful Coexistence" abroad, the PRC's artillery shelled
the offshore island of Quemoy and international tension mounted. This
act of violence requires an explanation because it seemed to contradict
the "peaceful offensive" that Peking was pursuing at that time.

In this section it will be argued first that the shelling of Quemoy
was actually a calculated and controlled move on the part of Peking
and was motivated by tactical rather than strategical reasons;29
second, that the declaration of a policy of "peaceful liberation" of
Taiwan in July 1955, by Chou En-lai following the shelling of Quemoy
deserves careful consideration; and third, that, even in its "liberate
Taiwan" campaigns, Peking tried to use the UN in such a way as to
make both its forceful and peaceful moves appear reasonable to the
Afro-Asians.

It was by necessity that in the autumn of 1954 Peking devoted
major attention to Taiwan. To begin with, attention must be paid to
the fact that, in a psychological maneuver, the Eisenhower administration had "unleashed" Chiang Kai-shek's forces during the Korean War.
When American military aid to the ROC forces was increased in the
spring of 1954, Peking watched with alarm and prepared for a Nationalist offensive across the Taiwan Strait. Next, as already mentioned,
intensive negotiations between the ROC and the US for a mutual defense
pact were in progress while Chou was endeavoring to help bring the
Indo-China War to a conclusion. Third, Chiang Kai-shek was in-
augurated for a second term as President of the ROC. Around the

time of his inauguration the Nationalist forces, according to Peking,
were "sending special agents by parachute and other means to carrying
out sinister activities" on the mainland.

Peking was uneasy because its leaders perceived that Taiwan
was becoming an active security threat as well as a damaging nuisance
to the PRC.[30] On July 26, an air battle between the PRC and the ROC
took place over Hainan Island. Peking called it an "extremely grave
provocation against the Chinese people."[31] In his August 11, 1954,
report on foreign affairs to the Central People's Government Council,
Chou En-lai paid special attention to Taiwan:

> . . . the aggressive circles of the United States . . . have
> continually attempted to intervene militarily in China and
> threaten us with war from three fronts: Taiwan, Korea and
> Indo-China. Now the Korean armistice and the restoration
> of peace in Indo-China have gradually reduced tension in
> Asia, and, precisely because of this the aggressive circles
> of the United States, to create new tension, seek to extend
> armed intervention by more intensive use of the Chiang
> Kai-shek traitor gang, hiding in Taiwan, to wage a war of
> harassment and destruction against our mainland and
> coastal areas.[32]

This "war of harassment and destruction" was obviously more than
annoying Peking. Chou continued:

> In true pirate fashion, this traitor group loots and holds
> up ships of various countries trading with our country.
> Shielded by United States naval and air forces and relying
> on training given by the United States "Military Assistance
> Advisory Group," it continues to reorganize its armed
> forces and boast of preparations to attack the mainland. . . .

Translated, this passage could mean that the blockade of the China
coast by the ROC and US forces had been effective to a significant
extent, and that American aid and support to the Nationalist armed
forces, particularly the modernization of their organization and
equipment in early 1954, could not be simply ignored.

It was under such circumstances that Peking took action in early
September against the offshore islands. The artillery shelling began
on September 3, the ROC retaliated with air attacks against the mainland on September 7, but discontinued them about a month later,
evidently at American request. In December, the Communists began

to blockade the Tachen Islands and, on January 18, conquered the
small Yikiangshan Island. In early February, the Nationalist forces
withdrew from Tachen under American protection. In March, as the
Bandung Conference scheduled for mid-April approached, Peking's
military pressure on the offshore islands eased.[33]

It seems that the primary purposes of Peking's military action
were to protest the US-ROC pact and to stop the "war of harassment
and destruction" along the coastal areas of the mainland. From the
beginning, Peking had no real intention of "liberating" Taiwan by force.
The shelling of Quemoy and the taking of Yikiangshan and Tachen were
a display of force and a warning that the ROC must stop its operations
against the mainland. No preparation was ever made to invade Taiwan.
A manifesto issued jointly by 19 Party and mass organizations, including the Taiwan Democratic Self-Government League, just before
the shelling of Quemoy began, "solemnly proclaimed to the whole
world: Taiwan is China's territory. The Chinese people are _determined_
to liberate Taiwan."[34] Significantly, it did not say when or how, only
"determined." On October 10, Chou En-lai sent a cable to UN Secretary-General Dag Hammarskjold.[35] The document enumerated no less
than seven "facts relevant to the armed aggression" committed by
the US government against Taiwan and demanded that the UN "stop
aggresssive action of the US government in interfering with the Chinese
people's liberation of Taiwan." Peking had not made such a formal
complaint against US aggression in Taiwan since 1951. If Peking
were "liberating" Taiwan itself, this demand upon the UN would seem
superfluous and counter-productive.

After the US-ROC pact was signed, Chou En-lai issued a statement
condemning it.[36] Interestingly, he again invoked the UN Charter in
doing so. He said that the so-called treaty of defense was in essence
"diametrically opposed to the purposes and principles which the UN
Charter proclaims . . . (and) cannot possibly promote peaceful coexistence between nations."

Apparently, Peking was effectively making use of the UN in
connection with its decisions about Taiwan. On every occasion, Chou
skillfully claimed the UN of the Charter for his side and accused the
US and her allies of being the violators of the purposes and principles
of the Charter. At the same time, he cast the PRC as a victim of
wrong-doing by the UN under US control to gain sympathy from Afro-
Asians.

On January 19, President Eisenhower told a news conference
he hoped the UN would exercise its good offices to obtain a cease-fire

in the Taiwan Strait. On January 24, Chou replied that a "so-called cease-fire between the People's Republic of China and the Chiang Kai-shek traitor gang" was "an intervention in China's internal affairs for the alienation of China's territory."[37] On January 31, the Security Council passed a resolution sponsored by New Zealand to invite Peking to discuss "hostilities in the area of certain islands off the coast of the mainland of China." In a cable replying to the Secretary-General's invitation, Chou En-lai stated that the New Zealand resolution constituted an interference in China's internal affairs and therefore was a violation of the Charter.[38] He complained that

> . . . the United Nations never took any action on the righteous charges by the People's Republic of China; on the contrary, it repeatedly slandered the People's Republic of China. What is especially intolerable is the fact that the People's Republic of China, representing the six hundred million Chinese people, is up to now still deprived of its legitimate position and rights in the United Nations. . . . Such an extremely unjustified situation makes it impossible for the representative of the People's Republic of China to take part in discussions of questions concerning China in the United Nations.

Further, he added:

> At the same time, it must be pointed out that without the representative of the PRC participating in the name of China. . . . all decisions taken in the Security Council on questions concerning China would be illegal and null and void. (Emphasis added.)

We have already mentioned in the previous sections Chou En-lai's explanation to his fellow diplomats at Bandung for not bringing up the question of "the tension created by the US in the area of Taiwan," and his overture to talk directly with Washington in order to "relax tension" in the Far East and the Taiwan area. In the spirit of Bandung, Chou announced on July 30 (three months after Bandung and five days after the agreement with the US on ambassadorial talks) at the Second Session of the First NPC another surprising move. He said:

> . . . there was no lack of precedents for peaceful liberation. Provided that the United States does not interfere with China's internal affairs, the possibility of peaceful liberation of Taiwan will continue to increase. If possible, the Chinese government is willing to enter into negotiations with the

responsible local authorities of Taiwan to map out concrete
steps for Taiwan's peaceful liberation. . . . 39

Thus, it was to be an all-out "peaceful offensive" including direct
negotiations with Peking's two arch enemies--the US and the ROC.

This "peaceful offensive" might have been encouraged by the
fact that Washington was determined to tolerate neither attacks by the
PRC upon Taiwan, nor provocation by Taiwan against the PRC. On
January 24, 1955, President Eisenhower sent a special message to
Congress requesting emergency authorization to use American armed
forces "to protect Formosa and the Pescadores Islands." The very
next day, the House adopted the Administration resolution with a
410-3 vote. Three days later, the Senate followed suit and the "Formosa
Resolution" was signed into law on January 29. It was also known
then that the US-ROC pact had been accompanied by an exchange of
notes whereby the ROC pledged not to invade the mainland without
prior consultation with the US.40

The corollary measures taken by Peking during this time also
tended to suggest Peking's seriousness about negotiations. There
was actually a cut in the military budget, an overall emphasis on
economic development. A new port, Tsamkong (Chankiang), to the
north of Hainan and out of reach of the blockade was built and a rail
line was extended to Amoy to facilitate trade. It would have been the
greatest triumph for Peking if the problem of Taiwan was actually
solved through peaceful negotiation. Once the Taiwan problem was
solved, so too would be the question of China's representation in the
UN. But things did not turn out that way. The Sino-American talks
bogged down not long after they started, and the overtures to the ROC
authority met a negative response.

In late 1955, the Hong Kong press reported rumors of secret
talks between Peking and Taipei. Shao Li-tsu, a member of Peking's
KMT Revolutionary Committee supposedly wrote to an intermediary,
residing in Hong Kong, regarding the peace terms. The intermediary,
who had worked under Chiang Ching-kuo before, in turn, wrote three
letters to his former boss in the latter half of 1955.41 Another
personality, Chang Shih-chao, a noted jurist and a National Committee
member of the CPPCC, reportedly appeared in Hong Kong as a "peace
envoy" and visited his old acquaintances.42 But these low-level attempts
did not succeed in getting the two sides together. Had the talks materialized in 1955 or early 1956, the specific terms offered by Peking reportedly would have embodied the following:

    1. Chiang Kai-shek would be Vice Premier of the PRC and his son, Ching-kuo, would be governor of Taiwan.

    2. Autonomous status for Taiwan and the Pescadores.

    3. Clemency for KMT officials.

    4. Taiwan-made goods would be treated as PRC products for customs purposes.

    5. In return, the Nationalist government would either concede its seat in the UN or agree with the Communist government on a delegation acceptable to both, for whose instructions Peking would assume responsibility.

    6. Closing of the ROC embassies and legations abraod.[43]

It should be pointed out that Peking's "peaceful offensive," though not successful as far as negotiating with either the US or the ROC was concerned, nevertheless had its harvest. There was an unmistakable trend in the General Assembly voting on the question of Chinese representation in favor of the PRC. In 1953, the voting was 10 in favor of seating the PRC, 44 opposed, and 2 abstaining. Thereafter, it changed to 11-43-6 in 1954, 12-42-6 in 1955, 24-47-8 in 1956 and 27-48-6 in 1957.

8

**ADVENTURISM,
PEKING
STYLE,
1958-61**

A RENEWED OFFENSIVE
AND ACTIVE APPROACH

The period 1958-61 seemed to characterize Peking's impatience
to move toward the second stage of the international protracted struggle.
In this chapter, it will be seen that Peking's leaders (1) mistakenly
perceived an increase in the capabilities of the PRC and its allies to
be a change in the world balance of power, (2) allowed their "revolutionary" zeal to lead them into abandoning the Soviet model and ventur-
ing with the "Three Red Banners," and (3) tried by force to discourage
the US from "plotting" to manufacture "two Chinas." But they met only
unexpected internal economic disaster and major external setbacks.

Between 1954 and 1957, Peking's grand strategy of "encircling
the developed areas from the underdeveloped areas" rested on the
assumption that the encircling camp to which Communist China belonged
was in a weak position. But from early 1958 on, the grand strategy
seems to have been pushed on the assumption that the encircling camp
was in a strengthened position. When the position of the PRC and her
allies was weak, Peking had to be humble and flexible; when their
position became stronger, Peking could also woo and command an
underdeveloped world. In other words, when the capabilities of the
international Communist forces were inferior, Peking's strategic
plays were moderate and reactive; when their capabilities became,
in Peking's own judgment, superior, an active militant approach was
called for.

Between 1958 and 1961, Peking's approach toward the UN was
comparatively aggressive. While the guiding principle remained
"work and wait" for the transformation of the UN, the push was

accelerated. During the couple of years after Bandung Peking had perceived that a degree of international status could be attained through association with the Afro-Asian forums, such as the Bandung Conference, apart from the UN. The tone and flavor of Peking's comments on the UN now seemed bolder and, at times, even arrogant. Obviously keeping a close watch on what was taking place in the UN, Peking now shrewdly played "the UN game" from a distance in such developments as the Middle East crisis, the Tibetan revolts, the U-2 incident, and the Congo crisis.

In the Middle East Crisis of 1958, Peking liberally praised a General Assembly resolution that it liked, but also tacitly disclosed its distaste for the Security Council where the "imperialists" dominated. The Assembly resolution was submitted by the Arabs, calling for the withdrawal of the United States and British "forces of aggression" from Lebanon and Jordan. On August 23, Ta Kung Pao, referring to this resolution, commented that "an outstanding characteristic of the (special) session was the isolation of the United States and British aggressors who appeared as defendants." It further pointed out that the fact that many Latin American countries manifested doubt and hesitation during the session was "a sign of the weakened United States influence in the UN and the loss of its international prestige." The next day, Chou En-lai said that the same session "reflected the characteristics of our era" because "the voice for peace and the safe-guarding of national independence gained supremacy" at the session. "With the support of the socialist and nationalist countries," he said, "the Arab states united in one" were not capable of frustrating "American attempts of aggression."[1] On the other hand, Peking reportedly persuaded Khrushchev to drop two proposals for holding an emergency summit conference on the Middle East Crisis. One of the proposals included India, but not China, as a participant; the other was an acceptance of President Eisenhower's counterproposal to hold the meeting within the framework of the Security Council where China was represented by the Nationalist government. It seems that a General Assembly session, though not considered favorable, was clearly preferable to Peking than either form of summit conference.[2] One suspects that the Assembly was, in Peking's evaluation at the time, closer to the UN of the Charter, while the Security Council was closer to the UN under US control.

In 1959, the Tibet issue was raised by Ireland and Malaya in the Assembly. Finding itself a direct target as in the Korean War, Peking again countered defiantly and offensively. A commentary of the New China News Agency (NCNA) called it "another farce aimed at slandering China, intervening in China's internal affairs and poisoning the

international atmosphere, solely directed by United States imperialism."
The article declared that "to allow the United States and its accomplices
to go on as they like, the United Nations organization will only lose
still more of its prestige." It further warned that

> all self-respected (sic) UN member states should discrim-
> inate between right and wrong, consider the advantages
> and the disadvantages and not place themselves in a posi-
> tion against the UN Charter and hostile to the Chinese
> people.[3]

On October 23, 1959, a formal statement by the government of the
PRC said that the General Assembly's adoption of the resolution that
found China guilty of violating the fundamental freedoms and human
rights of the Tibetan people was "100 per cent fabrication and slander,
reversing right and wrong," and that "the UN . . . again served as a
tool for interfering in China's internal affairs and creating international
tension."[4] Other Peking papers called the resolution "another shameful record for the UN," and "trampling on the UN Charter."[5] An
editorial of Kuang-ming Jih-pao said:

> What an irony! What are the fundamental freedoms of the
> Negro people and what are their human rights? What hu-
> man rights and freedoms are left in the United States when
> the American working class are being oppressed by means
> of the Taft-Hartley Law? They have the audacity to talk
> about human right and freedom for the Tibetans.[6]

The 1960 session of the General Assembly likewise received
few kind words from the Communist Chinese. On October 19, Jen-min
Jih-pao carried an editorial entitled "What Does the 15th Session of the
UN General Assembly Show?" In this editorial, it was said that the
session was in a "very favorable international situation characterized
by the prevailing of the East Wind over the West Wind," but because of
the "ferocious" doings of the United States, a "series of shameful
events" took place. The list of "shameful events" included, among
others, (1) refusal to admit the Lumumba government as the lawful
government of the Congo; (2) refusal to discuss the question of the
restoration of China's lawful rights in the UN; (3) passage of resolutions to put the so-called Tibetan question and Hungarian question on
the agenda; and (4) refusal to discuss "the criminal acts" of the
United States in sending its U-2 and RB-47 aircraft to encroach on the
Soviet territorial air. The same editorial went on to say that

the development of history is not determined by the main
UN voting machine. The majority in the UN can by no means
save imperialism from its inevitable doom. Further, even
this United States voting machine in the UN is becoming less
efficient. . . . Today we are in a minority, but tomorrow, as
we foretell you, you will be in a minority.[7]

What made Peking's leaders think that such a militant and arrogant approach was called for: Was there a significant increase in
Peking's (or its allies') capabilities in 1958? Were there other reasons
that explain Peking's sudden "confidence?"

The answers to these questions were found (1) militarily, in
a Soviet breakthrough in missiles and a Sino-Soviet secret agreement
on nuclear assistance, both in the autumn of 1957; (2) economically,
in the success of the first Five-Year Plan and the enthusiasm of the
"Three Red Banners"; and (3) politically, in Peking's fear of and
efforts to discourage the adoption of a "two-Chinas" or "one-China,
one-Taiwan" formula for solving the Chinese question by the US and/or
the UN.

RIDING WITH THE "EAST WIND"

In her book Communist China's Strategy in the Nuclear Era,
Alice Langley Hsieh demonstrated fairly convincingly that, prior to
1954, the PRC leaders had only an imperfect understanding of the
meaning of modern warfare and disparaged nuclear weapons; that a
new appreciation by these Chinese leaders probably took hold in the
autumn of 1954 following an open debate in the Soviet Union on the
implications of a nuclear war; and that Peking consistently exploited,
both politically and psychologically, Soviet strategic posture (particularly after the successful launching of an ICBM and the first earth
satellite in October 1957, established the alleged superiority of the
Soviet Union over the US).[8]

Peking's first reactions to Soviet achievements in 1957 almost
sounded jubilant. On August 26, the Telegraph Agency of the Soviet
Union (TASS) announced that the USSR had successfully tested an ICBM.
In the next few days, Peking's press described that an "epoch-making"
achievement that not only strengthened the national defense of the
Soviet Union but also added to the power of the socialist camp "in
defense of world peace," and would greatly change the balance of world
power.[9] On October 4, the Russians launched the first artificial earth
satellite, the Sputnik. Peking's Kuang-ming Jih-pao asserted that this

technological advancement was a powerful blow to the imperialist elements that boasted of having the most powerful weapons in the world.[10] Kuo Mo-jo suggested in Jen-min Jih-pao that "the American warmongers" might as well throw overboard their modern dream of war.[11] When Sputnik II was launched on November 3, Jen-min Jih-pao declared that the Soviet achievements were "important facts to show that the Soviet Union is speedily catching up with or surpassing the US in certain vital branches in industry, national defense, science and technology."[12]

In November 1957, Mao Tse-tung made his second and last trip abroad to Moscow to join in the celebration of the 40th anniversary of the October Revolution. Mao told Chinese students in Moscow, "at the present, it is not the West wind that is prevailing over the East wind but the East wind prevailing over the West wind."[13] It was subsequently learned that Mao was riding high with "the East wind" because the PRC had concluded on October 15 an agreement "on new technology for national defense" with the USSR. According to the Chinese, under this agreement the Soviet Union was to "provide China with a sample of an atomic bomb and technical data concerning its manufacture."[14]

This was of course a very significant event. Although Peking had signed an agreement with Moscow for the establishment of a Sino-Soviet Scientific and Technical Commission as early as October 1954, it required some special maneuvering to actually squeeze this promise of direct assistance out of Khrushchev.[15] In January 1955, the Soviet Council of Ministers stated that limited peaceful nuclear sharing would be undertaken with some of the nations of the Soviet bloc. In March 1956, an agreement for the establishment of the Joint Institute for Nuclear Research was signed by the Communist bloc members. In September 1956, a Statute was signed for that Institute. But these agreements only dealt with "peaceful nuclear sharing" in which the Soviet Union provided isotope-producing experimental atomic reactors and Soviet specialists in return for other members' contribution of raw materials to the Soviet atomic program. In June 1957, a group of the so-called anti-Party members of the Communist Party of the Soviet Union (CPSU) Presidium, headed by Molotov, made an attempt to remove Khrushchev from power. At the crucial moment in the struggle, Mao appears to have thrown his weight behind Khrushchev. It was this maneuver on the part of Peking that finally brought Khrushchev to sign the October 15 agreement on Soviet assistance for manufacturing the atomic bomb.

Thus, there were strong evidences that Peking's leaders felt in late 1957 and early 1958 that a new pattern of power relationship between East and West, including a changing position for Peking, was

emerging on the world scene. These were elements that contributed
to Peking's confidence. On July 1, 1958, Peking Radio reported that
the PRC's first experimental atomic reactor had begun operating
June 13. Peking was looking forward to becoming a member of the
exclusive nuclear club.[16]

This confidence was also supported by the general international
climate at the beginning of 1958. Peking's international position had
improved substantially after the Geneva Conference on Indochina and
the Bandung Conference. A keen student of Chinese politics observed
about this time that "the stigma of the United Nations indictment of
Peking as an aggressor in Korea could now be obscured or forgotten."[17]
The expected transformation of the UN was gradually materializing.
As more and more former colonies became independent and joined the
UN, the moratorium against the consideration of changing representa-
tion of China in the UN received less and less support. (See Appendix
A.) In July 1958, U Thant, then Burmese Ambassador to the UN,
estimated that 50 nations would establish relations with Peking if the
US changed her policy.[18]

THE "THREE RED BANNERS"

Domestically, 1958 was also a watershed year. On the one hand,
the unequivocal success of the first Five-Year Plan was most encourag-
ing. The advanced agricultural cooperatives had worked well. Production figures steadily soared. On the other hand, following the
"hundred flowers" episode, an anti-rightist rectification campaign
resulted in mutual mistrust between the Party and the intellectuals.
What ensued was a very unhealthy atmosphere that pervaded the nation.
The ruling circle adopted a new theme of "red and expert."[19] But the
really "red" elements were not very "expert" and the "expert" were
generally not quite "red" enough. The "red" seemed intoxicated with
the success of the first Five-Year Plan and tended to think that China
need not follow traditional economic principles in order to advance
rapidly in agriculture and industry because deficiencies in capital and
technical know-how could be overcome with unlimited human will and
labor. The "expert" knew better but refrained from offering their
knowledge for fear of being treated as ones who dared spread "fan-
tastic anti-socialist views."

In a sense we might say that the first generation leaders of the
PRC, led by Mao Tse-tung, have been a group of men whose temperament made them great revolutionaries but mediocre governors. To
use Mao's frame of thinking, Mao fully understands that to revolt is

not like having a banquet, or doing embroidery, or writing an essay or painting a picture; it cannot be so refined, gentle, restrained and magnanimous, etc. But he seems not to have an equal understanding of the fact that governing a nation is in a way like having a banquet, or doing embroidery, or writing an essay, or painting a picture; it requires those qualities of refinement, gentleness, restraint and magnanimity. For Mao, governing is a continuation of the revolution (politics is a continuation of war). When he called for open criticisms, he was perhaps imitating his own stereotype of good governors. When the open criticism became more than he could stand, he reverted to his familiar ways.

During 1958, Peking's leaders had to make a decision about the implementation of the second Five-Year Plan. They also had to find a way of acquiring the new wealth that building a nuclear weapons system would require once the Soviet Union came through with the promised assistance. Faced with this immense task, Mao and his close comrades chose to gamble rather than rely upon the mistrusted "experts"; they chose the revolutionary mass line. The Soviet model they had emulated hitherto was dropped. Recently acquired documents indicate that Mao said first at the Supreme State Conference on January 28, 1958, that "to revolt is to beat it while it's hot, one revolution after another, marching forward. . ." and later, on June 26, to a group of military cadres, that one must learn from the lessons of history and shed "the myths of old doctrines, foreign (particularly Soviet) methods and self (inferiority)."[20] In October 1957, there was already a call for a "great leap forward" when the Central Committee adopted a revised draft of "the National Agricultural Development Program, 1956-67." In May 1958, the Central Committee made another revision of that Program and gave the "Great Leap Forward" policy a great push. At the same time, the Committee also adopted the so-called General Line of Socialist Construction, which called upon the entire Chinese populace "to exert utmost efforts, press ahead and achieve greater, faster, better and more economic results." In April of that year, the first agricultural commune, significantly named Sputnik, was established in Honan province as a model of the "people's communes." In August, an enlarged session of the Politburo adopted a resolution to establish "People's Communes" in rural areas. Together, these three policies--the General Line, the Great Leap Forward, and the People's Communes--became the "Three Red Banners" of the PRC for the next three years, in place of an originally conceived second Five-Year Plan.[21]

In all, these three policies represented a new militant approach toward the solution of the PRC's domestic problems. The spill-over

of this militant approach into foreign affairs was, therefore, another
explanation of Peking's new boldness toward the UN in this period.
period.

TO DISCOURAGE
"TWO-CHINAS" CONCEPTS

Still another explanation relates to US policy and the situation
across the Taiwan Strait. What the US government had said and done
in response to Chou En-lai's peaceful overtures were most disheart-
ening to Peking. On June 26, 1957, Secretary of State Dulles made
what the State Department called a major speech of American policy
toward China.[22] He must have appeared unbelievably "reactionary"
to Peking. Dulles went down the most hostile line, declaring that the
PRC failed "to pass even those tests which . . . the Soviet regime
seemed to pass." He said the consequences of recognizing the Peking
government would be the following:

1. The many mainland Chinese, who by Mao Tse-tung's own
recent admission seek to change the nature of their government, would
be immensely discouraged.

2. The millions of overseas Chinese would feel that they had
no Free China to which to look.

3. The Republic of China would feel crushed by its friend. . .
and we are honor-bound to give our ally, to whom we are pledged by
a mutual defense treaty, a full measure of loyalty.

4. The free Asian governments of the Pacific and Southeast
Asia would be gravely perplexed.

Dulles added that American recognition would also "make it probable"
that Peking would obtain the seat of China in the UN which he said
was "a bad reformatory for bad governments."

That America's intentions for the PRC were overtly hostile
becomes even more evident when one reads in a State Department
memorandum that "one day (Communist rule in China) will pass" and
that by "withholding diplomat recognition from Peiping, (the US) seeks
to hasten that passing."[23]

In the Sino-American talks, Peking's initiatives to exchange
newsmen with the US and other proposals for increasing bilateral

contacts were all rebuffed by the US government. Furthermore, after
the 73rd meeting on December 12, 1957, Ambassador U. Alexis Johnson
who represented the US at those talks was reassigned to Bangkok.
Washington tried to reduce its representation at the Geneva talks to
below the ambassadorial level. As a result, the talks were suspended.

Meanwhile, unofficially, there were signs that the US was pursuing a de facto "two-Chinas" policy. This was clearly what Chou En-lai
had perceived. In his annual report on "the Present International Situation" to the NPC, delivered on February 10, 1958, Chou said:

> The United States holds ambassadorial talks with China, and
> yet at these talks demands that China accept the status quo
> of its occupation of Taiwan. This is in substance an
> attempt to create "two Chinas," which is of course abso-
> lutely unacceptable to the Chinese side. In the United
> Nations, the United States has met with growing opposition
> in obstructing the restoration to China of its legitimate
> rights, and it has come to see that it is impossible to bar
> China from the United Nations forever. That is why the
> method used by the United States is first to create where-
> ever possible a state of "two Chinas" in certain interna-
> tional conferences and organizations so as to establish
> gradually a fait accompli of "two Chinas" in international
> affairs.[24]

Chou pointed out that Peking had learned about US "plots" of "Two
Chinas" through experiences at the 16th International Olympic Games
in November 1956, from the Special Committee for the International
Geophysical Year in June 1957, and from the 9th International Red
Cross Conference held in October 1957. In every one of these cases,
the PRC withdrew its affiliation because it refused to accept any tacit
arrangement of "two Chinas." A government statement of June 30,
1958, stated that the American endeavor to bring about a situation of
"two Chinas" was "the crux of the reason for the failure" of the
Geneva talks.[25]

Across the Taiwan Strait, there were also causes for Peking's
misgivings in the ROC's moves. Programs of American military
aid to Chiang continued to expand, and most importantly, Chiang's
second term as President (the last under the ROC Constitution) was
due to expire in 1960. Peking might have suspected that Chiang would
attempt to carry out his promised "counterattack" on the mainland
within his remaining tenure.

On August 28, 1958, Peking initiated the second Taiwan Strait Crisis with a heavy bombardment of Quemoy. This action was taken presumably to discourage the manufacturing of "two Chinas" in international organizations and conferences, and to pre-empt or prevent any military assault by the ROC forces upon the mainland. Beyond that, it was probable, as Alice Langley Hsieh contends, that Peking wanted to test Soviet readiness to come to the PRC's aid when the stakes involved were primarily Chinese.[26] It was also reasonable to speculate that the creation of international tension would serve Peking's domestic needs. For Peking's leaders were then trying to arouse new patriotic fervor among the Chinese masses who were being asked to take a "Great Leap Forward" across China's socio-economic predicament.

DISASTER WITHIN, SETBACKS WITHOUT

All the reasons for Peking's jubilation and confidence at the beginning of 1958 were short-lived, however. As events unfolded, it became very clear that Peking's renewed offensive and active approach toward the UN was founded on unreal grounds. Peking's military, economic and political assessments were proved wrong by actual developments. During the years 1959 through 1961, Peking suffered many unexpected calamities, obstacles and failures both domestically and internationally. The results were not at all what Peking had hoped for: Economic disaster and a leadership crisis dominated the scene within; a fundamental Sino-Soviet rift, a display of Peking's impotency to "liberate" Taiwan and a "new trick" of the US to bar Peking's entry into the UN together shattered the basis of Peking's foreign operations without.

Domestically, the "Three Red Banners" boomeranged.[27] The General Line produced immense enthusiam but the mistakes that it generated were of such magnitude that the net result was grossly counterproductive. The Great Leap went backward instead of forward, owing to unusually bad weather and central as well as local mismanagement, among other things. The People's Communes met widespread resistance and productivity dropped drastically in practically all segments of the economy.[28] There was a serious shortage of food and other daily necessities, and the morale of the populace declined to an all-time low.[29] Before the end of 1959, some top-level Party leaders were already extremely perturbed by the grave situation. A number of them, namely P'eng Teh-huai, Huang K'eh-ch'eng, et al., boldly criticized Mao, and demanded changes, which led to an intra-Party leadership shake-up.[30]

During 1958 and 1959, there were three major changes in the top leadership. One was the appointment of Ch'en Yi on February 7, 1958, to the post of Foreign Minister (which had been concurrently held by Premier Chou En-lai up to that time) and to the newly created post of Director of the Staff Office of Foreign Affairs. In all likelihood, this was merely a reorganization intended to relieve part of Chou's heavy burden and to emphasize the importance of foreign affairs. The second was the retirement of Mao Tse-tung as the Chairman of the Republic in January 1959, and the nomination of Liu Shao-ch'i to succeed him in that capacity in April of that year. It is not yet clear whether Mao's retirement was entirely voluntary. At any rate, Mao obviously regretted this move, judging from the following statement that he reportedly made on October 25, 1966.

> In the last 17 years, one thing was not done right. In consideration of national security and in view of the Stalin lesson in the USSR, [we thought it wise] to set up the first and the second lines. I took the second line and other comrades occupied the first. Now I see that it has not been too good; the result has been divisive. Once [the two lines were] established, centralization became impossible; there have been the equivalents of several independent kingdoms. . . . I took the second line, relinquished the direction of daily works, let others do a lot of other things and cultivated others' authority, so that the nation would not experience a great shock when I left to see god. Everyone agreed with this opinion of mine. Later, the comrades on the first line disposed some matters badly. Some of the things I should have grasped but I did not; I too have responsibilities. . . .[31]

The third change of leadership was closely related to the retirement of Mao. In August 1958, Defense Minister P'eng Teh-huai was purged and Lin Piao, a faithful follower of Mao Tse-tung Thought was appointed as the new Defense Minister. P'eng was purged because he dared to attack Mao Tse-tung's mistakes and his authority. We now have clear evidence indicating that P'eng was not a very loyal follower of Mao or his thought. It was P'eng who proposed in 1956 to delete from the Party Constitution the special phrase referring to "Mao Tse-tung Thought," with the approval of Liu Shao-ch'i.[32] It was also P'eng who circulated a memorandum before the Eight Plenum of the Central Committee at Lushan on July 14, 1958, attacking the tragic mistakes of the Great Leap Forward policy, the People's Commune system, and the General Line of Socialist Construction. That Mao was greatly perturbed by P'eng's actions is a fact clearly reflected in the statement that Mao made in response to P'eng's charges. On July 23, Mao spoke to the Central Committee members for 40 minutes, in which he not only attempted to refute and indict P'eng and his associates but also made a half-hearted confession of two mistakes. After opening with a statement that he had "taken sleeping pills three times and still could not sleep," Mao said, inter alia, the following:

> Before August, last year, I put my main energy into the
> revolution; I was uninitiated at construction and did not
> understand industrial planning. . . . The main responsibility
> of 1958 and 1959 is mine. . . . "Was he not without posterity
> who first made wooden images to bury with the dead!" Am
> I not without posterity! A son died in war, another became
> insane. . . .[33]

Mao said that he had fired three great cannons: the Communes, the steel smelting and the General Line. He asserted that the General Line was "essentially a matter of more, faster, better and more economically," and could not be a mistake.[34]

> I have two criminal deeds: one is called 10,700,000 tons
> of steel, the campaign to produce steel en masse (mobi-
> lizing 90 million men), which you agreed to, and can share
> a little with me, but I am "the one who first made the
> wooden images" and cannot escape but to carry the main
> responsibility. [The other] is the People's Communes
> which the world, including the Soviet Union, opposed. . . .

The sequence and timing of events raises an important question: Was Mao politely "elevated upstairs" by the Liu-Teng elements in 1959? It was Mao who, soon after his return from Moscow, instigated the course of the "Three Red Banners." In June 1958, while Mao was calling upon the cadres to smash the three myths of old doctrines, of foreign (particularly Soviet) methods, and of self (inferiority), and plunge into the "Great Leap Forward," P'eng Teh-huai was collecting data on the "Three Red Banners" with which he disagreed.[35] At the Sixth Plenum, the Central Committee decided not to nominate Mao as the Chairman of the Republic when his term expired in January 1959. On July 13, P'eng wrote his critical memorandum that he addressed to Mao, but Mao did not receive until July 17, although copies of it were circulated among the participants of the Lushan Plenum on July 14. Mao counterattacked on July 23, and P'eng was purged on August 16 of that year. But that Lushan Plenum did not adjourn until the wrongs of the policy of the Three Red Banners were recognized, the production statistics adjusted and a call to "increase production and economize" was passed.[36]

This resolution calling for increased production and economy became a sort of mandate that gave the occupants of the "first line"-- Liu Shao-ch'i and his co-hosts of "revisionism"--the opportunity to adopt a moderate course geared to recovery and adjustment, buildup their own following and seize control of the Party organization during the next several years. Their "revisionism" was justified by the conditions of the PRC in 1960 and 1961. But Mao could not tolerate even this "revisionism" beyond the years of its absolute necessity. As we shall see later, in 1969, the Cultural Revolution would bring the downfall of Liu and Teng and reinstate Mao himself back on the "first line."

Through these storms of politics, Chou En-lai remained an indispensable master diplomat and administrator capable of co-operating with any leader in actual power. Chou was no doubt instrumental in helping the PRC sail through the rough seas of the late 1950's.

Internationally, in addition to the continuing struggle against US "imperialists," a serious rift developed between Peking and Moscow in 1959 and 1960. According to Mao, Khruschchev proposed to establish a "common fleet" with the PRC in order to "control the coast line and blockade us (the PRC)" when Mao visited Peking in July 1958. During the Sino-Indian border dispute of 1959, Khrushchev sided with Nehru instead of Mao.[37] On June 20, 1959, the Soviet government unilaterally nullified the 1957 agreement on nuclear assistance to the PRC without honoring its terms.[38] Khrushchev was presumably unhappy because Peking dared to abandon the Soviet model of economic development and launch the communes venture on its own. In September 1959, Khrushchev visited with Eisenhower at Camp David, Maryland, raising Peking's suspicion of possible Moscow-Washington deals at Peking's expense. In the autumn of 1960, Khrushchev ordered the withdrawal of all Soviet experts and technicians working in China. They were ordered also to bring back with them all the plans of enterprises under construction and to in no way facilitate the task of their Chinese successors. All deliveries to China of raw materials, manufactured goods and spare parts were suspended.[39] According to K. S. Karol, this Russian move was intended to compel Peking's capitulation to Moscow's authority as the leader of the international Communist movement. But Peking stood up to Moscow's economic "big stick."[40] From then on, the two Communist giants engaged in "shadow boxing" until the 22nd Congress of the CPSU in October 1961, when their quarrel became an open affair.

Inside Asia, American military aid to Southeast Asian countries gradually increased as the Laotian crisis and South Vietnamese situation became acute. Sino-Indian relations deteriorated over disputes on borders and the status of Tibet.

The Taiwan situation fared no better. Peking's bombardment of
Quemoy failed to discourage the de facto "two-Chinas" practice of the
US; instead it revealed Moscow's reluctance to come to the aid of
Peking. In the Sino-American talks, which resumed in Warsaw on
September 15, 1958, the US continued to elaborate a hidden "two-
Chinas" scheme. According to Young, the US position during the
second Taiwan Strait Crisis contained a two-staged proposal:

> First, a formal cease-fire so that real negotiations not at
> gunpoint could be made possible; and second, agreements
> on specific measures to relieve tensions in the Taiwan
> Straits, including thinning out of forces demilitarization,
> neutralization, trusteeships or a judicial settlement. It
> even hinted that a cease-fire and other arrangements
> could lead to a Foreign Ministers' meeting. . . .[41]

Peking called such proposals "preposterous" and accused the US of
deliberately creating a deadlock in order to mobilize diplomatic pressure to bear on the PRC "under the UN flag."[42]

Peking again tried to persuade Taipei to enter into direct
negotiations:

> The day will certainly come when the Americans will leave
> you in the lurch. . . . The clue is already there in the state-
> ment made by Dulles on September 30. . . . Of course, it
> would not matter so much even if the fighting should con-
> tinue for another 30 years. It is, however, better to secure
> an early peaceful settlement. The choice is up to you.[43]

Again, the reply was negative. After the Crisis subsided, Ch'en Yi
told a Canadian newsman in Peking:

> Quemoy, Matsu, Taiwan and the Pescadores must be lib-
> erated as a whole. We will not allow the handing over of
> Quemoy in exchange for placing Taiwan under trustee-
> ship. . . . Nor can we accept demilitarization or refer-
> ring the matter to the UN or the International Court of
> Justice.[44]

But the aftermath of the second Taiwan Strait crisis, in Kenneth T.
Young's words, "left Peking more restricted and less able than
before to 'liberate' Taiwan by any combination of means."[45]

Within the UN, changes unfavorable to Peking were also taking
place. In July 1960, the Soviet Union had reversed its previous attack

on the establishment of the UN Emergency Force (UNEF) and the UN
Observation Group in Lebanon (UNOGIL)[46] and voted along with the
United States to set up an international peace-keeping force in the
Congo.[47] For Peking, as long as the UN was seen as an organization
dominated by the US, the strengthening of its peace-keeping force
meant increased strength and additional alternatives for American
strategy.[48] Conversely, it could bring further difficulties to China's
grand strategy of "encircling the developed areas from the underdeveloped areas." Peking also feared that the UN would be turned into
a place where the Soviet Union might make deals with the US in order
to fend-off the PRC's invasion into their "superpower club." Although
the Russians renewed their opposition to "the formation of an international army before general and complete disarmament" a few months
later, Peking's fear was never completely erased.

     In early 1961, there were some favorable signs for Peking.
Fifteen African nations plus Cyprus were admitted to the UN in September 1960. The American public elected John F. Kennedy to the presi-
dency instead of Richard M. Nixon; there were reports that the United
States was finally going to drop the moratorium tactic on the question
of China's representation owing to mounting pressure of world public
opinion. However, these signs of hope turned out to be illusory. The
Kennedy Administration was not able to escape American domestic
pressure that blocked the introduction of a new China policy. The US
took up Nationalist China's position, namely that the question of
Chinese representation is a substantive question which, according to
Article 18, Paragraph 2, of the UN Charter, requires a two-thirds
majority vote of the General Assembly to make a change.

     According to Arthur Schlesinger, on one occasion President
Kennedy expressed his views regarding the Chinese question to his
newly appointed ambassador to the UN, Adlai Stevenson, in these words:

> You have the hardest thing in the world to sell. It really
> doesn't make any sense--the idea that Taiwan represents
> China. But if we lost this fight, if Red China comes into the
> UN during our first year in town, your first year and mine,
> they'll run us both out. We have to lick them this year.
> We'll take our chances on next year.[49]

     For four months, from August through December 1961, Peking's
propaganda machines concentrated on the denunciation of the new
"United States plot" to block Communist China from getting into the
UN. In between blasts, Peking tried in vain to persuade the Kennedy
Administration to negotiate some kind of a deal. On October 12, two

and a half weeks after President Kennedy delivered his "peace" speech in the UN and one week before the 22nd Congress of the Communist Party of the Soviet Union convened in Moscow, Foreign Minister Ch'en Yi made known that Communist China was willing to hold talks at the foreign minister level with the United States if the initiative came from Washington, and that if the US would abandon her attempt to block the PRC's entry into the UN, peaceful co-existence was "entirely possible." It was a long shot in vain.[50] On December 14, 1961, the General Assembly passed the five-nation resolution support- ing the US position with an unexpectedly large margin of 62 yes, 34 no, and 7 abstaining.

Reactions from Peking during the weeks immediately following the adoption of the five-nation resolution revealed a great deal about Peking's disappointment. On December 21, the Ministry of Foreign Affairs issued a statement in which it was "solemnly" declared that the resolution, "which tramples upon the UN Charter and infringes on China's sovereignty, is completely illegal and null and void."[51] The next day, Jen-min Jih-pao published a lengthy editorial that carefully answered a self-posed question--"Why is it that the United States should have acted so desperately to prevent the restoration of China's lawful rights in the UN and so obstinately clung to its policy of hostility to China?" It was charged that

1. The United States can never reconcile itself to the victory of the revolution of the Chinese people;

2. The United States wants to occupy China's territory Taiwan permanently;

3. The United States has regarded China as "wicked to the last degree" because the Chinese people, holding high the great anti-imperi- alist banner, have given a mighty inspiration to the revolutionary struggles of all oppressed nations and peoples of the world; and

4. The United States is extremely afraid of the international influence of new China, especially the expansion of this influence into the UN organization.[52]

With hindsight, it may be said that inexperience, wrong methods, bad management, foreign pressures and hard luck had all played their parts in making 1958-61 a dark period in Peking's records. But, one also suspects that the proud, self-righteous and defiant leaders of Peking had committed their disastrous mistakes because they lacked the ability (since the most dominant among them had been isolated from the outside world) to appreciate the indispensable services of their "expert" planners and advisors.

Whatever the explanations, one thing is clear: Peking's protracted approach toward the UN was surely protracted. So protracted that one could see no end in sight at all.

9

**A NEW
DIRECTION,
1962-65**

FROM POSITIVE TO NEGATIVE

After the 1961 Assembly resolution crushed its hope to take over China's seat in the UN, Peking's policy toward the world organization underwent another change. This time, the change was one of attitude, not just of approach; for the first time, Peking's basic attitude turned from positive to negative. In this chapter, the circumstances and the process of that change will be discussed, and a statement of Foreign Minister Ch'en Yi in September 1965, in which he stipulated some conditions of Peking's participation in the UN will be analyzed. The thesis here is that Peking turned its thinking toward finding or creating a substitute for the UN after 1961. Prior to January 1965, Peking searched in the Afro-Asian world for such a substitute. In January 1965, Peking plunged into that very idea, soliciting the Afro-Asians to quit the UN and join with the PRC in the creation of a new "revolutionary" world forum. But the world was not ready to accept what Peking had to offer. Again, Peking might have suffered internationally because, among other things, its top leaders did not fully understand the reality of the world situation; they seem to have assumed too much about the similarities between China's recent past and the Afro-Asian nations' present conditions and underestimated the sophistication and independence of many Afro-Asian leaders.

This change of attitude from positive to negative was, in retrospect, quite understandable. Circumstantial evidence in and out of the UN suggests that such a new direction was, from Peking's point of view, worth a try. To begin with, the UN controlled by the US seemed to perpetuate itself. As the non-Western forces grew stronger in the General Assembly, there were signs for a time that some pivotal functions of the UN were being shifted to the office of the Secretary-General.

By assisting in strengthening the office of the Secretary-General and
by exerting influence over its newly developing function of " preventive
diplomacy," the United States seemed able to by-pass the General Assembly when the latter organ became antagonistic toward the West.[1] Hence,
the "Troika" episode in 1960.[2]

Next, the role that the PRC could play in the UN had become a
dubious one. Peking now was struggling against not only "imperialist"
America, but also "revionist" USSR and "reactionary" India--the three
most influential members of the UN. In April 1961, an arcticle in the
top-secret military bulletin, Kung-tso Tung-hsun had this to say:

> If our country joins the United Nations, we cannot have a ma-
> jority in voting; formally the difficult situation may be mod-
> erated to some extent, but actually the struggle that arises
> will be more violent and we shall lose our present freedom of
> action. Though standing outside of the United Nations, we
> could still participate in the Bandung Conference. We made
> tremendous achievements in that conference. Last year we
> signed treaties of friendship with five countries (Cambodia,
> Nepal, Afghanistan, Yemen and Guinea), and settled problems
> about the boundary lines between China and Burma and between
> China and Nepal just because the United States had no chance
> to join in the negotiation or to exert pressure. . . . Outside
> of the United Nations, we have enjoyed a peaceful coexistence
> with the countries in Asia, Africa and Latin America, and the
> peaceful area is being enlarged.[3]

If further stated, ". . . some wished to limit the development of China
by dragging it into the United Nations in order to harness it," and then
warned its select readership, "The world is like a chessboard, and 'one
carless step will cause the loss of the whole game'."

Third, the prize of the UN seat had by now lost most of its important attraction. There was a realization on the part of Peking that
a seat in the UN even with the "veto power" would not add much to
China's already mounting power status. At the Geneva Conference on
Laos between May 1961, and July 1962, Peking was an acknowledged
major participant and was instrumental in bringing about the agreement
to neutralize Laos.[4] Peking had quite clearly realized the advantages
of staying outside the UN: it left Peking free to oppose or support the
actions of the UN and to advocate and encourage the national liberation
movements, as the above-quoted document clearly attests.

Outside the UN, the existing conditions also would support a
switch toward the new direction. First, there was little hope of

solving the Taiwan problem. It seemed every available means of taking
Taiwan in the short-run has been tried and found lacking. There was
no real choice left for Peking other than to wait. In the summer of
1962, a third Taiwan Strait Crisis developed because the KMT government in Taiwan tried to "recover the mainland" while the CPC Government was knee-deep in domestic and foreign troubles. Peking reacted
"vigilantly" but refrained from any action. After the crisis, rumors
travelled around the world that Peking-Taipei secret negotiations had
taken place and tacit agreements had been reached between them. But
such rumors remained rumors.[5]

Second, the impasse on the Taiwan problem was affecting Peking's
Afro-Asian policies. Afro-Asian nations that are sensitive to the
principle of self-determination tend to support the ieda of a plebiscite
for the inhabitants of Taiwan. Others that are more pragmatic seem
to respond to the ingenious "agricultural diplomacy" of the ROC rather
than to the ideological fanfare of the PRC.[6] As time passes, more and
more nations have come to stress the fact that Taiwan is actually larger
in the size of both its population and its national wealth than a great
majority of other members of the UN. As a result, it becomes more
and more difficult for Peking to advance its rigid claim to Taiwan. This
fact must have come to the attention of the attention of the PRC's leaders
over the years. The logical conclusion from this is that Peking might
be pressed by the Afro-Asian nations rather than just the US to accept
a "one-China, one-Taiwan" solution on the question of Chinese representation in the UN. Should that happen, Peking's position would be a very
awkward one: It would have to yield to that pressure or offend some
of the potential members of its contemplated "international united
front." Neither would be a happy choice.

Third, there was more evidence showing that Peking's fear of
political deals between the Soviet Union and the United States was not
unfounded. From Peking's point of view, the Russians had not only
failed to exploit their superior power after launching of Sputnik, but
under Khrushchev, had flirted with the United States at Camp David
in 1959 and voted for the Organisation des Nations Unies au Congo
(ONUC) in the UN along with the United States in 1960. Khrushchev also
had installed missiles on Cuba without consulting Peking. During
October 1962, Khrushchev committed the crime of "capitulating" to
American "blackmail" in the Cuban Missile Crisis. The following
year, Khrushchev further agreed with the Kennedy administration on
the installment of the "hot line" and signed the Test Ban Treaty with
Washington. All of these Peking took as evidence of Khrushchev's
betrayal. Such being the case, Peking might think it imperative that
effective measures be taken to prepare for the worst: a US-USSR

collusion against the PRC. A world forum in which the PRC rather
than either the US or the USSR dominated undoubtedly appeared attractive in Peking's imagination.

It seems probable, therefore, that the new tactic the United States
had successfully employed at the 1961 Session of the General Assembly
to bloc Peking's entry into the UN not only induced Peking to issue the
the editorial of December 22, 1961, quoted in Chapter 8 (see pp. 123
and 124), but also helped Peking make up its mind on the need to search
for a substitute for the UN. After the Korean War, the PRC had turned
to the Afro-Asian forums because the UN was not open to her. Then
the policy-makers of Peking, concluding that the Bandung Conference,
while a very fruitful creation, was not quite a substitute for the UN,
pushed for a transformation of the UN. When the United States successfully employed "the new trick" to block her entry into the UN, in spite
of increasing support for the PRC, Peking then turned seriously toward
a possible substitute for the UN.

The following two sections represent an account of the process
of Peking's switch from a positive to a negative attitude toward the UN.

IN SEARCH OF A UN SUBSTITUTE

After the editorial of December 22, 1961, there were a few scattered commentaries in the Chinese press repeating the same points,
and then all direct comments on the UN abruptly subsided. This silence
meant, perhaps, that the Chinese leaders were pondering another serious
change in strategy.[7] Because they had considered it wise to keep the
possible UN channel open, however, they made no open announcement
of their intention until January 1965.[8] It seems that the only important
comment on the UN during the two years after 1961 session of the General Assembly was an editorial of Jen-min Jih-pao dated December 18,
1963, which was a rebuttal of the Soviet Union's effort to link the question of Chinese representation with that of the broadening of Afro-Asian
representation in the Security Council and the Economic and Social
Council (ECOSOC).[9] The editorial expressed "greatest regret at the
improper tactics employed by the Soviet's delegate," affirmed Peking's
support for the Afro-Asian demand and suggested a readjustment in the
distribution of seats in the two organs as a simpler and easier method
to speedily meet the demands of the Afro-Asian countries. Beyond
this, however, the editorial tactfully declared:

Until the restoration of China's legitimate rights . . .

> China will undertake no commitment on any activity or
> decision of the United Nations including the revision or
> non-revision of the UN Charter. . . . The Chinese govern-
> ment has, however, always judged the activities of the UN
> on their intrinsic merits. We resolutely oppose all evil
> doings of the UN, but will have no objection to the good
> things, if any, done by the UN.

Significantly, Peking did not insist in this editorial, as it had before,
that any revision of the UN Charter without its participation would
be illegal and null and void. Clearly, this editorial was designed
to suit the taste of the Afro-Asians without jeopardizing its own
position regarding "the UN controlled by the US."

An investigation of the general domestic and foreign policies of
the PRC during 1962-63 reveals several interesting things, all tending
to support the proposition that Peking was stepping up its efforts to
win the support of the Afro-Asian and Latin American nations.

Internally, a retrenchment policy based on the doctrine of
"self-reliance" was introduced. Beginning in 1962, a policy under the
slogan, "Agriculture as a Foundation, Industry as the Leading Factor"
replaced the Great Leap. [10] To effectuate rapid recovery of the national
economy, the government of Liu Shao-chi'i and Teng Hsiao-p'ng introduced policies that emphasized " prudence, moderation, realism and
restraint." Concessions were given to land tillers in many areas.
Free market practices and private plots were allowed, and material incentives were utilized. Even the "capitalists" were encouraged to play
a greater part in the effort to accelerate economic recovery; the
government policies guaranteed them a high salary, a more favorable
political treatment, and even a bonus for superior performance. These
"revisionist" measures were taken by the Liu-Teng Party organization then in control of the "first line." While the primary motivation
behind such policies might have been the livelihood or just plain power
ambition, the outcome invariably helped Peking's other undertakings,
including a stepped-up nuclear program and an extended foreign aid
program, both of which are related to the idea of setting up a rival
UN with Peking as the leader.

Internationally, Peking stepped up its course of "people's diplomacy." It increased its aid programs toward the countries of the
"First intermediate zone,"i.e., Asia, Africa and Latin America, and
embarked on a new trade offensive toward the " second intermediate
zone,"i.e., Western European countries and Japan.[11] Its activities
in Africa and Latin America took on greater proportions. More major

delegations travelled to these regions from Peking, particularly from
the beginning of 1963.[12] Despite its own economic difficulties, Peking
made substantially increased aid promises to many African countries.[13]
The direction of its foreign trade drastically changed, reflecting a new
guideline of "leaning to all sides." Its trade with the non-communist
countries jumped while its exports to and imports from the communist
countries dropped.[14]

Events of 1964 proved the significance of these policy changes.
Between December 14, 1963, and February 29, 1964, Chou-En-Lai and
Ch'en Yi toured ten African countries, Albania and three Asian countries.
Peking was obviously wooing these countries in order to secure wider
support for another Afro-Asian conference and to win the support of
these countries in its struggle with India and with the Soviet Union.[15]
While the two men were in Africa, France recognized the government
of the PRC on January 9. In the following month, Peking took care to
repeat its support for Cambodia's "liberation" from American aid,
for the "restoration of the lawful rights of the Arab people of Palestine"
and for Indonesia's "confrontation" with Malaysia.

On May 26 Nehru died. India lost her leader with world influence.
On October 14, Khrushchev was ousted as Premier and First Secretary
of the CPSU. In November, Lyndon B. Johnson soundly defeated Barry
Goldwater in the American presidential election. Peking's leaders must
have watched these developments with satisfaction. On October 16,
Peking detonated its first atomic bomb, and called for a world summit
conference to ban the use of nuclear weapons and ultimately to eliminate them.[16] This nuclear achievement was a triumph of Peking's
"self-reliance," a victory in the socialist camp and a great boost for
the PRC's international prestige as the first non-white, non-Western
member of "The Nuclear Club."

These events must have reinforced Peking's self-confidence.
The idea of creating a substitute for the UN came alive. On December
4, 1964, an editorial of Jem-min Jih-pao pointedly queried:

> Since 1949, revolutions or coups d'etat have taken place
> in many of the UN member states, and the new regimes,
> irrespective of their character, have immediately and
> legally replaced the old regimes as representative of
> their countries at the UN. No objection has ever been
> raised in the UN to such changes, nor indeed should any
> be raised. . . . But why should the question of the legi-
> timate rights of the People's Republic of China be the
> only exception and even be described as an "important

question" whose settlement requires a two-thirds majority vote?[17]

Peking was obviously indignant about such a double standard. But there
is more. The editorial went on:

> Some well-intentioned friends would perhaps feel that
> China might as well recover its seat in the UN first and
> then have the Chiang Kai-Shek gang evicted. We appre-
> ciate the good intentions of these friends who are anxious
> to see China playing its proper role in the UN. But, we
> must point out that this would be falling into the U. S.
> trap of "two Chinas." China will, under no circumstances,
> accept this. If the UN does not evict the Chiang Kai-shek
> gang from all its organizations, the Chinese government
> will not have anything to do with it, nor undertake any respon-
> sibility toward it. . . .

Peking still had not quite said it, but this passage seems to suggest that
its leaders had already made up their minds not only to do without the
UN, but perhaps, also to create a rival UN.

THE CALL FOR ESTABLISHING
A "REVOLUTIONARY" UN

A sudden climax developed in January 1965. On December 31,
two days after the election of Malaysia to the Security Council, Indonesia's President Sukarno declared in a mass meeting in Jakarta that,
if Malaysia became a member of the Security Council Indonesia would
withdraw from the UN. A week later, despite the appeal of the Secretary-General and the Prime Minister of Japan for reconsideration,
Sukarno announced at another rally in Jakarta that "from now on Indonesia is no longer a member of the UN."[18]

The manner in which Indonesia withdrew seems to suggest that
Sukarno was merely an accomplice in staging a destructive blow against
the UN that would be the preparatory step toward setting up a rival
organization to be composed of the Afro-Asians and lead by the PRC.
If one recalls that the election of Malaysia to the Security Council on
December 29, 1964, was in accordance with an understanding reached
in the General Assembly in the previous year when Malaysia and
Czechoslovakia were deadlocked in competing for the seat, one cannot help but wonder if the Indonesian withdrawal was not a subsequent,
calculated move, and the objection to Malaysia merely a convenient
pretense.

The readiness and the vigor with which Peking welcomed the
Indonesian move also supports our reasoning. With Sukarno in the
front line, Peking took the opportunity to speak its mind. Its UN policy
turned swiftly into an active, negative, offensive and indirect approach.
During the week following January 7, Chairman Liu "expressed great
appreciation" for President Sukarno's statement that "the crown of independence of a country does not lie in membership of the UN, but in self-
reliance," and said that "in pursuing self-reliance, Asian and African
countries can rely on mutual assistance among themselves based on the
principle of equality, but not on the so-called aid from imperialism."[19]
Ch'en Yi called the Indonesian move "a lofty and just revolutionary move"
and "the first spring thunderbolt of 1965 which resounded throughout
the world," which "shocked and dismayed" the "imperialists," but
"inspired and brought joy to all countries and peoples fighting imperialism and colonialism to safeguard their national dignity."[20] A government statement of January 10 said:

> It is quite understandable that newly independent Asian
> and African countries should have placed some hopes in the
> the UN. However, more and more facts have shown that
> the UN has been increasingly reduced to a tool of imperial-
> ism and old and new colonialism headed by the United
> States. . . . In the development over the past 20 years, the
> UN has reached a stage where a reappraisal of it in the
> light of its actual deeds has become necessary. The People's
> Republic of China representing the 650 million Chinese people
> has all along been excluded from the UN and now Indonesia
> representing 104 million people is compelled to withdraw
> from it. Is this not adequate proof that this so-called world
> organization needs to be thoroughly remolded? . . .
>
> The UN is by no means sacred and inviolable. We can live
> on very well without it. . . . President Sukarno has kicked
> the backside of this tiger. This is a great help in ending the
> blind faith to the UN.[21]

The Jen-min Jih-pao editorial of the same day counted the "shameful
records" of the UN one by one and said:

> The increase in the number of Asian and African members
> in the UN has by no means brought about any fundamental
> change in the fact that the UN has become a United States
> imperialist instrument for agression. . . . The UN is not
> the place where the Asian and African countries can uphold
> justice; it is the place where United States imperialism

bullies and oppresses people. Can this be tolerated any
longer?

It then condemned "the cult of the UN," and called the world organization a "paper tiger."[22]

On January 24, Premier Chou declared:

The UN has committed too many mistakes. It has utterly
disappointed the Asian and African countries. It must
correct its mistakes. It must be thoroughly reorganized.[23]

He did not stop there; he let out a trial balloon.

In these circumstances, another UN, a revolutionary one,
may well be set up so that rival dramas may be staged in
competition with that body which calls itself the UN but
which is under the manipulation of United States imperialism and therefore can only make mischief and do nothing
good.

About this time, Mao Tse-Tung granted an interview with Edgar Snow,
of which Snow wrote in February:

Indonesia had withdrawn from the United Nations, I
observed, accompanied by applause from China. Did
Mao Tse-tung think the move would set a precendent
and that other withdrawals would follow?

Mao said that it was the United States which had first
set the precedent, by excluding China from the United
Nations. Now that a majority of nations might favor
China's seat despite US opposition, there was a new
scheme to require a two-thirds majority instead of a
simple majority. But the question was, did China gain
or lose by being outside the UN during the past 15 years?
Indonesia had left because she felt that there was not much
advantage to remaining in the UN. . . .

Is it now practicable [Snow asked] to consider forming a
union of nations excluding the United States?

Mao pointed out that such forums already existed. One
example was the Afro-Asian conference. Another was
GANEFO--Games of the New Emerging Forces--
organized after the United States excluded China from the
Olympics.[24]

Snow elaborated that "it had been obvious for some time that the Afro-
Asian Conference is also viewed as a potential permanent assembly
of the have-not nations, to exist independently from the American-domi-
nated United Nations." One rationale behind this thinking was supplied
by Mao to Snow, and it also explains in part the quarrel between the
Chinese and the Russians:

> ... The gap between their (Afro-Asian) ever-falling standard
> of living and that of the affluent countries is rapidly widening.
> Under such conditions, will time wait for the Soviet Union
> to demonstrate the superiority of the Socialist system--
> and then wait a century for parliamentarianism to arise
> in the underdeveloped areas and peacefully establish Social-
> ism? Mao thought that it will not wait so long.[25]

There were signs that Peking believed in this reasoning. The push
for the Second Afro-Asian Conference was all too clearly a major step
towards setting up "a revolutionary UN." In fact, Peking was so anxious
for it that when Algeria's Colonel Boumedienne staged the untimely
coup d'etat ten days before the Conference was to convene in Algiers,
the Chinese "put their face in their pocket, . . . hastened to embrace
him, in the hope of salvaging the summit." They did not even consider
that "a city where further shooting may occur is hardly the place to
assembly the heads of 50 governments."[26] When the Preparatory
Meeting finally decided to postpone the Conference until October or
November 1965, because only 35 delegations (out of close to 70 expected) and arrived in Algiers on the eve of June 29, and because material preparation" required more time, Peking again quickly agreed,
explaining that the postponement was necessary for a more successful
conference.[27]

       However, Peking's "rival UN offensive turned out to be a great
diplomatic blunder. Mao Tse-tung might have "that sense of history"
that marks a strong political leader, but his lack of understanding about
the ups and downs of the international climate and his timing could not
have been worse. When Ben Bella was ousted in Algeria in June 1965,
Peking suffered the first of a series of serious setbacks. Its effort to
court Boumedinne obviously did not succeed. As October 28, 1965--
the rescheduled date of the beginning of the Second Afro-Asian Confer-
ence--drew near, Peking found itself arguing with the new Algerian
regime. The government of the PRC now opposed convening the meeting
at that time because "it will create a split" between the Afro-Asian.[28]

The real reason, however, seems to be Peking's perception that she was losing support. Peking wanted to exclude the Soviet Union, which was "neither an African nor an Asian country," from attending the Conference. It also wanted to have the Conference condemn "US imperialist aggression against Viet Nam." Further, she requested the cancellation of "the illegal invitation to United Nations Secretary-General U Thant, 'because "to invite a representative of the UN or anyone from it. . . would mean, in effort, to bring the United States into the Conference."29 But Chou En-lai's team was not at all sure that these Chinese positions could be pushed through the Conference successfully. The Conference was eventually postponed again, indefinitely. But it was hardly a victory for Communist China.

In the months following the Algerian coup d'etat of June 1965, Peking experienced more sharp reverses in its diplomatic fortunes. There was a political upheaval in Indonesia in September that led to a military takeover and a bloody purge of the Indonesian Communist Party (PKI), and eventually, the stripping of Sukarno's political power in March 1966.30 In Latin America, Comrade Castro turned against Peking and bitterly attacked the PRC at the opening of the Afro-Asian-Latin American Solidarity Organization's conference held in January 1966.31 In Ghana, Nkrumah was outsted on February 24 by his own people while en route to visit Peking.32 It was Sukarno's Indonesia that dealt the first blow upon the UN in response to Peking's calls by withdrawing from the world organization. Peking had hoped to built its "revolutionary UN" on Sukarno's pilot project of the NEFO (New Emerging Forces) assembly.33 It was Nkrumah who served as the mouthpiece of Peking in Africa, and to a lesser extent, Cuba's Castro in Latin America. Peking expected to sell its theory of revolution--that the real salvation of the "have-nots" lay only in unrelenting revolutionary struggle by the NEFO against the OLDEFO (Old Established Forces), and not in non-alignment--with the help of Sukarno, Ben Bella, Nkrumah and Castro to the three continents.34 However, Peking lost these important friends one by one in close succession.

There were other disappointments. From Peking's point of view, the war in Viet Nam had not been going well since the summer of 1965. Despite Peking's flirtation, Pakistan cooled off after the Tashkent settlement tended the renewed fighting between Pakistan and India.35 Leaders of Kenya and the Ivory Coast expressly denounced China as "a long-term danger for Africa."36 And the Organization of American States went on record protesting a resolution in support of "wars of liberation"adopted by the Afro-Asian- Latin American Solidarity Organization's conference in Havana.37

Ironically, it seems that the UN was the only place where Peking
had experienced not a reverse but an advance in 1965. Despite Peking's
continued attack on the UN at the 20th Session of the General Assembly,
12 nations jointly sponsored a resolution calling for the restoration to
the PRC of its "legitimate seat" in the UN. The result of the voting
was a 47 to 47 tie. Some observers speculated right after the voting
that Peking might get a majority support at the 21st Session.

Yet, even that favorable development was not a cause for Peking's
rejoicing. For the feared US-USSR collusion was extending into the
meeting rooms of the UN. The UN was "becoming more and more a
place where the Soviet Union and the United States made their deals."[38]

CH'EN YI'S "CONDITIONS"
FOR PARTICIPATION IN THE UN

On September 29, 1965, Foreign Minister Ch'en Yi stipulated
several stiff demands upon the UN at a press conference. [39] He said:

> How can China be expected to take part in an international
> organization which calls her an aggressor? Calling China
> an aggressor and asking the aggressor to join, would not the
> United Nations be slapping its own face? The question now
> is how to reform the UN in accordance with the purposes and
> principles of its Charter and to free it from the control of
> the United States and other big powers. If the task of re-
> forming the UN cannot be accomplished, conditions will
> no doubt gradually ripen for the establishment of a re-
> volutionary United Nations. . . . The United Nations must
> rectify its mistakes and undergo a thorough reorganization
> and reform. It must admit and correct all its past mistakes.
> Among other things, it should cancel its resolution con-
> demning China and the Democratic People's Republic
> of Korea as aggressors and adopt a resolution condemning
> the United States as the aggressor; the UN Charter must
> be reviewed and revised jointly by all countries, big and
> small; all independent states should be included in the
> United Nations; and all imperialist puppets should be
> expelled. [40]

There have been various interpretations of these demands. These
words have led some American observers to conclude that Peking has
challenged the right of the UN to exist as a world organization,[41]
while others view them as signs of Peking's abandonment of the Charter

principles.[42] In retrospect, it seems quite probable that this statement expressed Peking's disinterest rather than stipulated the necessary
conditions of its participation in the UN. The Indonesian withdrawal
from the UN in January 1965, followed by Cambodia's withdrawal from
the UN Special Committee of Decolonization seems to have led Peking's
decision-makers to mistake their own wishful thinking for a realistic
hope--the hope that a substitute for the UN was not out of reach.[43]
Peking decided to accelerate its cultivation of the Afro-Asian Conference
and the New Emerging Forces where it intended to stage and direct its
own drama of world politics. Perhaps a decision was reached in Peking
that the cautious approach prior to 1965 should be abandoned in favor
of a more aggressive and frontal one that would discredit the UN and
promote Afro-Asian solidarity at the same time. If such was the case,
it is understandable that Peking's utterance during and after 1965 turned
openly hostile toward the UN and the Special Agencies. The Ch'en Yi
statement of September 1965, is thus a set of intentionally impossible
conditions for Peking's participation in the UN. This interpretation
is supported by the fact that prior to 1965 the only condition for Peking's
participation in the UN was the expulsion of the Nationalist representatives and the complete restoration of China's legal right to the PRC.
As late as December 4, 1964, Jen-min Jih-pao was still asserting that
"the day will certainly come when China's legitimate rights in the UN
will be restored," and "US obstruction will fail."[44]

Actually, what is of interest is that Ch'en Yi bothered to stipulate
these conditions at that time. On August 3, 1965, after two weeks of
talks with Chinese leaders in Peking, the French Foreign Minister,
André Malraux, told a Hong Kong press conference that the Chinese
leaders were "still keeping one window open to (joining) the UN that now
exists" while "keeping one window open to a new UN."[45] If that was
true, perhaps Ch'en was trying to keep the door ajar while Peking worked
on the "revolutionary" UN; it was his way of saving that Peking was
"not interested" in the existing UN for the time being.

Thus, if it is kept in mind that Ch'en Yi was intentionally stating
Peking's toughest conditions, and the reasons behind the words are considered, it may be possible to analyze his statement meaningfully.

Logically, the statement includes three conditions: (1) the UN
as "an aggressor," (2) the UN must "admit and correct all its past
mistakes," and (3) the UN must "undergo a thorough reform and reorganization" in order to "free itself from the control of the United
States and other big powers."

The first condition, if realized, would be tantamount to the UN's

self-destruction. It is entirely unrealistic. As long as Peking holds
on to this condition, one can only conclude that the PRC is not really
interested in joining the UN.

With regard to the second condition, Peking had in mind specifically the cancellation of the earlier Security Council resolutions that
condemned the PRC and North Korea as "aggressors" and imposed
embargoes upon them. Perhaps the rectification of this "mistake" as
an added condition of the PRC's participation in the UN should be considered. For, as the representative of a self-protrayed "New China,"
Peking has been jealous of its prestige; it has been "face conscious."
This is clearly expressed by the first paragraph of the above quoted
Ch'en statement.

Whether the relevant Security Council resolutions actually constitute a "mistake" or not, it may be pertinent to observe here that, until
now, the PRC and North Korea have been the only governments officially
condemned by the UN as "aggressors" even though serious offenses
by other actors have not been lacking. [46] The nullification of the said
resolutions, in effect, would not lead to further complications and may
even inject a new sense of fairness into the world organization. It is
quite probable, therefore, that the UN may find it both necessary and
useful to search for a way out that is satisfactory to Peking should it
decide to seat the PRC in its chambers.

As to the numerous "other mistakes" of the UN, they need not
be dwelt on here. Peking's insistence would perhaps only indicate its
disinterest. Once the UN has made the gesture of nullifying its earlier
condemnation of the PRC, we may find Peking not quite so unyielding
on rectifying other "mistakes" of the UN, if its interest in taking advantage of the services and facilities of the UN system has revived.

The third condition is more complicated. It states that the UN
must be thoroughly reformed and reorganized in accordance with the
purposes and principles of its Charter. That Peking has always supported the Charter can be considered as a propaganda gimmick designed
to woo the Asian-African nations. But, more than that, the Charter also
represents a hope for Peking. For, according to the Charter, the PRC
can aspire to play the role of an equal with the other "big four" in the
world arena. If the Charter is faithfully adhered to, the veto power
will serve to safeguard Peking's vital interests as it has for the
Soviet Union. In 1963, when Peking gave its support to the Afro-Asian
quest for greater representation in the Security Council and ECOSOC,
it also painstakingly suggested that a readjustment in the distribution
of seats in two organs rather than a revision of the Charter was more

appropriate. To be sure, Peking did not argue against a revision of
the Charter, but it certainly showed reluctance in supporting any revision of the Charter without its participation.[47]

As to "reform and reorganization," the specific demand was
that the UN must "free itself from the control of the US and other big
powers" so that it may "better reflect the balance of forces in the
world and present international realities."[48] To free the UN, the expansion of Afro-Asian representation alone is not enough; for it has
"by no means brought any fundamental change."[49] Peking suggests
further that all "independent states" must be included and all "imperialist puppets" excluded. However, it has not identified those it
considered as "imperialist puppets." Broadly interpreted, this may
mean all UN members who follow the lead of the US, including all
the Latin American countries other than Cuba. It is hard to believe that
this is what Peking wants. Narrowly interpreted, one can identify only
the ROC, South Korea, and South Vietnam as the "imperialist puppets"
that Peking will not consider as states. What causes concern here, therefore, is the question of admitting the divided states, namely South
Korea and South Vietnam. North Korea, North Vietnam, and the two
Germanys are presumably just "independent states."[50] If Peking insists
on excluding the former and including the latter, a stalemate may result.

These conditions incorporated in Ch'en's 1965 statement, some
simply impossible and some difficult and improbable, are Peking's
calculated strategic demands. They also can be considered as Peking's
"preferred" conditions for participation in the UN, which normally
would not have been "necessary." In other words, they are negotiable,
if and when Peking changes its attitude and regains an interest in entering the UN.

10

**IMPACT
OF THE
GREAT PROLETARIAN
CULTURAL REVOLUTION,
1966-69**

Peking's approach toward the UN was particularly hostile and offensive during the Great Proletarian Cultural Revolution (GPCR). Its direct comments on the UN were sometimes on the verge of being insulting.

In this chapter, the hypotheses are that Peking's militant and hostile pronouncements on the UN during the prelude and the destructive phases of the GPCR reflected more the abnormal work of overly enthusiastic and/or insecure zealots in the midst of a political storm than the calculated, true position of the PRC; that Peking's foreign policy stance, including its position on the UN, began to return to the pre-GPCR level in late 1967 after the "Rebel and Seize Power" campaign was replaced by another of "Struggle-Criticism-Transformation;" and that there were preparations to turn toward a conciliatory line during the third, reconstructive, phase of the GPCR.

These hypotheses imply that domestic (as opposed to foreign) events carried a much greater weight in influencing Peking's foreign policy-making during the GPCR. Preoccupation with the extraordinary internal crisis seemed to have brought out an unusually irrational foreign policy stance. There was a wider than usual discrepancy between official words and thought.

A PERSPECTIVE ON THE GPCR

Soon after the GPCR became a focal point of world attention in 1966, a student of Chinese affairs observed that what was unfolding inside the PRC was neither proletarian, nor cultural, nor revolutionary,

but a great power struggle. As we look back, the name coined by the
Mao-Lin group was not as superficial as it seemed. This latest of
great experiments in the PRC might well be a phase of development
in China called for by the preceding historical events; it has been
literally a proletarian cultural revolution. It is proletarian because
the values espoused are proletariat as opposed to either bourgeois or
reactionary. Proletariat, meaning "the property-less class" (wuch'an
chiehchi), which includes the peasants, artisans, etc., rather than just
"the working class" (kungjen chiehchi). It is cultural since its targets
are the old "thought, culture, customs and habits" of men instead of
just socio-economic status or political power. In other words, it aims
at the minds, not the stomachs or skins, of men. It purports to rev-
olutionalize the Chinese way of life. Its ultimate goal is a fundamental
change in the thinking of man, or even the creation of a new man. That
new man is to be molded in line with the so-called Mao Tse-tung
Thought. It is revolutionary in the sense that it calls for the conscious
and violent overthrow of the old established cultural patterns and the
willful and immediate adoption of new patterns based on the "proletarian
culture" a la Mao Tse-tung Thought.

This proletarian cultural revolution is, from Mao's point of view,
a necessary sequel to the anti-imperialist national revolution, the
anti-feudal democratic (political) revolution and the anti-capitalist
economic revolution that preceded it in China's recent history.

The Chinese people's "liberation" has progressed from the more
tangible to the more intangible. Each step represents a partial revolution: first the foreign over-lords, the imperialists and the colonialists, were driven out; next, the feudal dynasty and the "reactionary"
KMT regime were overthrown and "anti-revolutionary" elements within the country purged; then a "revolutionary" effort was made to get
rid of the capitalist and neo-capitalist system and the PRC was guided
by the General Line of Socialist Construction toward an economic
"great leap." At this juncture, the failure or shortcoming of the previous sequences of revolution was discovered to be closely linked to
the "cultural" obstacles that stood in the way. Mao and his "revolutionary comrades" have come a long way. They cannot stand by and
let the results of their lifetime endeavor gradually evaporate into thin
air. Another resolute effort must be made to carry through this last
sequence of the revolution. A cultural revolution must follow.

Yet, to his great dismay and disappointment, Mao discovered
that the USSR under the leadership of Khrushchev had begun to revive
what he considered a "revisionist" capitalist line, abandoning the
international Communist movement in the process. It was an even

greater shock to realize that within the PRC, his own deputies had been treading the same route of "revisionism" that Khrushchev and other Eastern European Communist countries, particularly the "traitorous" Yugoslavia, had been travelling during the years while he was occupying "the second line." It became clear then that a struggle to regain "the first line" positions had to be won first before a cultural revolution could be staged. In other words, the GPCR and the seizure of power from the "first line" occupants who had cleverly betrayed him became intertwined; Mao decided that the GPCR could be waged both as a means to remove the "revisionists" in power and as a means toward the final completion of the revolution of modern China.

For Mao at least, the stake of the GPCR was not just the fate of certain political leaders named Mao Tse-tung or Liu Shao-ch'i, but beyond that to China's future after his passing from the scene. The power struggle was necessitated by the fact that "the number one Party person in authority" was leading the revolution astray on "the capitalist road."

This perspective on the GPCR is not yet commonly accepted; it is indeed speculative. However, it comes closest to a satisfactory explanation of the events that have taken place in mainland China during the last decade, including the outbreak of the GPCR.

PHASE I: A SELF-IMPOSED
ISOLATION POLICY

The first phase of the GPCR, approximately from October 1965, to July 1966, can be characterized as the prelude to a violent political storm. In this phase, Peking's foreign policy was essentially one of self-imposed isolation. Its attitude and approach toward the UN was a continuation of the preceding period, only more offensive and more arrogant. The self-imposed isolation policy was itself a sign of Peking's preparation for the coming events inside the country. Its offensive and arrogant UN policy was a sign that no new decision was made regarding the UN.

Internal Development

The origin of a cultural revolution in the PRC can be traced back to the mid-1950's.[1] But the current outburst of the GPCR was obviously initiated by Mao at a session of the Standing Committee of the Politburo held in September and October 1965, which was also

attended by "the leading comrades of all the regional bureaus of the
Central Committee."2 It took hold first with the publication of Yao
Wen-yuan's article, "On the New Historical Plan 'The Dismissal of
Hai-jui'" in Shanghai's Wen-hui Pao on November 10, 1965. From that
time on, the internal structure of the PRC became preoccupied with a
nation-wide campaign against the leading literary, art and educational
figures and the "poisonous weeds" that they had produced.3

In February 1966, P'eng Chen, Mayor of Peking, submitted an
"Outline Report on the Current Academic Discussion Made by the
Group of Five in Charge of the Cultural Revolution," which was approved
by Liu Shao-ch'i and distributed in the name of the Central Committee
on February 12, 1966.4 In it, apparently P'eng and the Liu-Teng "group
in power" tried to "whitewash" Wu Han's "mistakes." During the next
three months, Mao probably planned the course of action for the next
phase to come.

On May 16, 1966, Mao issued a circular (known as the May 16
Circular) in the name of the Central Committee to all units of all
levels of the Party's hierarchy which revoked P'eng Chen's Outline
Report.5 In particular, the Circular said:

> it [the Outline Report] obscures the aim of this great
> struggle, which is to criticize and repudiate Wu Han and
> the considerable number of other anti-Party and anti-
> socialist representatives of the bourgeoisie (there are a
> number of these in the Central Committee and in the Party,
> government and other departments at the central as well
> as at the provincial, municipal and autonomous region
> level).

Such a statement undoubtedly sounded the alarm for all who were not
sure of their alignment with the Mao-Lin line at that time.

At any rate, there followed the purge of P'eng Chen and his
associates in the Peking Municipal Party Committee. Lu Ting-i,
Director of the Propaganda Department of the Central Committee,
became the next victim. In a matter of weeks, propaganda, education,
literary and art units became common targets for their critics.
Severe criticisms were directed not only at ideas but at personalities.
A massive "Study Mao Tse-tung's Thought Movement" quickly permeated the country as word of the GPCR spread.

During June and the first half of July, Liu Shao-ch'i and Teng
Hsiao-p'ing dispatched their own "work teams" to college campuses

where extreme leftists were most active. This was Liu's last direct
attempt to wrestle politically with Mao. His "work teams" were almost
immediately identified and accused by the Red Guards, who began to
appear in Peking, of blocking the GPCR.

On July 16, Mao reportedly "had a good swim in the Yangtse
River, braving the wind and waves," taking part in the 11th Cross-
Yangtse Swimming Competition. However, the outlandish report of
that event and the feverish supporting editorials of Peking's leading
newspapers did not appear until July 26.[6] There is little question
that "Mao's good swim" was a political rather than a sporting event.
On July 18, Mao returned to Peking from Shanghai and Liu was de
facto removed from his daily central work duties by Mao.[7]

Foreign Relations

With the internal situation so tense and uncertain, it was no
wonder that Peking's foreign policy practically lapsed into a suspended
state as soon as the GPCR took hold. The New Year's Day message
of Jen-min Jih-pao emphasized the theme of "international class
struggle" and the program of "international united front." Regarding
the former, it said:

> . . . the focus of the counterrevolutionary global strategy
> of the US is being shifted from Europe to Asia. . . . We
> must maintain sharp vigilance and arrange all our work on
> the basis of coping with the eventuality that US imperialism
> will launch an early and large-scale war.

Regarding the latter, it said:

> We shall unite still more firmly with the people of the coun-
> tries in the socialist camp, with the people in Asia, Africa
> and Latin America, with the people of all countries in the
> world, including the American people, and with all peace-
> loving countries and all forces opposed to US imperialism,
> to form a broad international united front and struggle to
> the very end for the defeat of US imperialism and its
> lackeys.[8]

Nonetheless, the most outstanding characteristic of Peking's
foreign relations during the first phase of the GPCR was an isolationist tendency.[9] Peking was typically withdrawn, undoubtedly owing to
its preoccupation with domestic development. This isolationist tendency

was largely necessitated by the internal situation, even though there
were serious difficulties with the USSR at the 23rd Congress of the
CPSU[10] as well as fear of war with the US.[11]

A UPI dispatch from Paris reported on February 18, 1966, that
in some 40 capitals around the world, the PRC ambassador was "en
route to Peking."[12] Subsequently it was revealed that Peking's ambassadors were all being summoned back home, presumably for "re-
education" among other things. Since Peking maintained diplomatic
relations with only 46 countries then, recalling most ambassadors
left the embassies without constant on-the-spot direction. Since
Peking was anticipating a political struggle, it was doubtful that the
Foreign Ministry could have kept the embassies in a normal state of
operation.[13] In early March, Jen-min Jih-pao published a series of
articles explaining to the Chinese people that they must expect "temporary reverses" in the world-wide revolutionary movement and that
there would be "many ebbs and flows" and "twists and turns" before
the final victory was reached.[14] Peking's leaders were perhaps preparing the stage for the oncoming showdown between the Mao-Lin and
Liu-Teng groups. It is not difficult to understand why they would have
temporarily closed the gates to the outside world.

UN Policy

In this context, we see that Peking's UN policy--the appeal to
establish a "revolutionary" UN--was not revised, even though it received no audible echo among the Afro-Asian nations during 1965.
Peking's commentaries on the UN during this phase of the GPCR
were mostly platitudes. On December 27, 1965, a lengthy editorial of
Jen-min Jih-pao denounced the UN as "a marketplace for US Soviet
political deals."[15] The 20th Session of the General Assembly, the
editorial said, "was an anti-China conference, . . . a conference for
pursuing the policy of American-Soviet co-operation for the domination
of the world." The session's "shameful record" included the following:

1. Behind-the-scenes bargaining over the Vietnam question.

2. Endorsing US imperialism's armed intervention in the
Dominican Republic.

3. Shielding Indian aggression against Pakistan.

4. Authorizing Britain to "pacify" the situation in Southern
Rhodesia.

5. Working actively to set up a permanent UN force.

6. "Preventing nuclear proliferation" and consolidating nuclear monopoly.

7. Anti-China Clamor.

On the last item, the editorial had this to say:

On the question of restoring to China its legitimate rights
in the UN, the US lined up its hirelings to raise a ballyhoo,
slandering China as adopting 'belligerent attitudes,' being
committed 'to the use of force' and working to disrupt UN
'mediation' of the Indo-Pakistan conflict and to 'weaken'
and 'subvert' the UN.

Under the manipulation of US imperialism, the UN
again used what it called the 'Tibet question' to smear
China. . . .

During the debate on China's representation, Goldberg poured forth a stream of slanders against China.
But Soviet delegate Fedorenko spoke perfunctorily for
only 12 minutes. . . . Besides, . . . Gromyko said that
'certain persons' assumed a 'nihilist' attitude toward the
UN and spread 'pessimism' about disarmament. . . .

If Peking seemed to be denying its intention to "weaken" and "subvert"
the UN or its "nihilist" attitude toward the UN, the editorial did not
help to clarify Peking's true position. It ended with this new assault
upon the UN:

For many years, the UN under the thumb of US imperialism,
has done a lot of bad things. At present, with the leadership
of the Soviet Union working hand in glove with US imperialism for their joint control and greater misuse of the UN,
this organization is bound to do more evil. Today, both the
US imperialists and Khrushchev revisionists are going all
out for 'upholding' and 'strengthening' the UN. But the more
evil it does, the quicker it will go bankrupt. Such is the
dialectics of history.

On January 31, 1966, the Security Council adopted a resolution
submitted by the US recommending that the UN offer mediation to
organize a peace conference on Southeast Asia on the basis of the 1954

and 1962 Geneva agreements. On February 2, Jen-min Jih-pao said "the UN has no right whatsoever to discuss the Vietnam question."16

On April 19, US Ambassador Goldberg, speaking at the National Press Club in Washington, outlined the minimum conditions under which the US would agree to seating the PRC in the UN.

> Peking would have to abandon its demand for expulsion of
> Taiwan, withdraw its demand that the UN rescind its con-
> demnation of Red China for aggression in Korea and brand
> the US as the aggressor, withdraw its demand that the UN be
> reorganized and that unnamed 'lackeys' of the US be expelled,
> and promise to observe the provisions of the UN Charter.17

Peking did not respond to this unofficial US statement. Perhaps few besides Mao knew what to say even if a reply was attempted. The violent political storm was approaching; the prelude was almost over.

PHASE II: "THE CENTER OF WORLD REVOLUTION" AND "RED GUARD DIPLOMACY"

The second phase of the GPCR, approximately from August 1966, to October 1968, was one of ferocious power struggle between followers of the two lines led by the Mao-Lin and Liu-Teng groups. From the perspective of Mao's GPCR, this was the phase of seizing power from the "first-line" Liu-Teng authority, of destroying the Liu-Teng Party (and State) organization, and of establishing a "provisional" structure of power before the destroyed Party apparatus was rebuilt. This phase lasted over a year longer than Mao himself had anticipated. It actually consisted of two parts: The first part (roughly from August 1966, to September 1967) was characterized by Mao-Lin's campaign to "Rebel and Seize Power" by armed struggles of the masses; the second part (from October 1967, to October 1968) was characterized by a retreat to the campaign of "struggle-criticism-transformation."

Peking's foreign policy during this phase seemed overshadowed by an almost fanatic claim that Mao Tse-tung Thought was the banner of a new era of world revolution and that the PRC had replaced the USSR as the center of world revolution. In the first part of this phase, the characteristic foreign operation of Peking was one of "Red Guard diplomacy." Its pronouncements on the UN were insulting and invidious. In the second part, "Red Guard diplomacy" was stopped, but Peking had become even more isolated from the rest of the world.

Peking's approach toward the UN seems to have mellowed a little, but there was no discernible shift in attitude.

Internal Development

Internally, Mao called a meeting of the Eleventh Plenum of the Eighth Central Committee, which met from August 1 to 12, 1966. Half-way through the Plenum, Mao put up a big-character poster with the caption, "Bombard the Headquarters," which ignited a new flame of the GPCR.[18] From that day on, Liu ceased his official functions altogether. The Eleventh Plenum elected Lin Piao as the sole Vice-Chairman of the CPC, and dropped the others who had previously occupied the same position. It also adopted a Resolution Concerning the GPCR (known since as the 16 points) which called for "daring" struggle, among other things, and authorized the Ministry of Culture to work out plans to print and distribute Mao's works on a mammoth scale.[19]

In a matter of weeks after the Eleventh Plenum, Red Guards were on the rampage, first in Peking and soon all over the country, wrecking the "four olds" (old thinking, old culture, old customs and old habits) wherever they went. In October, Liu and Teng were severely criticized at the Central Work Conference of the Party and submitted their "self-criticisms" asking for "corrections." Mao half-heartedly blamed himself for leaving "the first line" to them, but did not pardon his two rivals.[20]

In January 1967, the "Rebels" backed by the Mao-Lin group took over most of the Ministries under the State Council, the press and the CPPCC.[21] The Foreign Ministry was not taken over at this time, but Minister Ch'en Yi was forced to submit his "self-criticism" on January 24.[22]

It took more than 20 months and an unknown amount of bloodshed before the seizure of power and the establishment of the so-called "Revolutionary Committees of Three-in-one Combination" were finally accomplished in all of the 29 provincial-level administrative units.[23] It seems the use of Red Guards was a move that brought many unexpected and uncalculated difficulties. Although the Red Guards were all over the country" "seizing power," only six "Revolutionary Committees" were established in the first four months of 1967.[24] In the next four months or so, there were many fights and even bloodshed in various parts of the country but no successful results. During the summer months of June-August, the Foreign Ministry, which had been carefully protected by Chou En-lai from radical

leftists, was attacked anew. In early August, the anti-Ch'en Yi leftists
led by Yao Tengshan (the Charge d'Affaire ad interim in Indonesia
until April when he was declared persona non grata and returned as
a hero to the PRC) made their move to take over the Foreign Ministry.
For two full weeks, Yao, obviously with the backing of Wang Li, an
ambitious member of the Cultural Revolution Group, functioned as
Foreign Minister and "sent cables to the embassies in foreign countries
without the permission of Chairman Mao and Premier Chou," en-
couraging the promotion of the PRC's revolution overseas.[25]

In that same month, Mao reportedly toured various parts of China
and issued a statement on the strategy of the GPCR.[26] On September
1, 1967, the leading members of the Central Committee suddenly issued
an urgent call (without using the names of Mao or Lin), instructing that
all proletarian revolutionaries should "closely follow the strategic
plan" of Mao, and redirect their fire to "the handful of top Party persons
in authority taking the capitalist road headed by China's Khrushchev."
It ordered "students and others of the revolutionary masses now exchanging revolutionary experience in other places" to return immediately to their own places and their own units to carry out the campaign
of "struggle-criticism-transformation."[27]

This urgent call was the signal of Mao's retreat; it declared the
end of the first part and the beginning of the second part of Phase II.
The "Rebel and Seize Power" campaign was terminated because it
had not really worked, rather than because it had accomplished what
Mao had intended. Clearly the continuing chaos and bloodshed had
brought the situation to an intolerable state, which prompted Mao to
concede to the military leaders who were already beginning to take
things into their own hands. As the campaign to "Criticize and Repud-
iate China's Khrushchev" and the campaign of "struggle-criticism-
transfromation" were launched, the Red Guards were suppressed.
Thence, the PLA (People's Liberation Army) was more or less in
charge of the tasks of establishing the "provisional organs of power"
in the provinces. Many local PLA leaders whose political leaning
might be considered "rightist" by Mao, emerged as the power wielders
while paying lip service to the Mao-Lin line. Between September 1967,
and June 1968, 18 "Revolutionary Committees" were established one
after another, mostly under the control of local PLA leaders. In June
1968, the GPCR group under Mao tried to instigate a new "Anti-Four-
Rightist Struggle" movement (anti-rightist reversal, anti-rightist
splittism, anti-rightist capitulationism, and anti-rightist opportunism).
It only led to more armed fighting and sacrifice of Mao's supporters,
and was quickly halted. During August and September, "Revolutionary
Committees" were established in the remaining five provincial-level
units.

Between October 13 and 31, the "Enlarged" Twelfth Plenum of
the Central Committee met. The Plenum ratified the "Report on the
Examination of the Crimes of the Renegade, Traitor and Scab Liu
Shao-ch'i" submitted by a special group under the Central Committee,
and "unanimously adopted" a resolution "to expel Liu from the party
once and for all, to dismiss him from all posts both inside and outside
the Party and to continue to settle accounts with him and his accomplices for their crimes in betraying the Party and the country."[28]
But the short communique of this Plenum and its single, hurried
reference to "the reactionary bourgeois theory of 'many centers'"
betrayed the difficulties that the Central Committee had tackled prior
to and during the session. Phase II of the GPCR was now concluded,
but Mao's "cultural" revolution through power seizure was only a
partial success.

Foreign Relations

The foreign policy of the PRC during Phase II of the GPCR was
first and foremost the glorification and the spread of Mao Tse-tung
Thought in the world. Beginning with the August 1966 Communique
of the Eleventh Plenum of the Eighth Central Committee, an abstract
and vague claim for Mao's supremacy as a spokesman of the world's
revolutionary peoples seemed to overshadow all else in Peking's
public statements. In that Communique, it was said:

> Comrade Mao Tse-tung is the greatest Marxist-Leninist
> of our era. Comrade Mao Tse-tung has inherited, defended
> and developed Marxism-Leninism with genius, creatively
> and in an all-round way, and has raised Marxism-Leninism
> to a completely new stage. Mao Tse-tung's thought is
> Marxism-Leninism of the era in which imperialism is
> heading for total collapse and socialism is advancing to
> world-wide victory.[29]

A sort of annotation of this statement was made in the 1967 New Year's
editorial of <u>Jen-min Jih-pao</u> and <u>Hung Ch'i</u>.[30] According to that
editorial, the October Revolution solved the question of seizing power
from suppressive authorities and establishing the dictatorship of the
proletariat for the first time, but failed to answer the question of
maintaining that dictatorship after it has been established. The PRC's
GPCR "started and led by Chairman Mao Tse-tung himself has set
a new and great example for the whole world proletariat in the solution of this question of great historic significance." However, by far
the most astonishing statement that indicates the extent of Peking's

claim was contained in a very long editorial jointly printed by Jen-min Jih-pao, Hung Ch'i and Chien-fang-chun Pao on the occasion of the 50th anniversary of the October Revolution on November 6, 1967.

> The world has now entered a revolutionary new era, with Mao Tse-tung's Thought as its great banner. France was the center of revolution in the late 18th century, and the center moved to Germany in the mid-19th century when the proletariat entered the political arena and Marxism came into being. The center of revolution moved to Russia early in the 20th century, and Leninism came into being. The center of world revolution has since gradually moved to China and Mao Tse-tung's Thought has come into being. Through the great proletarian cultural revolution, China, the center of world revolution, had become more powerful and consolidated.[31]

Because of this almost fanatic self-claim, Peking's foreign relations during this phase met even greater difficulties all around the globe. In the first part of this phase, the most outstanding feature of Peking's contacts with the outside world were described by observers as "Red Guard diplomacy."[32] The contents of that "diplomacy" consisted of imposing the new gospel of Mao's thought upon foreign envoys to China and of spreading the same in other countries by Peking's own foreign service personnel abroad. Such "diplomacy" was carried out by rampaging Red Guards and radical members within the foreign policy apparatus both at home and abroad by all available means, including physical coercion. Because of this very unorthodox, undiplomatic diplomacy, Peking became even more isolated from the rest of the world. When the paranoiac "Red Guard diplomacy" was halted in September 1967, it had already done irreparable damage to the PRC's image and prestige abroad. Peking had antagonized many former friends and created new enemies; relations with several countries had hardened. Within a short time, the PRC's reputation changed from that of a formidable challenger of the US throughout Asia and of the USSR inside the Communist bloc to that of a dissent-ridden, convulsing giant that was capable of neither self-assertion nor sustained growth.

The prospects of "US-USSR collaboration" at the expense of the PRC received continuous and repetitious treatment in Peking's press during the whole phase, including the most chaotic months. Peking was understandably nervous. On April 20, 1967, a Jen-min Jih-pao editorial said:

To encircle China, US imperialism has made large-scale
military dispositions and built many military bases in Japan
proper, Okinawa, Taiwan, south [sic] Vietnam and Thailand
which form a crescent east and south of China. Soviet revisionism, on its part, has formed another crescent west
and north of China. Now they are working to make the vast
territory of India their military base to link up the two
crescents and turn them into an anti-China ring.[33]

That Peking was very sensitive to this "US-USSR collaboration" idea
even at the height of the "Rebel and Seize Power" campaign was a
fact amply testified to by its nuclear policy. While the Party and
government organs were generally subjected to rectification, Peking's
nuclear program was not only unaffected but accelerated instead.
On May 9, 1966, the PRC conducted its third nuclear test, using some
thermonuclear materials. On October 27, a guided nuclear missile
test was successfully conducted and on December 28 another test
similar to the one on May 10 was made. On June 17, 1967, Peking
surprised many foreign observers with a hydrogen bomb test that was
in the several-megaton range. A series of other advanced technological
achievements were yet to come in the next three years, including an
earth satellite that was to broadcast the music of "East is Red" while
orbiting in space in late April 1970. All these were attributed to Mao's
inspiration, among other things. In every case, Peking's announcement
carried a statement to the effect that China's bombs were strictly for
defense, and that the PRC's bombs were good news for revolutionary
people the world over who should not have to subject themselves to
the "nuclear blackmail" of the US or the USSR now that the PRC had
them too.[34] On the other hand, the Nuclear Non-Proliferation Treaty
and the Treaty on the Peaceful Use of Outer Space were both written
off as "dirty deals" between the two "nuclear overlords" for the purpose of insuring their joint world domination.[35]

In respect to Afro-Asian countries, Peking was able to hail the
first Games of Newly Emerging Nations (GANEFO) held in Cambodia
in November 1966, as a symbol of closer "friendship and unity" among
the 17 participating countries. But a second GANEFO scheduled for
September 1967, in Peking never materialized. Likewise, the fifth
conference of the Afro-Asian People's Solidarity Organization (AAPSO)
had also been scheduled to meet in Peking during 1967, but Peking's
GPCR pre-empted it. On March 18, Peking severed its ties with the
Cairo-based Secretariat of the AAPSO because that organization failed
to exclude the Soviet Union who was neither an Asian nor an African
nation.[36] A number of non-aligned Asian and African nations were
now increasing their contacts with the ROC, and Peking's press was

protesting over and over again that countries like India,[37] Tunisia,[38] Japan,[39] Kenya[40] and Indonesia[41] were scheming to create "two Chinas." Perhaps the only significant exception to the proposition that Peking's foreign policy during this period was isolation-oriented was the agreement that Peking and two African nations--Tanzania and Zambia--had reached in September 1967. In that agreement, Peking promised to help build a major railroad within the next ten years. Peking's relations with these two nations improved considerably after that agreement was signed. But that was an exception to the general pattern.[42] If we also take into consideration the break of relationships between the CPC and the Japan Communist Party and other similar cases, Peking's "zigzags and reversals" were indeed very real.

UN Policy

While "Red Guard diplomacy" reigned, the UN was one of the main targets of abuse in Peking's propaganda. First, in November 1966, there was a reversal for the first time in the General Assembly's voting trend on the question of Chinese representation. The resolution to seat the PRC in place of the ROC received 45 yeas, 57 nays with 17 abstentions, compared to 47-47-20 the previous year. Reacting to this added frustration, the December 2 editorial of Jen-min Jih-pao, captioned "China Asks the UN for Nothing," said:

> The result of the voting on the question of China's re-
> presentation at the current General Assembly session shows
> once again that, unless the UN rids itself of US control, it
> is impossible to expel the Chiang Kai-shek gang and restore
> to China her legitimate rights in the UN.
>
> Therefore, the fundamental question now, as it has
> been in the past, is one of freeing the UN from the control
> of the US and its collaborators, thoroughly reorganizing
> it and completely rectifying all the mistakes it has com-
> mitted.[43]

Both the Italian draft resolution, which called for the establishment of a non-partisan study committee, and the Canadian "three-point-plan," which proposed concurrent seating of Peking and Taipei, were dubbed "two-Chinas" plots instigated by the US.[44] UN discussion on the Vietnam War and the Korean question were also denounced as illegal undertakings that inevitably would have corrosive effects on the UN flag.

In the summer of 1967, when the extreme leftists were in command of Peking's Foreign Ministry, a commentary appeared in Jen-min Jih-pao on July 8.[45] The tone of this commentary was most unrestrained. After calling the emergency session of the General Assembly on the Middle East "an ugly farce" and "spurious show," it said:

> What kind of thing is the UN? It is the tool of US imperialism, number one overlord, and the Soviet revisionist ruling clique, number two overlord, to press ahead with neocolonialism and big-nation power politics. . . . The aggressors get protection as usual and the victims of aggression have to put up with it. Such a UN can only be a refuge for imperialists, revisionists and counterrevolutionaries, and a chain binding the oppressed nations hand and foot.

It went on to offer a piece of advice to the Arabs:

> In order to safeguard their independence and defeat the aggression by US imperialism and its flunkey, the Arab people must rely on their own struggle. Pinning their hopes on the Soviet revisionists and the UN is like asking the tiger for its hide, and that will only bring on more catastrophes. Never should the bloody lesson of the Middle East events be forgotten!

After "Red Guard diplomacy" was terminated, Peking's denouncements of the UN became less invidious, although still spiteful. On November 20, 1967, Jen-min Jih-pao's commentator wrote:

> The annual voting at the UN General Assembly on the so-called question of China's representation has become a regular occasion for the exposure of the nature of the UN. . . .

> The UN has long been discredited as a result of the treachery of US imperialism and Soviet revisionism. Speaking frankly, the Chinese people are not at all interested in sitting in the UN, a body manipulated by the US, a place for playing power politics, a stock exchange for the US and the Soviet Union to strike political bargains and an organ to serve the US policies of aggression and war.[46]

From there, it went on to repeat the demand of rectification and reorganization and the "right" of wronged nations "to set up a new and revolutionary UN." After this commentary Jen-min Jih-pao published no more special comments on the UN for almost a year.

PHASE III: REBUILDING THE
PARTY AND THE
GOVERNMENT

Phase III of the GPCR is the phase of rebuilding the Party and
the government. It began after the 29 provincial Revolutionary Committees were established and the call for Party and government rebuilding was issued in October 1968, by the Twelfth Plenum of the
Eighth Central Committee. But there is no clear indication as to
whether it has ended. Technically, the GPCR will not conclude until
the tasks of "Party Consolidation and Party Building" at all levels
have been accomplished, the Fourth National People's Congress has
been convened and new State organs of power re-established according
to a new Constitution of the Republic based on the "proletarian line."
However, Peking's own pronouncements have been rather vague on this.
Campaigns and movements for the building of the Party "ideologically
and organizationally" continue, yet official documents have been content to "hail the victory" of the GPCR instead of calling all concerned
to "carry the GPCR through to its ends." The Central GPCR Group
has never been officially dissolved, yet that group made no report to
the Second Plenum of the Ninth Central Committee, at least not according to the Plenum's Communique.[47]

By and large, this third phase of the GPCR was characterized
by an anxiety to convene the Ninth Party Congress in order to bring
the chaotic and sometimes bloody power struggle to an early close.
As the dust from Phase II began to settle, it appeared that the Mao-Lin
group had not won a clear-cut victory in the struggle to gain "first
line" power. Instead, a moderate group of leaders seemed to have
effectuated in the name of Mao and Mao Thought certain policies bearing the marks of "revisionism." Behind radical propaganda, a relatively conciliatory foreign policy loomed, hinting at things to come.
Commentaries on the UN became less spiteful, giving the impression
that Peking's interest in the world organization might be reviving.

Internal Development

Thus far, the highlights of Phase III consist of (1) the Ninth Party
Congress, which adopted a new Party Constitution and elected the
Ninth Central Committee, (2) the establishment of new Party Committees in 24 of the 29 provincial-level units (at the end of May 1971),
and (3) the consolidation of several Ministries of the State Council
and other administration structures.[48] Still to come are, among other

things: (1) organization of new Party Committees in the remaining 13
provincial-level units and similar reorganization of local Party Committees, (2) the convening of the Fourth National People's Congress to
adopt a new State Constitution and to elect the "first line" office holders,
including a Chief of State to replace Liu Shao-ch'i, and (3) the rebuilding of provincial and local State organs of power in place of the provisional "revolutionary committee," as well as the consolidation and
reorganization of the Communist Youth League and other mass organizations.[49]

Nominally, the materialization of the Ninth Party Congress might
be interpreted as proof of Mao's success in attempting to recapture
"first line" power. In reality, however, the success or failure of Mao's
attempt, like the success or failure of the GPCR itself, depends on
which group--those who subscribe to the "proletarian culture" or those
who pursue "revisionism" or "bourgeois reformism"--actually gained
power. If the "proletarian culture" group headed by Mao-Lin had gained
total control, the GPCR would probably have progressed according to
Mao's vision and the question of "first line" power would have been
solved. But, if that group succeeded in capturing only partial control,
then the GPCR would likely to be delayed and/or diluted and the question
of who would control the "first line" of central power would become
an important function of the Fourth National People's Congress.

In specific terms, the goal of Phase III of the GPCR, as stipulated
in the Communique of the Twelfth Plenum of the Eighth Central Committee, was

> to establish the dictatorship of the proletariat in the super-
> structure, including all spheres of culture, to fulfill the
> tasks of all stages of struggle-criticism-transformation
> put forward by Chairman Mao and to carry the GPCR
> through to the end![50] (Emphasis added)

"The dictatorship of the proletariat" as envisioned by Mao, however,
seems to have been usurped by a group of leaders who pay lip service
to Mao and Mao Thought but implement policies that incorporate "revisionist" ideas.

There are a number of unmistakable signs that the military has
ascended to the position of power, nominally following the Party's
instructions but actually holding the key to both policy decision and
policy implementation. Furthermore, circumstantial evidence suggests
that the prevailing sentiment of the army leaders who actually command

troops favor moderate, pragmatic policies rather than the vehemently "revolutionary" Mao-Lin line.

The ascendance of the military is shown in the following: First, in October 1967, the practice of publishing joint editorials by Jen-min Jih-pao and Hung Ch'i was altered. For the first time, a third medium, the PLA's Chien-fang-chun Pao was added to the other two as publishers of the most authoritative Party policy.[51] Second, in Part III of Lin Piao's Report to the Ninth Party Congress, there was a paragraph that began with the following words:

> The People's Liberation Army is the mighty pillar of the dictatorship of the proletariat. Chairman Mao has pointed out many times: From the Marxist point of view the main component of the state is the army.[52]

This passage is most unusual and significant. Since the GPCR had taken hold in late 1965, all quotations of Mao that appeared in print had been in salient bold type. This passage, as analyst Chang Man points out, was a conspicuous exception. Moreover, "the main component of the state" may be sovereignty, people, territory or government, but not "the army."

Third, a policy of "three supports and two militaries" (support industry, agriculture and the masses of the Left; military administration of factories, schools, communes, etc., and military and political training of Red Guards and others) was imposed in early 1967.[53] Equipped with this policy, which legitimatized its actions, the army effectively permeated the whole nation at the provincial level and below. This policy is still being propagated as of June 1971.

Fourth, it is estimated that the composition of the Ninth Central Committee included 123 full and alternate members from the military (44 percent plus), compared to 77 from the leading revolutionary cadres (27 percent plus) and 79 from the mass organizations (28 percent plus).[54] At the provincial level, 43 percent of the 220 chairmen and vice chairmen of the Revolutionary Committees were military representatives.[55]

That the moderates hold the key within the military is suggested by the following: In March 1968, Huang Yung-sheng was appointed the Chief of Staff following the purge of Yang Ch'eng-hu. This event was significant for several reasons.[56] One, Yang was a loyal aide of Lin Piao who appointed him to the post of Acting Chief of Staff after Lo Jui-ch'ing was purged. He was purged in March 1968, despite his open blandishment of Mao. In contrast, Huang had been known not for his support of the Mao-Lin line but for the fact that he commanded the most formidable military units in the southern part of the country--the Kuangtung military district. His politics were definitely more "revisionist" than "proletarian." Two, when Lin Piao announced Yang's "mistakes," he mentioned that Yang clandestinely maneuvered to oust a number of other PLA leaders, including Huang Yung-sheng. The individuals named by Lin Piao on that occasion were commanders of other major military districts. Subsequently, all those named were elected to the Politburo at the Ninth Party Congress. Three, when Huang was appointed as the Chief of Staff, he was not "acting" as was Yang. Moreover, Huang's confidant, Wen Yu-ch'eng, was concurrently summoned form Canton to become the new Commander of the Peking Garrison Command. At the October 1 National Day celebration, Huang and Wen were listed in the tenth and fourteenth spots respectively, i.e., ahead of notables in the Politburo. Four, Huang spoke on Army Day on August 1, and scaled down the PRC's verbal attack on the USSR for the first time. On September 11, Chou En-lai, together with Li Hsien-nien, Hsieh Fu-chih, and Huang were able to meet Kosygin and agreed upon border talks with the Kremlin. Five, on the list of 29 slogans released for use at National Day celebrations, there was a slight but significant change between a September 17 version and the October 1 version. In the September 17 version, slogan 16 read "Down with Soviet revisionist social-imperialism!" but in the October 1 version, the word "Soviet" had been deleted.[57] All these suggest that the downfall of Yang Ch'eng-hu and the rise of Huang Yung-sheng in March 1968, was a compromise reached between Lin Piao and the real power holders of the PLA led by Huang Yung-sheng.

This analysis of the moderates within the military is also supported by the trends of both domestic and foreign policies since the Ninth Party Congress. One analyst calls their ways one of "revolutionary pragmatism," about which we shall have more discussions in Chapter 11.

Foreign Relations

With moderate elements operating at the center, Peking's foreign policy began to turn toward conciliation. Glorification of Mao Thought was considerably de-emphasized and greater attention was now paid to normal state-to-state intercourse.

In a content analysis of Peking Review based on the number of pages given to several select areas of attention relating to foreign affairs, Daniel Tretiak tabulated some of his findings as shown in Table 4.

Particularly noteworthy in this table are: (1) the abnormally large increase of general statements on foreign policy between July 1966, and June 1968, reflecting the claim of the universality of Mao Thought at the height of the GPCR; (2) the significant decrease of such general statements after late 1967 and again after the summer of 1968; (3) greatly increased attention to the USSR during the destructive phase of the GPCR in contrast to decreased interest in the US in that same period, suggesting that "the US was less of a valid ideological target within the rhetoric of the Cultural Revolution" and that "Chinese officials did not wish to risk hostilities with the US";[58] (4) the relative importance of Asia to China compared to Africa, Latin America or the Middle East; and (5) the lack of attention to Taiwan throughout most of this entire period.

Relations with the Soviet Union were at their worst just before and after the Ninth Party Congress of the CPC. Border clashes over Chenpao (Damansky) Island in the Ussuri River in March followed by other skirmishes along the Sinkiang-Kazakhstan borders threatened to drawn the two Communist giants into war.[59] In early June, the Conference of Communist Parties was held in Moscow at which Brezhnev severely criticized Peking's revised Party Constitution. By proxy, Peking attacked the Conference as a "despicable plot of the Soviet revisionist renegade clique to convene a counterrevolutionary conference of revisionist parties."[60] Later that month, Moscow proposed the creation of a "system of collective security in Asia," which Peking branded as "Soviet revisionism's tattered flag for anti-Chinese military alliance."[61] However, on September 11, Chou and Kosygin met at Peking airport and an agreement to hold vice-minister-level talks was reached. Tension began to relax afterward. Both sides played down their differences for the remainder of the year.

Relations with the US saw interesting restraints on the Peking side as well, although it was Washington that took initiatives to accelerate the thaw. The Warsaw Talks had been suspended after January 1968. In November, Peking proposed to resume the talks on February 20, 1969, and specified two items for discussion: (1) US withdrawal from Taiwan and the Taiwan Strait, (2) an agreement on peaceful coexistence. Washington was encouraged by the second item proposed.[62] But in January 1969, Peking's Charge d'Affairs to the Netherlands, Liao Ho-shu, defected and Peking cancelled the 135th Warsaw Talk

again on the pretext that Liao's defection was incited by the US Central
Intelligence Agency.63

When the US succeeded in the first landing on the moon, Peking's
press made no mention of the event. But there was a reaction to
President Nixon's announcement of a new Asian policy (the Nixon
Doctrine) in July 1969. A New China News Agency (NCNA) article
accused Nixon of trying to play the role of behind-the-scenes boss
who lays out money and guns for "Asians to fight Asians." Significantly,
however, this article was printed on the inside pages of <u>Jen-min Jih-pao</u>
and not as an editorial.64

At any rate, it is probable that Peking was already preparing to
"turn out" around the time of the Ninth Party Congress. Soon after
that event, Peking's ambassadors were returning or being reassigned
to foreign posts. Relations with Afro-Asian and other countries would
begin to normalize and expand. The direction was now outward, not
isolation-oriented.

UN Policy

Peking's official commentaries on the UN during Phase III of
the GPCR were few but relatively conciliatory. In contrast to the
invidious assault of the previous two years, the commentary on the
23rd session of the General Assembly took the form of repeating what
the delegations to the UN had said on the question of Chinese repre-
sentation.65 An appreciation was expressed for the countries who
submitted the resolution to seat the PRC in place of the ROC and
spoke favorably for Peking at the session. There was no rancorous
cry that "China asks the UN for nothing" or that the UN protects only
its overlords. The US and the USSR received the blame rather than
the UN itself, although there was an assertion that the session "reveals
the political and moral bankruptcy of the so-called UN Organization."
What made Peking particularly unhappy was the behavior of the USSR.
According to <u>Peking Review</u>:

> The representative of the Soviet revisionist renegade
> clique again played the despicable role of a double-dealer
> in the recent 'debate.' At the November 13 meeting,
> Yakov Malik hypocritically expressed 'support' for
> restoring China's legitimate rights in the UN and 'opposi-
> tion' to the idea of 'two Chinas.' But, immediately after-
> ward, he put the 'question of restoration of China's repre-
> sentation' on a par with that of admitting the two German

TABLE 4

Changes In Peking's Foreign Attention Reflected In Peking Review,
January 1966-November 1969

(Figures are the percent of total attention over a six-month period
to the international system that is devoted to a particular
area or country. Total may exceed 100 percent since
some categories are counted twice)

	1966		1967		1968		1969		
	January-June	July-December	January-June	July-December	January-June	July-December	January-June	July-November	Semi-annual Average
Asia[a] (all countries)	35.27	24.27	24.35	43.90	27.53	30.98	22.71	32.35	30.18
Soviet Union	5.90	6.82	18.75	14.05	12.70	13.54	34.29	19.59	15.71
Africa	3.62	3.27	3.30	5.60	7.44	5.12	3.09	6.36	4.73
United States	10.66	10.28	6.25	6.55	16.33	7.85	7.51	12.78	9.77
Communist Parties[b] (misc.)	10.70	8.07	5.60	4.80	9.11	13.87	17.69	8.25	9.78
Latin America	7.2	3.18	.40	1.30	4.15	2.82	6.37	2.31	3.59
Foreign Policy Gen. Statements[c]	7.5	13.19	22.40	11.90	13.87	7.53	6.16	5.27	10.98
Albania	14.00	12.16	9.30	11.70	2.64	18.66	5.04	4.66	9.77
Southeast Asia[d]	25.64	16.79	11.06	27.68	20.96	16.36	11.60	18.13	18.53
China[e] State-State Relations (misc.)	8.80	21.82	3.60	6.70	6.73	4.62	2.47	11.27	8.25
Japan	3.80	2.49	4.00	5.10	3.85	5.83	4.94	3.67	4.21
India	2.20	1.33	2.80	5.30	1.48	2.49	3.06	6.06	3.09
Taiwan	.18	.36	na	na	-	.70	.67	1.03	.49
Middle East	.50	.20	4.80	1.60	2.55	2.77	3.51	3.82	2.47

[a]Does not include Middle East.
[b]Data omitted from Laos, Indonesia, Malaysia, Thailand, Burma and Vietnam, Japan and India and Albania.
[c]Includes mainly statements on general world problems and relevance of Mao's thought for other countries.
[d]Includes Burma, Laos, Indonesia, Thailand, Malaysia, North and South Vietnam.
[e]Includes relations with miscellaneous Asian non-Communist and Communist regimes, East European ones, Africa, international Communist organizations; excludes relations with Japan, India, all Southeast Asian governments, the USSR and Albania.

Source: Daniel Tretiak, "Is China Preparing to 'Turn Out'?: Changes in Chinese Levels of Attention to the International Environment," Asian Survey March 1971 (Vol. XI, No. 3), 224.

164

states. The Soviet delegate was thus openly serving US imperialism's scheme of creating 'two Chinas'[66]

It seems Peking had kept a very close watch and did a very careful analysis of what was going on at the UN. There is more:

> Furthermore, on the eve of the 'debate,' personnel of the Soviet revisionist clique distributed much anti-China material in the UN to prepare public opinion, in co-ordination with US imperialism, for obstructing the restoration of China's legitimate rights in the UN.

Were Peking a direct participant, it would not have been more observant of what was going on in the UN. It was as if Peking had confessed that it was interested in the UN again.

11

ACCELERATING
THE END
OF THE "B.C." ERA
IN THE UN,
1969-71

The following quotation appeared in the November 27, 1960, issue of Peking Review, one week after the General Assembly approved with 51 votes for, 49 against and 25 abstentions the draft resolution of 18 countries that demanded "the restoration to the PRC of its legitimate seat in the UN," and the expulsion of the ROC delegation.

> Our great leader Chairman Mao pointed out 14 years ago: 'The present situation in which the United States controls a majority in the United Nations and dominates many parts of the world is a temporary one, which will eventually be changed.'

After 21 years, that "temporary situation" seems to be approaching its end.

Most observers will perhaps agree that Peking's entry into the UN has been a matter of time whether Mao said so or not. However, the speculation that 1970 would be the year 1 B.C. (Before China)[1] might have had something to do with the significant policy change on Peking's part after the Ninth Party Congress of April 1969.

Although it is still too early to evaluate the exact nature of this policy change, it is surmised (1) that a number of decisions made at the top level (probably the Politburo) between the First (April 1969) and the Second (August 1970) Plenum of the Ninth Party Congress, in effect, have directed Peking's domestic and foreign policies toward a sort of "revolutionary pragmatism"; (2) that, following the Ninth Party Congress and particularly after the Second Plenum of the new Central Committee, the State Council under Chou En-lai's leadership, possibly with the approval of Mao-Lin and certainly with the backing of the moderates within the top hierarchy, began to implement a new foreign policy, a policy of coexistence and negotiation with all but a few carefully identified and narrowly defined "enemies"; and (3) that a goal

was set about the time of the Second Plenum in August 1970 to push
for an early acceptance of the PRC by the General Assembly of the UN.

POSITIVE ATTITUDE, ACTIVE APPROACH

Peking's new interest in the UN came through quite clearly after
the Ninth Party Congress. A Canadian Foreign Ministry spokesman
disclosed on September 16, 1969, that Peking wanted Canada to support
its bid to China's seat in the UN.[2] In November, Peking's commentary
on the 24th session of the General Assembly included this passage:

> Budo [Albanian representative to the UN, Halim Budo] emphasized
> that the government of the PRC alone was qualified to enjoy the
> legitimate rights [of China] in the UN. Without the participation
> of socialist China, no important international problem could find
> just solution in the interest of the peoples and of peace.[3]

If one recalls Peking's previous comments on the UN and thinks in
terms of what other things Peking could have said, one cannot fail to
understand the meaning of this special reference to Budo's "emphasis."
The commentary from which this passage was taken was interestingly
composed as well. Fully 15 paragraphs were devoted to the positive
things that Peking's supporters had said at the Assembly and only
four paragraphs were used to denounce the US and the USSR. The
commentary ended with a statement declaring that "no force in the
world can prevent the great socialist China from playing her tremendous role and exerting a tremendous influence on the international
arena." There was no resentful attack on the UN itself.

Nonetheless, revival of interest in the UN did not necessarily
mean taking bold steps to knock at the UN's front door immediately.
It was not until the fall of 1970 that such an active UN policy was
adopted and the machinery of conciliatory diplomacy put into operation
to win support for a renewed UN bid. The timing suggests the possibility that a decision to do so was reached at the Second Plenum of
the Ninth Central Committee in August–September 1970 where the
pragmatic leaders probably won the hand against the more radical
elements.[4] For, immediately after that Plenum, a number of events
signaled Peking's new thaw. Most notably, diplomatic relations were
established with Canada in October 1970, on the basis of a formula
relating to the Taiwan issue that Peking had not found completely
agreeable throughout the preceding 18 months of continued negotiations.[5]
Following that, formal diplomatic relations were established with a
number of other nations, without even mentioning the Taiwan issue

in the communiques.[6] When Albania and other sponsoring countries submitted their resolution on Peking's behalf, they received cables of thanks--a formality that was not observed in previous years.[7]

Two weeks before the General Assembly voted on the China question, Peking Review noted that the 25th anniversary session of the UN, rather than being a cheerful commemorative occasion, was more a "platform for denouncing US imperialism."[8] Leaving the denunciation of "the crimes of US-manipulated UNO" to Cambodia's Prince Samdech Norodom Sihanouk, the Chinese statement pointed out that

> The United Nations under the domination of the two superpowers has been steadily on the decline with a complete loss of prestige. This instrument has become more and more ineffective.[9]

The statement went on to imply that such a pitiful fate for the UN had something to do with the unlawful deprivation of the PRC's legitimate rights in the UN and the "schemes" of the two superpowers to dominate or partition the world.

A week after the China question had been voted upon, Peking Review returned to the subject with a jubilant report.[10] Referring to the General Assembly's approval of the Albanian resolution "amid thunderous applause," it said:

> This is a big defeat for the policy of US imperialism. . . . It is an important victory for the Chinese people and the people of various countries upholding international justice. It proves that a just cause enjoys abundant support while an unjust cause finds little support, and that the dyke of hostility towards China built by US imperialism in the UN has begun to collapse.

The same report also noted that the "illegal" draft resolution making the China question an "important" one was adopted with 66 votes for, 52 against and 7 abstentions, but that, compared with 1969, the votes for the draft dropped by 5, those against it increased by 4 and the abstentions increased by 3, and that "silence prevailed at the Assembly when the draft was passed." This calculation of changes in votes on the "important question" resolution was of pivotal importance. For the final result of UN debate on the China question can be reversed in 1971 if only eight nations are persuaded to switch their votes in favor of the PRC on that resolution.[11]

Apparently, the China seat in the UN is within Peking's reach in the next year or two. Unless the US comes up with another new "plot" as it did in 1961 (e.g., a formal proposal based on the "two-Chinas" concept offered as an alternative to the Albanian resolution, or a threat to withdraw from the UN if and when the PRC enters), Peking can probably sway the needed votes with a new concerted application of the Bandung spirit, if entering the UN is its goal. This probability certainly did not escape Peking's calculation. It seems Peking has been working toward that end since the autumn of 1970. So much so that some observers now suggest that entering the UN has become Peking's "overriding purpose in recent maneuvers,"[12] and that Peking's leaders have "embarked on a systematic world-wide campaign" aimed at entry in the fall of 1971.[13] Ironically, and to the surprise of many, such campaigns have now extended to the United States.

There can be no doubt that Peking's UN policy has drastically changed again since the Ninth Party Congress of April 1969. Its attitude is now definitely positive, its approach, active and intensive.

What are the explanations of this interesting turnabout in Peking's UN policy at this juncture? The full story will have to wait until this current development completes its course and more information becomes available. In the meantime, some answers might be found by a closer examination of two areas: (1) the "revolutionary pragmatism" of the ascending moderates within Peking's leadership and its foreign policy ramifications; and (2) the unmistakable and accumulative overtures of the Nixon administration and Peking's calculated responses.

REVOLUTIONARY PRAGMATISM

The hypothesis here is that, within the top echelon decision-making circle in Peking, pragmatic reason prevailed over revolutionary ideology in the wake of the GPCR, giving rise to a sort of second Bandung period in the evolution of Peking's UN policy. Conceivably, Peking's leaders have been aware of the tarnished reputation that the GPCR and the Red Guard diplomacy had wrought for the PRC. By the same token, it seems reasonable that when Peking decided to break out of its self-imposed isolation from the rest of the world in the third phase of the GPCR, it must have considered its strategy regarding the UN. Past efforts to create a rival "revolutionary" UN bore no fruit for the PRC. Instead, they taught Peking the futility and costliness of such endeavours. If Peking can utilize the UN in its national purposes, that world organization still is the most useful organ available. Why should Peking not give it another try?

This hypothesis is closely related to the fact that moderate elements led by army Chief of Staff, Huang Yung-sheng, might have gained substantial power during the GPCR and have further ascended in power status since that time.[14]

In a recent article, Harry Harding characterized the developments in China during 1970 as a move toward revolutionary pragmatism. Harding explained that

> the major issues currently facing Chinese leaders can be represented as . . . sets of contradictions, each with a 'revolutionary' aspect, stressed during the Cultural Revolution, and a more 'pragmatic' aspect. The programs pursued during the past year are efforts to resolve each of the contradictions--not by establishing the dominance of one aspect over the other, but rather by creating the proper balance between the two.[15]

This perspective is a useful one and Harding used it effectively in explaining a number of major policy changes in the PRC.

In the analysis of this writer, however, the accent of the new "revolutionary pragmatism" in the PRC during the post-Ninth Party Congress period, particularly since the Second Plenum of the Ninth Central Committee in August 1970, has been on "pragmatism." In a simplified way, one might say it has been "revolutionary" in words but "pragmatic" in deeds.

The strengthened position of the moderates is reflected in a number of events. Among them are (1) substantially increased representation of the moderate figures such as Chou En-lai, Huang Yung-sheng, Li Hsien-nien, Chiu Hui-cho and Yeh Chien-ying in public ceremonial occasions contrasted with the less and less frequent appearances of the more "revolutionary" such as Lin Piao, Chiang Ch'ing, Ch'en Po-ta, K'ang Sheng and Yao Wen-yuan;[16] (2) the public trial of Yao Teng-shan, the former Charge d'Affaires to Indonesia, in June 1971, for leading a raid on Peking's foreign ministry, burning down the British chancellery and plotting a personal assault on Premier Chou in the summer of 1967;[17] (3) the implied attack on Ch'en Po-ta in the joint editorial commemorating the 50th anniversary of the CPC;[18] and (4) the prominence of reportedly moderate military figures in the new provincial Party Committees established since December 1970.[19]

It is not our suggestion here that the moderate leaders have been coercing Mao and Lin into their line of thinking by sheer military force. Contrary to certain assertations that Mao and Lin have become mere puppets, it would seem unthinkable that central policy measures can be effectively implemented in spite of Mao's or even Lin's active opposition. Our suggestion is that the moderates, because of their substantial power, have succeeded in gaining greater representation in the Central Committee and its Political Bureau, and thereby have become capable of expressing their strong sentiment favoring pragmatic programs within the decision-making organs. This point has already been discussed in Chapter 10. We also suggest that Mao and Lin have come to recognize and respect the voice of the moderates both by reason and by necessity. The necessity stems from Mao-Lin's recognition of power reality; after all, they are veterans of power struggle. The reason is based on a realistic assessment of China's needs and possibilities at the present stage; for the excess damages and costs of the GPCR have been recognized by Mao himself, and both Mao and Lin are confirmed patriots.[20] In short, we see the new "revolutionary pragmatism" as a summary result of domestic political compromises between the Mao-Lin group and the moderates; it bears the approval of both.

The accent on pragmatism is manifested in turn in the following policies and developments: (1) an emphasis on decentralization and the importance of the middle-level Party committees where most of the military's strength is seated; [21] (2) a greater attention to some facets of professionalism and increased investment in the development of more sophisticated weapons systems; [22] (3) a new policy on intellectuals emphasizing that even the "die-hard capitalist roaders and bourgeois technical authorities who have incurred the extreme wrath of the masses . . . should be given a way out," on the ground that most intellectuals are "patriotic and . . . willing to serve the people; . . . to be remolded . . .";[23] and (4) unmistakable hints that, while adhering to the principle of "maintaining independence and keeping the initiative in our own hands and relying on our own efforts, we do not reject learning from other countries," in order to develop the PRC's agriculture and economy.[24]

In foreign affairs, the impact of the moderates is even more visible. Trends of conciliation and negotiation continued and expanded. A number of foreigners held in the PRC since the second phase of the GPCR were released, and high-level delegations from various countries visited Peking. Publicly and privately Peking repeatedly expressed its willingness to establish or resume diplomatic relations with all nations, their differing social systems notwithstanding, on the basis of the five principles of peaceful coexistence. Relations with Yugoslavia and with the United Kingdom took a turn for the better for

the first time in many years. On November 20, 1969, a Yugoslav
Foreign Ministry spokesman announced that an agreement had been
reached on exchanging ambassadors with Peking.[25] As of this writing,
negotiations are progressing between Peking and London on upgrading
their embassies, a step that Peking resisted for two decades.[26]

Between April 1969, and June 1971, formal diplomatic relations
were established with Canada, Italy, Equatorial Guinea, Ethiopia,
Chile, Kuwait, Cameroon, Nigeria, San Marino and Austria. No less
than 40 ambassadors and 10 charge d'affairs heading missions have
returned or been reassigned to overseas embassies.[27] Aid agreements
were signed with North Vietnam, Albania and North Korea and assistance in the construction of the Tanzam railroad made world headlines.
Expanded trade deals were made with many countries, including several
with whom no formal diplomatic relations existed. Efforts were made
to mend past wounds in regard to India and Burma.

Relations with the USSR changed most drastically. Border talks
that began during October 1969, in Peking seem to have produced no
formal agreement, but both sides have called back some of their troops
stationed along borderlines, toned down their rhetorical polemics and
expressed good will for each other. In July 1970, an announcement
was made that the two nations would exchange ambassadors and in
November, Liu Hsin-chuan, a trusted aid of former Foreign Minister
Chen Yi, was appointed Ambassador to Moscow. Since then trade
between the two Communist giants has increased significantly.

Relations with Japan had a unique twist. Because of increased
reference in the world press to Japan as Peking's potential rival in
Asian affairs, of genuine fear of resurgent Japanese militarism, and
of the Sato government's relative hostility toward the PRC, Peking's
official press consistently condemned the Sato government's "collusion
with the US imperialism", its "reviving militarism" and its "plot to
create two Chinas." Strict conditions (the so-called Four No-Trade
Principles[28]) were imposed on Japanese Trade organizations, obviously as a means of pressuring them to help bring about a change in
Japan's China policy. Despite such treatment, trade with Japan expanded from a value of $625 million in 1969 to $825 million in 1970.
This figure, though relatively small for Japan, actually represents
about one fifth of Peking's foreign trade and makes Japan the number
one trade partner of the PRC, ahead of Hong Kong and West Germany.
It is note-worthy that Central Daily News reported on July 3, 1971,
that Premier Sato told Chiang Kai-shek's Secretary-General, Chang
Ch'un, in Seoul that Japan will not sponsor the "important question"
resolution in the UN in November.

Relations with the United States during this period constitute one of the most interesting of international love-hate stories and we shall discuss it in some detail in the next section of this chapter. Suffice it to say here that, in this instance too, it is love that prevails over hate.

To be sure, these signs of conciliatory and pragmatic foreign policy since the Ninth Party Congress cannot, and should not, be construed to represent the totality of Peking's international posture. More accurately, it must be added that the revolutionary aspects of Peking's foreign strategy--support to world revolutionary movements and the opposition to imperialism, revisionism and reactionaries-- have by no means been abandoned. Rather, they have been delegated to the background for the time-being, in the interest of an earlier entry into the UN and of giving the PRC's tarnished prestige a brush up. In other words, the influence of the moderates within Peking's top leadership has created an emphasis on pragmatism but not a total forsaking of China's long-term revolutionary programs, either domestic or foreign. Nonetheless, the ascendance of the moderates in power and the emphasis on pragmatism made Peking so much more susceptible to circumstantial changes and inducements. When such inducements came in the form of persistent friendly gestures from the US government while a Soviet threat to the north was heavily felt, Peking's temptation to accommodate them would have been strong indeed.

PEKING-WASHINGTON LOVE-HATE GAME

The second explanation for Peking's new UN policy, therefore, is based on the hypothesis that Peking's leaders concluded in the fall of 1970 that the time was ripe to "embark on a systematic world wide campaign" in order to gain entry into the UN, primarily because of persistent overtures from Washington. The love-hate syndrome in the recent Sino-American relations should be a political cartoonist's fertile soil. It had been the US, as the gate keeper as well as the master of ceremonies of the UN, who manipulated the UN's rejection and condemnation of the PRC. It had been the US who prevented Peking's liberation of Taiwan by giving military protection and aid to the ROC. And, it is the US who alone has the capability and will to come to Peking's help in case of a military threat from the USSR. Should it be possible to come to terms with Washington on a mutually acceptable basis, would that not be the most effective way to solve the PRC's most troublesome foreign problems? Were that an actually managable course of action, why should Peking not take advantage of it? Specifically in relation to the UN question, what else could possibly obstruct Peking's entry into that body if Washington had been "persuaded" to render its explicit or tacit support?

If this line of reasoning is sound, one need only document the conditions in support of the hypothesis stated above. This will be done in a chronological narrative, beginning with the inauguaration of the Nixon Administration in January 1969.

It is an ironic yet not unforeseen twist in the international love-hate story involving the United States and China that Richard M. Nixon, the shrewd politician who built his early political career on a hard-line anti-Peking stand, should become the American president who would bring a turnabout in Sino-American relations and thereby help to modify the course of world political development. In his inauguration speech, President Nixon made "an era of negotiation" his main theme. Soon afterward, he ordered a full-scale review of America's China policy and instructed his National Security Advisor, Henry Kissinger, and his Secretary of State, William Rogers, to make discrete hints to some third-country sources that Washington was seriously interested in working toward a normalization of relations with Peking. Earlier, in a Foreign Affairs article, Nixon had called a new tune, asserting that "any American policy toward Asia must come urgently to grips with the reality of China."[29] As the President, he seems determined to move toward that direction. It is not certain whether these earliest overtures had any impact upon the deliberations of Peking's leaders who were then preoccupied with the preparations of the Ninth Party Congress called for April 1969. At least, there is no reason to believe that Peking's top leaders were unaware of such overtures.

When the Warsaw Talks, scheduled to resume on February 20, 1969, were cancelled by Peking 48 hours before their reopening because of the Liao Ho-shu incident, US Secretary of State Rogers expressed hope that the two governments might still hold talks soon regarding "peaceful coexistence" and the exchange of reporters, scholars and scientific knowledge.[30] In March, Senator Edward Kennedy made a major speech urging the government to adopt a new liberal policy toward Peking. His speech was to be followed by those of other Congressional leaders from both Democratic and Republican parties in the following months.[31] This Congressional agitation probably contributed to Nixon's plans for China. In mid-year, Nixon undertook a major trip to Southeast Asia. Just a few days before his departure, Nixon announced the first concrete step taken by his administration aimed at easing tensions between China and the US. American tourists were now allowed to buy and bring back home up to $100 worth of goods

made in mainland China and the travel ban to the PRC was lifted for
American scholars, doctors, scientists and journalists.[32] At Guam
he proclaimed a new Asian policy--the Nixon Doctrine--emphasizing
the need for America's Asian allies to defend themselves.[33] He also
made a detour to Rumania where he let his host know that he would
welcome overtures from Peking.

    Since that time, a series of additional steps were taken by the
Nixon administration, culminating in the visit of a US Ping-Pong team
to the PRC in April 1971. Such steps included the following:

    1.   In December 1969, the American Ambassador to Poland
"mingled" with the Charge d'Affaires from Peking and suggested the
resumption of the Warsaw Talks. Peking's response was happily an
affirmative one. Two weeks later, Washington announced that, effective December 22, 1969, the embargo on the PRC would be partially
lifted so that subsidiaries and affiliates of American corporations
abroad might sell certain non-strategic goods to the PRC and buy
Communist Chinese goods for resale on foreign markets. Concurrently,
the ceiling of goods to be brought into the US by tourists for non-
commercial purposes would be abolished.[34]

    2.   In his first "State of the World" message, President Nixon
spoke of a US desire to improve relations with Peking because "a
lasting peace will be impossible so long as some nations consider
themselves the permanent enemies of others."[35] A low-keyed approach
was assumed regarding the PRC-Canadian talks during 1970.

    3.   At the 1970 session of the General Assembly, Christopher
H. Phillips, US Deputy Permanent Representative to the UN, openly
stated on the Assembly floor that "the United States is as interested
as any in this room to see the People's Republic of China play a con-
structive role among the family of nations."[36] Without changing its
voting position on the China question, the delegation of the US labori-
ously explained to the Assembly audience that the US was only opposed
to the Albanian resolution because it would admit the PRC at the expense of expelling the ROC, a conscientious and loyal supporter of
the UN.

    4.   In February 1971, Nixon stirred the world press and caused
the ROC to lodge a "strong protest" by using the term "the People's
Republic of China" in his second "State of the World" message.[37]

    5.   On March 15, 1971, the notation "not valid for travel into or
through" the PRC was removed from passports issued by the US
State Department.[38]

    While these measures were being announced, behind-the-scenes
diplomatic moves were also being made. According to Edgar Snow,

during 1970 a number of go-betweens had been delivering messages
to the Peking government on behalf of Washington.[39] Among them
were Andre Bettencourt, the French minister of planning, and Maurice
Couve de Murville, the French premier under the late Charles de
Gaulle. "It was to General de Gaulle, I was authoritatively informed,
that Mr. Nixon had first confided his intention to seek a genuine detente
with China," Snow reports. Furthermore,

> other diplomats had been active. The head of one European
> mission in Peking, who had already made one trip to see
> President Nixon, returned to Washington last December.
> He bypassed the State Department to confer at the White
> House, and was back in China in January. From another
> and unimpeachable diplomatic source I learned, not long
> before my departure from Peking in February, that the
> White House had once more conveyed a message asking how
> a personal representative of the President would be received
> in the Chinese capital for conversations with the highest
> Chinese leaders. About the same time, I was enigmatically
> told by a senior Chinese diplomat who had formerly main-
> tained quite the opposite, 'Nixon is getting out of Vietnam.'

As if to convey the importance of such developments, Snow twice
stressed that such "background information" was not provided to him
by Mao Tse-tung.

In spring 1971, a Nixon Administration aide said that the US was
led to expect "a dramatic gesture by Peking this spring in response
to the US overtures."[40] That dramatic gesture, to the surprise of
all, turned out to be a "private" invitation extended on April 7, 1971,
to the American Ping-Pong team in Japan to tour the mainland of
China, a most unusual but imaginative diplomatic move that one reporter said "constituted a breakthrough of historic proportions."[41]

Actually, Peking's decision to respond to American overtures
had taken shape in late 1970. In early December 1970, Chou En-lai
had already told Edgar Snow that Peking was ready to negotiate with
Washington and that visas would soon be issued to those American
friends of China who wished to visit the mainland. "The door is open.
The question is whether the US is sincere about solving the problem
of Taiwan," Chou said.[42] Similarly, Mao had also informed Snow on
December 18, 1970, that "the foreign ministry was studying the matter
of admitting Americans from the left, middle and right to visit China."[43]

The American Ping-Pong team and the reporters who accompanied

them were treated royally while in China. Premier Chou declared:
"You have opened a new page in the relations of the Chinese and
American people. I am confident that this beginning again of our
friendship will certainly meet with the majority support of our two
peoples."[44]

The immediate repercussions of the Ping-Pong diplomacy have
been felt far and wide. The more so because, about this time, Snow
wrote in Life magazine about his December 18, 1970, interview with
Mao which included this passage:

> Should rightists like Nixon, who represented the monopoly
> capitalists, be permitted to come? Mao explained, at
> present the problems between China and the USA would
> have to be solved with Nixon. Mao would be happy to talk
> with him, either as a tourist or as President.[45]

Witness the Nixon Administration's responses: First, on April 14,
President Nixon announced five measures in a single package to show
his pleasure.[46] They were: (1) A relaxation of the 20-year-old
embargo on US trade with the PRC (a list of items placed on the general
license was subsequently made public on June 10).[47] (2) A pledge to
"expedite" visas for Chinese citizens wishing to visit the US. (3) A
relaxation of US currency controls to permit the PRC to pay for
imports with dollars and to allow American citizens to send checks
to China without first obtaining permission. (4) Permission for
American oil companies to sell fuel to ships or planes bound to or
from the PRC, except for Chinese craft heading to or from North
Vietnam, North Korea or Cuba. (5) Authorization for US ships or planes
to carry Chinese cargoes between non-Chinese ports, and for American-
owned carriers that operate under foreign flags to visit the PRC
itself.

Then, on April 16, the Washington Post reported a Nixon remark
that he would like to visit Peking during his tenure as the President
of the US. Later, on April 20, it was announced that Peking has accepted an American invitation to send a Ping-Pong team to visit the
US.[48]

As this chapter was being finalized for publication, news of the
secret Kissinger trip to Peking between July 9 and 11 was disclosed
by President Nixon. "I will go to China," the President told the
world. Thus Peking has now come to make deals with the head of the
American "imperialists." Not long ago its own propaganda machine
had accused the Russians of engaging in "collusion" with the Americans

in the UN and in other places. How could this be satisfactorily explained? The answer is not immediately clear.

Meanwhile, Peking's leaders seem to have made many remarks
about the need to expel Taiwan from the UN. The Algerians checked
with Peking whether the 18-nation (i.e., Albanian) draft resolution
on Chinese representation in the UN should adopt a modified formula
just before the 1970 session and were told no.[49] Yet, Peking specifically thanked the Algerians and others for having sponsored that
draft resolution. According to Yoshikatsu Takeiri, chairman of the
Komeito of Japan, Chou En-lai told his group visiting Peking in June
1971, that Peking would participate in UN activities, but first the legal
position of the PRC must be restored, and Chiang Kai-shek driven
out of that body.[50] "That is all that needs to be done," he reportedly
said. Moreover, he added:

> It is the responsibility of the United Nations, of the various
> member countries. We are grateful to countries and par-
> ties that advocate restoring the legal position of the People's
> Republic of China in the United Nations. But we ourselves
> do not make any demands.

Whatever other motives there might be in Peking's "collaboration" with the Nixon Administration thus far, can there be any
serious doubt that Peking has been endeavoring to accelerate the end
of the "B.C." era in the United Nations?

SUMMARY OBSERVATIONS OF PART II

In Part II, the actual records of Peking's international behavior
during the period 1949-71 were examined in order to find out when, how
and why Peking's attitude and approach toward the UN have changed.
The findings can be summed up as follows.

First, in terms of Peking's UN policy, the 22 years under examination seem to divide into seven periods. We have traced a development of Peking's approach from (1) an initial period (1949-50) characterized by an active, direct and defensive approach to (2) a shift to
offensive in the period, 1950-53, to (3) an almost totally new approach
characteristically defensive, reactive and indirect in 1954, which continued through 1959, to (4) an adventurous offensive and active approach
during 1958-61. (5) A change in attitude, not just approach, took place
after 1961; the period 1962-65 actually representing a change from
positive to negative, with the approach remaining offensive, active

and indirect. (6) During the GPCR (1966-69), preoccupation with internal crises overshadowed Peking's foreign operations; Peking's UN policy, like its general foreign policy was temporarily suspended. (7) Since the Ninth Party Congress (April 1969), however, Peking has not only renewed its interest in the UN but seems to be embarking on a systematic program to push for an early entry into that organization.

It would be presumptuous to suggest that there is a rhythm or a cycle in Peking's UN policy or its international strategy, but one might note in passing that our periodization, without attempting to do so, has cut the 22 years under consideration into a series of three-to-four-year periods following the initial year of the PRC.

Second, it is interesting that Peking did not adopt a negative attitude toward the UN until 1961, and that that negative attitude has changed back to positive after the spring of 1969. This point is of particular interest because it is a direct evidence that a "UN angle" exists in Peking's foreign policy deliberations. Even during the interval when Peking's attitude was negative, it seems clear that Peking was searching for a substitute to the UN rather than just forgetting about the UN altogether.

Third, Peking's approach changed from direct to indirect in 1954 and has remained indirect since that time. At the beginning of Part II, the direct-indirect aspect of adjustment was described as one relating to the tactfulness in strategic maneuver. A direct approach implies confidence; an indirect approach implies doubt or mistrust. It seems Peking's mistrust of the UN (or doubt about its own ability to gain entrance into the UN) became a basis of its UN policy (and presumably its foreign policy in general) in 1954 and has remained unchanged since then.

Fourth, Peking's approach changed from active to reactive in 1954, and back to active in 1958 and has remained active since. One may say that its approach was consistently active with the exception of the 1954-57 period. The active-reactive aspect of adjustment relates to the matter of strategic initiatives. An active approach implies strength; a reactive approach implies weakness. This finding suggests, therefore, that Peking's approach has been based on the assumption that the PRC was in a position of strength. This is a questionable practice. There can be three interpretations of this finding: (1) the finding is wrong. Peking's leaders certainly had not been blind to the fact that they were dealing with superpowers like the US and the USSR. (2) Peking's leaders had been unrealistic in their approach toward the outside world, including the UN. It was pointed out in Part I that the foreign policy-makers of Peking as a group have been characteristically isolated from the outside world and tended to see the world through the prism of their past experiences. (3) Peking's leaders had been unconventional and innovative. Mao's personal style, as was also pointed out in Part I, is characterized by activism among other things. His "paper tiger" thesis, his idea that men, not weapons or machines, win the final war and his revolutionary zeal all make him appear "irrational" in conventional eyes. It is not inexplicable that Mao's foreign policy had been active all along. At this time it is not clear just which of these three interpretations is the correct one. Perhaps a combination of all three interpretations comes the closest. In any case, it is also interesting to note that 1954-57 was the one period during which Peking's international behavior appeared "normal" in terms of the conventional theory of power politics. This is true whether the findings on other periods turn out to be correct or not.

Fifth, Peking's approach also changed back and forth between defensive and offensive no less than three and perhaps four times. The offensive-defensive aspect of adjustment, by the definition at the beginning of Part II, relates to strategic posture, i.e., the terms a nation proposes or is ready to accept. An offensive approach implies determination and/or one's just position; a defensive approach implies lack of will or acknowledgment of the opponent's just position. In 1950, Peking's approach shifted from defensive to offensive. It was found that that shift was an expression of Peking's defiance against the US, which in Peking's view had threatened the national security of the PRC under the guise of the UN flag. In 1954, Peking returned to a defensive approach. It was found that this was actually Mao's concept of "strategic defensive"--the first stage of protracted war-- which Peking seems to have adapted to its international revolutionary movement; it was actually a move in preparation for a later offensive. In 1958, there was another switch from defensive to offensive. This was found explainable in terms of Peking's mistaken perception about the world balance of power and its impatience to move toward the second stage of the "international protracted war." Since April 1969, Peking's approach has again changed from offensive to defensive. This time, it was hypothesized that the change may have been effectuated by a group of moderate, and more realistic, leaders in the name of Mao and Mao Thought. Thus, with the exception of the last case about which there is rather limited information at this time, in every other case when Peking adopted a defensive approach, there was actually neither a lack of will on the part of Peking, nor an acknowledgment that its position was less "just" than that of the UN. There may be a lesson here: The deduction of the implications of a defensive approach is incomplete. Aside from signalling a lack of will or an

acknowledgment of the opponent's just position, a defensive approach
may also imply other things, such as a temporary retreat (1954-57)
or simply naivete (1949-50).

Sixth, Peking's attitude and approach at any given time depend
partly on its perception of the fundamental nature of the UN with which
it is dealing. There seem to have been five different kinds of UN's
in Peking's perception. Conceptually they can be labelled: (1) the
UN of the Charter, (2) the UN under US control, (3) the UN of parliamentary diplomacy, (4) the "revolutionary" UN, and (5) UN of US-USSR
collusion. In Chapter 13, more space will be devoted discussing each
of these five kinds of UN. For now, the distinguishing characteristics
of each will be sketched.

1.   The UN of the Charter. This is the UN according to its
founders' intent, where important political decisions are made on the
basis of a concert of the five permanent members of the Security
Council. It roughly corresponds to Ernst Haas's concept of a "concert
of big powers" type of collective security. This UN existed in Peking's
realistic thinking only in the brief initial period of the PRC. After the
UN police forces threatened the PRC's border security in 1950, the
UN of the Charter became but a convenient prototype that Peking
freely invoked for its own political purposes.
2.   The UN under US Control. This is the UN in which a big
power, the US, controls an "automatic majority" necessary for the
passage of resolutions in either the General Assembly or the Security
Council. It is similar to what Haas calls a "permissive enforcement"
type of collective security in which a big power is capable of carrying
out its national policy in the name of the organization even over the
objection of one of the other big powers. This UN is, for Peking, the
real UN, which prevented it from taking China's seat. It came into
being during the Korean War and has been a target of Peking's propaganda attacks ever since.
3.   The UN of Parliamentary Diplomacy. This is essentially
Haas's "balancing" type of collective security. In this UN, the
adoption of important resolutions cannot be swayed by the decision of
any single power. Resolutions are adopted on the basis of the successful conduct of diplomacy by supporters in the General Assembly.
It differs from the UN of the Charter in that the veto power of the big
five is set aside. It was conceived in 1954 and more or less discarded
in 1961 by Peking.
4.   The "Revolutionary" UN. This is the UN that Peking turned
to after 1961 and proposed to establish in January 1965. It was conceived to be anti-imperialist and pro-revolutionary, presumably with
the PRC at the helm. In it the socialist and the "new emerging"

forces would stage their own drama in competition with the UN that had fallen to the imperialists, the modern revisionists and the reactionaries. But it never gained any momentum and might have already had its stillbirth.

5. The UN of US-USSR Collusion. This is the UN in which the two superpowers allegedly conspire to bolster their advantageous status by collaborating to control the decision-making in the UN organs through their combined influence, to the detriment of lesser powers. It appeared in Peking's propaganda implicitly during the Congo crisis and explicitly after 1964. It has received the most verbal abuse from Peking.

III

EMPIRICAL ANALYSIS: CONTINUING CHARACTERISTICS AND PATTERNS OF PEKING'S UN POLICY

At the beginning of Part II, the term "continuity" was defined as relative persistence and constancy in the position, direction or posture of a policy for the period under consideration. By this we mean not the total lack of interruption or modification in details, but the existence of certain threads that string together the scattered events and explain their common characteristics. A study of changes concentrates on the parts, particularly the joints between parts; a study of continuity focuses on the whole, particularly the veins that run through the parts. From a study of policy changes, one learns about the dynamics of a foreign policy system; from a study of policy continuity, one learns about the orientation and behavior patterns of a foreign policy system in its international interactions with other systems.

Part III is concerned with the articulation of the aspects of continuity in Peking's UN policy over the last 22 years. A few steps back will be taken and a look at the empirical data as a whole in order to discover the continuing threads of Peking's UN policy and to attempt an interpretation of Peking's behavior patterns and orientations.

In the last three chapters, three main lines that appear to characterize Peking's UN policy throughout the 22-year period under consideration will be identified. They are (1) a legal line, couching Peking's unyielding claim as the sole representative government of the whole of China (including Taiwan) in the UN; (2) a political line, showing Peking's constant expedient practice of evaluating the UN in terms of the instrumental value of that organization; and (3) an ideological-psychological line, reflecting the ever-present imprint of the thought and psychology of Mao Tse-tung and his "Maoist" followers.

12

LEGALISTIC STAND
ON THE QUESTION
OF CHINESE
REPRESENTATION

The most salient aspect of continuity in Peking's UN policy is legal. Succinctly stated, Peking's official position on the question of Chinese representation in the UN has never departed from the claim that the government of the PRC is the sole legitimate government of the whole of China and that the UN is obliged legally to restore to that government all legitimate rights to which China is entitled. Implied in this claim is the assertion that Taiwan is an integral part of China that Peking sooner or later will "liberate" from the discredited regime of the ROC. All variations of "two-Chinas" or "one-China, one-Taiwan" formulae have been rejected. In effect, non-participation of a rival Taiwan in any form other than through the PRC has become a precondition of Peking's participation in the UN.[1]

THE LEGAL STATUS OF TAIWAN

The origin of the problem of Taiwan was outlined in Chapter 5. The main concerns here are the complicated problem of Taiwan's legal status and the fundamental position on Taiwan that Peking has unfailingly adhered to since 1949.[2]

Doctrines on Taiwan's International Status

There are at least six different views on Taiwan's present international status. These views have been expressed by scholars of international law, on the basis of their interpretations of three documents: (1) the ROC's Declaration of War on Japan, December 8, 1941; (2) the Cairo Declaration of November 26, 1943, as incorporated in the Potsdam

Proclamation and the Japanese Instrument of Surrender; and (3) the Treaty of Peace with Japan, September 8, 1951. The six views are as follows:

1. Taiwan has been a <u>de jure</u> Chinese territory since December 8, 1941, by the abrogation of the Shimonoseki Treaty.[3]

2. Taiwan has been a <u>de facto</u> Chinese territory since September, 2, 1945, by conquest.[4]

3. Taiwan has been a condominium of the Allied Powers since April 28, 1952, by the Peace Treaty with Japan.[5]

4. Taiwan has been a Chinese (ROC) territory since October 25, 1945, by prescription.[6]

5. Taiwan has been a Chinese (ROC) territory since October 25, 1945, by occupation.[7]

6. Taiwan has become a separate state independent from the PRC since October 1, 1949, by state succession.[8]

It is not the purpose of this study to discuss the arguments and merits of these different views. Suffice it to say that, except discovery, all means of territorial acquisition that traditional international law recognizes have been invoked by someone to justify one of the six positions. The fact is that none of the six positions has been commonly accepted. Each seems legally unsatisfactory when all facets of the Taiwan problem are taken into consideration. It may be said that a situation exists regarding Taiwan's legal status that no observer has been able to explain satisfactorily in terms of the prevailing concepts of international law. Perhaps precisely because of this ambiguity, many commentators, practitioners and academicians alike have resorted to making propositions for solving the Taiwan problem without necessarily justifying their formulae on the basis of existing principles of law.

Alternatives for Solving the Taiwan Problem

The alternatives for the solution of the problem of Taiwan can be summarized on the basis of methods and outcomes suggested in the following chart.

Methods	Outcomes
1. Freezing the status quo	A. Two Chinas[13]
2. Military conquest of the ROC by the PRC	B. One China--PRC
3. Recovery of the mainland by the ROC	C. One China--ROC
4. Negotiations between Peking and Taipei[9]	D. One-and-a-half Chinas[14]
5. Plebiscite in Taiwan[10]	E. One China, One Taiwan[15]
6. Formosan declaration of independence[11]	E. One China, One Taiwan
7. UN resolution on Taiwan[12]	F. UN trusteeship or administration of Taiwan[16]

The correlations between methods and outcomes of solutions are suggested as likely but not necessary. Specifically, the outcomes of methods 1 and 7 are entirely open. Freezing the status quo means to continue the present impasse and allow changes inside either the PRC or both to take their courses. Any significant change--the passing from the scene of Mao Tse-tung or Chiang Kai-shek, a major confrontation between the PRC and the USSR, substantial civil strife in either domain, etc.--may open up one or more of the other methods. Should the status quo persist for a very long period of time, it may by itself lead to a fait accompli of "two Chinas," which may eventually become acceptable to all parties concerned. But that possibility is very remote. Similarly, utilizing the UN's authority to solve the problem may end up with any of the six outcomes, depending on the alignment of the supporters of each position at the time a UN decision is made. Judging from past performances of the UN it probably cannot impose any particular solution upon either the PRC or the ROC. The possibility of a UN trusteeship or temporary administration will be realistic only when the contending parties themselves first agree to that solution.

The correlations between methods 2 and 3 and outcomes B and C are logical. So is 6 and E. Method 4, "negotiations between Peking and Taipei," is likely to lead to D, a "one-and-a-half Chinas" solution,

i.e., with the PRC having suzerainty or residual sovereignty over
Taiwan and simultaneously guaranteeing Taiwan's autonomy. But this
too is not a necessary correlation. Finally, a plebiscite supervised by
an international authority may lead to E, the "one-China, one-Taiwan"
solution only if the plebiscite is held after the Taiwanese masses have
been informed of their options and their personal freedoms guaranteed.
Otherwise, the outcome is not predictable.

Peking's Fundamental Position

Amidst all these doctrines and proposals, where does Peking
stand? Following the outbreak of the Korean War, in his statement
of June 28, 1950, Chou En-lai said:

> On behalf of the Central People's Government of the
> People's Republic of China, I declare that, . . . the fact
> that Taiwan is part of China remains unchanged forever.
> This is not only a historical fact; it has also been con-
> firmed by the Cairo and Potsdam Declarations and the
> situation since the surrender of Japan.[17]

Since then, this same position has been repeatedly stressed by spokesmen of the PRC government.

Briefly, this fundamental position of the PRC government regarding Taiwan's legal status can be described along the following
lines: (1) Taiwan is historically a part of China; (2) even though Taiwan
was temporarily "stolen" by Japan, China resumed its de jure sovereignty by the unilateral abrogation of the Shimonoseki Treaty in 1951;
(3) this was confirmed by the Cairo and Potsdam Declarations; (4)
when the Chinese government accepted the Japanese surrender and
occupied Taiwan on October 25, 1945, Taiwan became, not only de jure,
but also de facto, an inalienable part of Chinese territory; and (5) when
the KMT regime was "overthrown by the Chinese people," as a result
of the Communist-led revolution in 1949, the sovereignty of the Chinese
government, including the jurisdiction over Taiwan, passed from the
old ROC government to the new PRC government.

It follows from this position that (1) the ROC, being a government "repudiated by the Chinese people" and "representing nobody"
must be removed from the roster of the family of nations; the representatives of the PRC government should be recognized in place of
those of the ROC in international organizations and conferences; (2)
the "liberation of Taiwan," peaceful or otherwise, is a matter of China's

sovereignty and her internal affair--no outside interference is allowed; (3) President Truman's statement on June 27, 1950, and the American military presence on the island of Taiwan and in the Taiwan Strait is tantamount to an armed aggression against China; (4) all schemes devised to "create two Chinas" (two successor states theory, one-and-a-half Chinas, or one China and one Taiwan) or attempts to split Taiwan from China (UN trusteeship, plebiscite, etc.) can only be interpreted as a conspiracy to violate China's territorial integrity and cannot be tolerated.

In concrete terms, Peking's practice seems to have been consistent as to the status of Taiwan within the PRC system. The Taiwan Democratic Self-Government League was one of the consistent bodies represented at the 1949 Plenary Session of the CPPCC.[18] Although the "province of Taiwan" was not included in the domain of the six military and administrative regional committees established by the Organic Law of the New Regional Government Committees on December 16, 1949,[19] Article 2 of the Common Program of the CPPCC did state that the new regime "shall undertake to wage the people's war of liberation to the very end, to liberate all the territory of China, and to achieve the unification of China."[20] In 1954, when the government was reorganized in accordance with the new Constitution, special care was taken to reserve seats for delegates from Taiwan.[21] Similarly, the result of the 1953 population census did not fail to include an entry of 7,591,298 for the Province of Taiwan.[22] In Part II it was shown how the Taiwan question was the stumbling block in the Sino-American Talks. In the last two years, a number of different formulae have been adopted in Peking's communiques announcing the establishment of diplomatic relations between the PRC and Canada, Chile, Italy, Equatorial Guinea, Ethiopia, Cameroon, Nigeria, Kuwait, Austria, San Marino and so forth.[23] Such formulae demonstrated Peking's flexibility in its diplomatic actions. But in no case can one say that Peking has yielded its sovereign claim to Taiwan. Quite the contrary, when Libya unilaterally announced its "full recognition" of the PRC on June 11, 1971, it received no official response from Peking, presumably because Libya failed to sever its ties with the ROC.[24]

In short, as far as Peking is concerned, the problem of Taiwan is one of liberation, not of legal status. Peking will try to "liberate" the island by peaceful means if possible, and by force if necessary, even if the "liberation" is only nominal.

FUNDAMENTAL NATURE OF THE QUESTION
OF CHINESE REPRESENTATION

Doctrines on China's Participation in the UN

The legal nature of the question of China's participation has been debated by many scholars of international law and delegates to the UN. In general, their arguments can be classified in one of three schools of juridical interpretation.[25] One, the membership school, considers the question one of admitting the PRC as a new member. Two, the representation school, argues that the question is one of determining which of the two contending governments can legitimately claim the right to represent China. Three, the credentials school, sees no problem in either China's membership or the representation of its government, but contends that the question is merely one of approving the credentials of a delegation.

Arguments for these three schools of interpretations are advanced usually in support of one or the other of the two contending Chinese parties. Each school of interpretation invokes a special set of legal principles. Opponents of the PRC frequently adhere to the membership school and invoke Article 4 of the Charter, which stipulates the qualifications of a new member. Supporters of the PRC tend to subscribe to the representation school, invoking traditional principles of international law regarding succession of states. Advocates of the credentials school, usually favoring the status quo, cite the relevant Rules of Procedures of the organs concerned as the law to be applied.

In this analysis, the credentials school will not be considered as pertinent to the question of Chinese participation in the UN. In the fianl analysis, a genuine question of credentials can arise only when two delegations claim to represent one government. That is clearly not the case regarding China. The case of China is either a question of admission or representation, depending on one's assumption as to the legal status of Taiwan. In a way, one may say that the legal solution regarding the question of Chinese participation is, in general, dependent upon two sets of assumptions: (1) about the legal status of Taiwan and (2) about the philosophy of the United Nations organization.

Assumptions about the legal status of Taiwan determine whether the question is procedurally one of admission or of representation.

1. If Taiwan (ROC) is considered a sovereign state separate from the PRC, then one must further determine whether the state personality of China, an original member of the UN and a permanent member of its Security Council, is continued in either the PRC or the ROC. The one that is deemed the continuing state will continue to represent China; the other will then have to apply for admission.

2. If Taiwan is judged to be a part of China, the question is a matter of representation. The government that is denied the right to represent China will also be denied participation in the UN activities, except through the government that is recognized.

3. Finally, if Taiwan's status is considered undetermined, it would seem necessary to examine whether the ROC government still legitimately represents China, after a revolution has exiled it to the island and a new government has taken control of Chinese territory. The question is also one of representation.

Collaterally, assumptions about the philosophy of the UN determine the criteria by which the problems of admission or representation are solved.

1. If the UN is considered universal in scope and purpose, the "objective" criteria prevail--whether an applicant for admission meets the qualifications of a sovereign state, or whether a contending government has effective control of the territory and command of its people's habitual obedience.

2. If universality is not the rule, the organization is deemed a selective club with restricted participation, then the "subjective" criteria take precedence over the "objective" ones. Whether an applicant for admission or a contending government actually possesses the capability and willingness to meet its obligations.

That the legal status of Taiwan has been in a nebulous state, despite the ROC's de facto rule has already been discussed. No particular doctrine has been found capable of explaining the legal status of Taiwan satisfactorily. Such an ambiguous situation inevitably casts a shadow over any legal interpretation on the Chinese question at the UN.

Similarly, the philosophy of the UN is by no means clear. Whereas the provision of Article 4 emphasizes the "peace-loving" quality of a membership applicant and its ability and willingness to carry out the Charter obligations, the practice of the organization reflects the part of its general membership that universal participation is essential for the successful operation of the UN.[26] It is not surprising, therefore, that arguments on the legal solution to the question of Chinese participation in the UN have been diverse and ambiguous.

Alternatives for Solving the Question of China's Participation in the UN

In the last section (see p. 191), six alternative solutions were identified for the problem of Taiwan in terms of possible outcomes. Each of the six also suggests a specific mode of solution for the Chinese question at the UN, as the chart below shows.

Taiwan Problem	Chinese Question in UN
A. Two Chinas--PRC and ROC	1. PRC (or ROC) represents China and admission of ROC (or PRC) as a new member; or admission of both as new members
B. One China--PRC	2. PRC represents China
C. One China--ROC	3. ROC represents China
D. One-and-a-half Chinas (PRC and autonomous Taiwan)	4. PRC represents China, and admission of Taiwan as a member with status comparable to Ukraine
E. One China, One Taiwan	5. PRC represents China, and admission of Taiwan as a new member
F. UN trusteeship or administration of Taiwan	6. PRC represents China, and UN determination of Taiwan's status in the future

In solutions 2 and 3, there is no question of admission involved The question is one of representation. To the government that is given the right of representation belong all the privileges and obligations of China's membership in the UN, including the permanent status in the Security Council. The same applies to solution 6, where Taiwan's status is temporarily deferred. The ROC government presumably will be replaced by the administration appointed by the UN. The Chinese

seat will simply be taken over by the PRC. There will be no question
of either admission or representation for the time being. At the end
of UN trusteeship or administration, Taiwan may be admitted as a new
member or it may participate in UN activities through the PRC, depending upon the terms of such trusteeship or administration. At that
time, however, the question of Chinese representation will have been
solved. The question will have become one of Taiwan's rather than
China's participation.

In contrast, solutions 1, 4 and 5 cannot avoid the question of
admission. In solution 1, there are logically, three possibilities of
Chinese participation in the UN: admitting the PRC, the ROC or both
of them as new members. To admit the PRC (ROC) as a new member
implies the recognition of the ROC (PRC) as the legitimate representative of China, the original Charter member. To admit both the PRC
and the ROC as new members implies the disintegration of China, the
original Charter member, and the cancellation of its permanent seat
in the Security Council. It is an academic exercise, but interesting,
nevertheless, to point out that in the first two possibilities, the one
applying for new membership may find the other casting a veto against
it at the Security Council, unless prior agreement of a two-Chinas
solution binding the recognized Chinese government has been reached.

Solution 4 is evidently a compromise favoring the PRC. One
probable variation of it is a special arrangement patterned after
the Soviet-Byelorussia-Ukraine representations at the UN. The PRC,
which controls the mainland, will represent China. The province of
Taiwan within the greater China will enjoy an autonomous status
and concurrently be represented in the General Assembly as a voting
member, taking directives from Peking. Finally, solution 5 is a clear-
cut case of admitting Taiwan as a new member with a separate and
independent identity of its own. The China seat is passed from the
ROC to the PRC.

The legal procedures involved in each of these six alternative
solutions are simple enough to decipher. But agreeing on one of these
solutions is a matter of political struggle beyond any analysis on paper.
The PRC and the ROC are likely to hold onto solutions 2 and 3 respectively and resist any deviation, unless an extraordinary urgent and
threatening situation forces them to yield. In either case, the territory
under the government that is denied recognition by a one-China solution will be misrepresented by the favored government. The third
parties who do not align their positions with either the PRC or the
ROC will favor one of the other four solutions as a means to overcome
the dilemma. For them, solutions 1, 4, 5 and 6 are more acceptable

in that they reflect the reality of international society more closely.
But the same solutions are also less realistic because all of them contradict the basic positions of both the PRC and the ROC, and are unequivocally opposed by both governments.

From the UN's point of view, each of the six approaches is also
a note of commentary on the philosophy of the organization. Adopting
one of them to the exclusion of the others may have repercussions on
the future development of the UN. For instance, solution 2 tends to
underscore the principle of universality. Its adoption is likely to promote the development of a UN incorporating all members of the family
of nations, including the divided states of Germany, Korea and Vietnam.
Solution 3, conversely, will bolster the conservative values of the
established Western members and contribute to the growth of a less
realistic, if not "virtuous," world organization. Solution 1 represents
a tacit acceptance of the "two successor states" doctrine, together
with a more or less coercive approach geared to forcing one of the
contending governments to acquiesce in the perpetuation of its rival.
Outsiders may see this as the ROC's "greatest insurance for continued membership in the UN,"[27] but the ROC government certainly will
not swallow this bitter pill with ease. That it is an unacceptable solution
for Peking seems clear. Consequently, this approach will likely de-
prive the UN of the PRC's cooperation for an extended period. Solution 4 means approximately the opposite, i.e., the sacrifice of the
ROC, a smaller but faithful member of the UN, to appease the PRC,
a big and threatening power. Whatever Machiavellism one employs to
explain world politics, it is reasonable to speculate that smaller nations
will come to mistrust the UN if such a solution is effected. Both solutions 1 and 4 ignore the principles of national self-determination as
stipulated in Article 73 of the Charter. This too is not likely to add
to the UN's prestige. Solution 5 seems to be a preferable arrangement. Granting Taiwan a separate membership independent from that
of the PRC presumably will be a result of a plebiscite supervised by
the UN or an impartial international authority. If this can be done, it
will benefit both the inhabitants of Taiwan and the UN. It is even conceivable that, in the long-run, a fait accompli of an independent Taiwan
may become acceptable to a new generation of leaders in Peking.
Solution 6 also possesses some features that will enhance the prestige
of the UN if successfully executed. However, in both of these last two
solutions, there is the paradox that they need prior cooperation of the
ROC government, if not that of the PRC as well. The UN cannot make
Taiwan an independent state or place it under trusteeship or a UN
appointed administration just by a resolution. Any such UN resolution
will undoubtedly meet determined resistance from the KMT forces
actually controlling the island. Without local cooperation, the UN

cannot function effectively. In the views of the two contending Chinese governments, any attempt to create a "two-Chinas" solution is also a violation of Article 2 (7) of the Charter, which propagates the principle of non-interference in the domestic affairs of a member state. Again, few nations are ready to encourage the UN's interference in their domestic affairs.

Thus, uncertainty again is the rule. Pending a political solution, either through negotiations or through war, there exists workable legal solution to the question of Chinese participation in the UN.

Peking's Fundamental Position

In his first cable to the UN Secretary-General and the President of the General Assembly, Chou En-lai asserted that the Central People's Government of the PRC "is the sole legal government representing the entire people" of China. From this assertion, Peking's basic legal position concerning the question of Chinese participation in the UN is deduced. Briefly, the logic of it can be summarized as follows: (1) China is one of the founding members of the UN; (2) the ROC government that signed the Moscow Declaration of 1943, the UN Charter of 1945 and other related documents was overthrown by the Chinese people in 1949 and replaced by the PRC; (3) the PRC is the same "pre-liberation" China and its Central People's Government is the sole legal government of China; (4) the UN should, therefore, expel the delegation of the ROC and "restore" China's seat and legitimate rights to the PRC; (5) all decisions adopted by the bodies without the participation of "the lawful representatives of the PRC" are illegal and, therefore, null and void; (6) the prolonged delay in expelling the representatives of the ROC is "a violation of the purposes and principles of the UN Charter; it makes a mockery of the UN itself, and is an insult to the members of that body."[28]

Many fine points of this position are elaborated by Chou Keng-sheng, a noted Chinese authority on international law, in an article published in Jen-min Jin-pao in 1961.[29] This important article is by far the most authoritative legal argumentation put forth by the Communist Chinese regarding China and the UN. For this reason, it is worth quoting at length in order to organize a succinct statement on Peking's fundamental legal position on the question under scrutiny.

Point by point, Chou Keng-sheng discussed the legal problems involved in the Chinese question in the UN, covering such topics as the effect of a revolution on the international personality of a State,

the linkage of representation in an international organization and recognition of a government, Article 18 (2) of the Charter dealing with
the procedures of the General Assembly, Article 23 dealing with the
official names of China, the Charter revision in relation to Chinese
participation, and so on.

On the subject of the effect of revolution on a State, the article
argued that changes in the form of a state or political regime of a
country that has experienced a revolution do not affect its international
personality. This, it said, is a universally acknowledged principle of
international law confirmed in the UN Charter and international practice.

> In the United Nations Organization, there are member states
> in which new regimes were established as a result of <u>coups</u>
> <u>d'état</u> or revolutions. Their seats in the United Nations
> were not affected. Iraq and Cuba are notable examples.[30]

In other words, a revolution is essentially an internal affair. The question of who represents China is a matter for the Chinese people to
decide, and decided it they have. The UN must follow their decision.

The question of the representation of a State in the UN should not
be confused with the question of the recognition of a government by
another. Confusing the two institutions "would appear to be legally
inadmissible." This was the opinion of the legal department of the
UN Secretariat in 1950, the article said. The article further reasoned:

> As a matter of fact, it has never been the case that all UN
> members are recognized by all other members. A number
> of newly independent nationalist countries have not been re-
> fused admission into the United Nations merely on the
> ground that for the time being only a few UN members have
> recognized them.[31]

Since China is a founding member, the question is not one of
admission. In fact, it is not even a question of representation because
that too is already solved. The real question is the "restoration" to
the PRC of what rightfully belongs to China. The author was very
careful on this point, emphasizing that

> there should be a correct understanding of how the ques-
> tion of "China's representation" should be presented. . . .
> The Soviet delegate has submitted . . . a resolution propos-
> ing that the General Assembly discuss the question of re-
> storing to the People's Republic of China its legitimate

rights in the United Nations and drive out (sic) from all UN
organs the representatives of the Chiang Kai-shek clique
who are in illegal occupation of China's UN seat. This way
of presenting the question is perfectly correct; it gets
straight to the gist of the matter.[32]

Such being the case, the correct procedure for the UN to follow is to
deal strictly and only with the mechanism of restoring the rights of
China to Peking and of driving out the illegal delegation of the "Chiang
Kai-shek clique." The question is one of procedure, i.e., the procedure
of nullifying the credentials of the representatives from the ROC and,
in their place, recognizing the representatives appointed by the Peking
government.

The article dwelled at length on Article 18 (2), evidently because
the application of the so-called important question formula to the
Chinese question was first proposed that year in the General Assembly.
Several sharp argumentations were articulated in this connection. First
it was alleged that the Five-Power Resolution of 1961 was a pretext
being used by the US and its followers to continue to obstruct the PRC's
participation in the UN. Then it was pointed out that for a number of
years, the Assembly had decided to postpone discussion of the question
of Chinese representation by a simple majority vote. In the author's
view, this postponement was an extremely important question, as it
prevented "the restoration of China's legitimate rights in the UN."
Now, all of a sudden, the question of representation, another procedural
question, was declared "important" and under the jurisdiction of Article
18 of the Charter. Of the two procedural questions of importance, one
was dealt with by a simple majority vote, while the other was singled
out as requiring a two-thirds majority vote. Why? "This is self-con-
tradictory and untenable from the standpoint of law," the author declared.

As to Paragraph 3 of Article 18, which provides that "Decisions on the questions, including the determination of additional categories of questions to be decided by a two-thirds majority, shall be
made by a majority of the members present and voting," the article
observed that "only categories of questions not individual specific
questions, are referred to" in that paragraph. Citing Oppenheim's
International Law, Chou Keng-sheng contended that to interpret it
otherwise would lead to repeated misuse of the provisions of that
Article by the "imperialists." The question of "restoring" China's
rights in the UN is a specific question that could not be classified as
one requiring a two-thirds majority decision, unless a general provision for creating an additional category covering that matter was
first approved by the Assembly.

Since Article 18 does not apply to the Chinese question, the normal procedures of the UN relating to procedural matters (Article 21 on the Rules of Procedure of the General Assembly and Article 30 on the Rules of Procedure of the Security Council) should be followed. As far as the Security Council is concerned, there is a consensus that the veto cannot be applied in regard to a decision as to what regime should represent a member. The article noted that this view was expressed by both Trygve Lie and Dag Hammarskjold and by Western experts in international law. The reason is clear. For

> if the examination of credentials of representatives is regarded as a non-procedural matter and at the same time the veto can be applied in the Security Council on the question of the right of representation, then, after the government of a state has undergone a revolutionary change, the person still acting as representative of the overthrown government of a state having a permanent seat in the Security Council would be able to exclude the representative of the new government by veto while himself (sic) forever illegally occupying his seat in the Security Council. Should this be allowed, wouldn't it lead to preposterous results and paralyze the organization of the United Nations?[33]

It is difficult to refute this observation. Having expounded this point, Chou Keng-sheng made his query:

> Now, if a procedural question can be decided by a simple majority in the Security Council, why then should this self-same question require a two-thirds majority decision in the General Assembly? What kind of logic is this?[34]

The attempt by the United States to tie the question of Chinese representation with that of broadening the membership of the Security Council and the Economic and Social Council was also attacked. Even though the two questions were related in that revision of the Charter without the approval of the PRC as a permanent member of the Security Council would be considered illegal by Peking, the article nonetheless demurred to the tie between the two questions on the ground that the two questions were of an entirely different nature--one being a substantive question and the other a procedural one--and therefore should not be dealt with together.

There was also a rebuttal of the argument that an amendment to Article 23 of the Charter, which specifically named "the Republic of China" as a permanent member of the Security Council, would be

necessary in order for the PRC to replace the ROC in the Council.
This argument was denounced as being "completely divorced from the
essence of the question," and "a deliberate misinterpretation of the
provisions of the Charter." It was argued that the signatory to the
UN Charter simply represented a state. Quoting Hans Kelsen, it pointed
out: "Under general international law a state has the right to change
its name, and the Charter does not restrict this right of a member state
of the United Nations, even if this state is a permanent member of the
Security Council mentioned under a definite name in Article 23 of the
Charter." No re-writing of the Charter would be necessary.

Chou Keng-sheng's article was published in the offical party paper,
obviously with central approval. As presented, it seems clear that
Peking's legal position on the question of Chinese participation in the
UN is consistent in itself. The problem is that its basic position does
not agree with that of the majority of the UN (led by the United States)
who consider the Chinese question to be one as yet unsettled and who
find it expedient, pending its final settlement, that the ROC should be
allowed to continue to represent China. Peking is not unaware of this
difference. But political expediency dictates that it should remain unyielding on its own fundamental legal position. The strategies for gaining China's seat, on the other hand, are a different matter about which
Peking has not been slow in adjusting to political needs, as has already
been shown in Part II of this book.

13

THE UN
AS AN INSTRUMENT
OF
NATIONAL
POLICY

Politically, Peking's UN policy displays another aspect of continuity, namely, the propensity to consider the UN in terms of its instrumental rather than consummatory value. Peking consistently tried to utilize the UN as an instrument of national policy, either to secure China's own national interests or to promote the international revolutionary movement. Even though the nature of the operational UN changed from period in its perception, Peking never ceased to look upon the UN (particularly, UN the arena) as a tool for obtaining political gains—either from within or from without.

When the instrumental value of an international organization becomes questionable, either because of an unfavorable political climate or because of the absence of institutional safeguards, Peking's practice has been to postpone or terminate its participation in that body. From Peking's vantage point, the instrumental value of an international organization such as the UN depends largely upon its membership composition and its institutional arrangements. If the majority of the members of the UN were not friendly toward the PRC, Peking would find the political climate therein difficult to tolerate. Similarly, if the operational structure and procedures of the organs of the UN discriminated against the PRC, Peking would probably choose not to participate.

INSTRUMENTAL VALUE OF THE UN

Since its creation in 1945, the UN has been regarded by its members, large and small, as an important and useful instrument for their own national purpose. Most members have come to expect the UN to perform certain functions and, accordingly, assigned to it certain roles.

In many respects, the great powers have found the UN almost indispensable. For example, despite the fact that the Soviet Union has played the part of a "permanent minority" thus far, the Kremlin seems to have concluded through its experience that membership in the UN has been beneficial. As Alexander Dallin puts it, it has given the Soviet Union opportunities

1. for the settlement of relatively minor disputes;

2. for international contacts, both to exchange views and to initiate and pursue negotiations, often informally rather than at offical sessions;

3. for gathering information, political intelligence, technical know-how, scientific data, and securing economic and other goods and services, as a matter of self-interest;

4. for gaining prestige and respectability as a major power in the family of nations; and

5. for engaging in propaganda, in the broadest sense of the term, and attempting to influence the views, attitudes, political alignments and actions of other states.[1]

For the United States, who enjoyed a dominant position until the mid-1950's, and has continued to exert strong influence even after its control of a two-thirds majority was lost, the UN has been all this: a ready forum for the dissemination of propaganda; a convenient center for intelligence gathering; an arena for formal and informal parliamentary diplomacy; an assembly to demonstrate American power and prestige; and a mechanism for settling minor disputes. But more, it has also served as a testing ground where a trial balloon can be released and observed in order to measure the international climate at a given time relating to certain policy steps; as an organ that can be called upon to give an American policy the flavor of international legitimacy; as a lever, in the form of ostracism, against adversaries of the US to be used to force their compromise or even conformity with an American policy; and finally, on occasion, as a scapegoat--a convenient structure on which hot and difficult issues can be temporarily unloaded.[2]

As to the smaller states, their stakes in the UN are no less real if somewhat different. Particularly for the newly emerging Afro-Asians who lack both trained diplomatic personnel and the financial resources necessary to establish a network of diplomatic missions in the capitals

of most other countries around the world, the UN is actually the most
important diplomatic center as well as a decision-making organ on
foreign affairs outside their own homelands. It is the chief arena where
they place their best talents to carry out much of their externally ori-
ented activities, including the formulation, the execution and also, at
times, the control of their external policies. For many, it also serves
as a good training ground for their future diplomats and national leaders.
There is no denying that within the UN system, the small powers can
speak and vote on a basis of equality with the greater powers. Further,
it is through their caucusing groups within the UN system that these
small powers actually derive a great deal of their organized strength
and extract substantial deference from superpowers such as the United
States and the Soviet Union.[3]

These advantageous features of membership in the UN have been
generally recognized. To date, all members have seen fit to remain
within the UN system.[4] Similarly, almost all non-member nations who
are not restricted by special commitments such as neutralized status
have made continuous efforts to enter the organization.[5] This clearly
attests to their expectations that the UN would serve their own national
purposes favorably. They obviously expect to gain, not to lose, from
associating with the UN.

This pattern of behavior among nations also characterizes Peking's
UN policy, despite some isolated signs pointing to the contrary. What
is peculiar in the case of the PRC is perhaps the fact that she has always been excluded from the UN and that, in Peking's perception, there
is not just one UN but as many as five, as was sketched at the end of
Part II of this book. Consequently, the instrumental value of the UN for
Peking has not been the same as for other countries.

VARIED USES FOR FIVE KINDS OF UN

Briefly, the following paragraphs will demonstrate that each of
the five UN's conceptualized in Peking's deliberations actually could
be and had been assigned certain utilitarian roles in Peking's foreign
policy operations.

The UN of the Charter

In Part I, it was concluded that the PRC can benefit from associating with the UN in many ways, even though, at first glance,

the objectives of the PRC appear to be incompatible with the principles and purposes of the UN Charter.

In the empirical analysis in Part II, it was found that, from the beginning, Peking's leadership has always voiced formal support for the UN of the Charter. Mao himself wrote in April 1945, that the CPC "fully agrees with the proposals of the Dumbarton Oaks conference and the decisions of the Crimea conference on the establishment of an organization to safeguard international peace and security after the war."[6] As soon as the PRC was proclaimed, Peking cabled and requested the various organs of the UN to seat its delegations as representatives of China.

From the UN of the Charter, Peking had three great expectations: One, it hoped to gain international recognition of the new government. Two, it hoped to play the role of a veto-wielding power alongside the other big four. Three, it hoped to gain a world forum for its propaganda. In other words, if things went smoothly, Peking entertained the idea that the UN could play at least three instrumental roles: (1) an international authority that would underwrite the legitimacy of the Communist regime; (2) an arena where Peking would be able to exert its influence upon other nations and, perhaps, to prepare for future independence from the "big brother"--the Soviet Union; and (3) a forum where Peking could reap advantages of its "peace offensive."

These expectations turned out to be too optimistic. Nevertheless, Peking recognized the importance of the UN to many Afro-Asian nations and continued to use the UN of the Charter as a tool to demonstrate its "peaceful intentions," in order to gain support from them. In its dealings with these developing countries, Peking frequently announced its support of the Charter. Up to 1960, at least, the Charter was cited with approval in most of the bilateral treaties of friendship concluded between Peking and other countries.

The UN under US Control

In 1950, when the UN endorsed President Truman's swift action in Korea, and the military forces of the UN under General MacArthur's command crossed the 38th Parallel northward, Peking began to speak of a UN that had become "an appendage of the State Department" of the United States, which "violates its own Charter" and the wishes of "the peace-loving peoples of the world."

This UN controlled by the US, it is to be recalled, is the UN that
threatened to bomb China's important industrial sites across the Yalu
River and, in Peking's view, endangered China's security. It is the UN
against which Peking's "volunteers" fought vicious battles. It is the
UN that humiliated the PRC by insisting on the voluntary repatriation of
prisoners of war, branded the PRC as an "aggressor" and imposed an
economic embargo upon it. By Peking's logic, all these "evil deeds"
were, of course, not the doing of the UN of the Charter. They were,
indeed, only deeds done under American "coercion."

That Peking took the pains to make the technical distinction between the UN of the Charter and the UN under US control is a fact that
indicates Peking's desire to keep a door open for her future association with the former while attacking the US as the one who must be
responsible for the consequences of the latter's wrongs. Peking had
"excused" the UN for the wrongs, presumably because it still expected
to utilize the UN in its foreign policy where possible.

How can this UN under US control be of use to the PRC? As a
rule, the UN under US control was seen as a threat rather than a means
to secure China's national security or to increase its power and prestige.
Since the Korean War, Chou En-lai has repeatedly declared that all
decisions made by the UN organs without the direct participation of
the PRC are "null and void" as far as Peking is concerned. Peking
has also consistently refused any UN discussion on questions that
it deemed "domestic affairs" which, in effect, included most questions
relating to China's security such as Tibet, Taiwan and the "civil wars"
in Laos and Vietnam. Since it was impossible to utilize the UN from
within, Peking used it from without. First, the UN served as a good
example of US imperialism. The US "imperialist," i.e., the "enemy
of the peace-loving peoples of the world," had "usurped" the world
organization for its own evil purposes, and Peking points to the UN to
prove it. Second, the UN served as a barometer of the sentiments of
the Afro-Asian nations and of the general international climate.
Peking could assess the world situation by following the general debates
and the voting trends on major issues in the annual sessions of the UN.
Third, the annual voting on the Chinese question became a useful yardstick for measuring Peking's world status, for testing the attitudes
of certain countries toward the PRC along a friendship-hostility con-
tinuum, and for evaluating the degree of success or failure of its
strategies toward the countries whose support Peking sought.

The UN of Parliamentary Diplomacy

As the process of decolonization accelerated and new members were admitted, Peking began to hope for a transformation in the UN itself. In 1954, as was pointed out in Chapter 7, Peking adopted a grand scheme of "surrounding the cities from the countryside," which entailed the organization of an international united front and the application of the strategy and tactics of protracted war. In that connection, Peking envisioned the coming of a UN of parliamentary diplomacy.

From this UN of parliamentary diplomacy, Peking expected many things. First, it would restore Peking to its "legitimate place" in the UN. In this expectation, Peking obviously saw a new role for itself. The veto power would not mean as much in this kind of a UN as in the UN of the Charter, but the PRC, the most populous and most revolutionary nation in the whole world, could not help but play the role of a leading power. In other words, the UN would be very useful for enhancing Peking's prestige and influence. Second, it would be the most efficient and economical propaganda forum readily available to Peking. In fact, it could be the most convenient place to disseminate anti-imperialist ideas and propagandize the "virtues" of the "progressive" international Communist movement. Third, it could well be the right place to organize the international united front and carry out some of the strategic and tactical operations of the international protracted war against the "imperialists."

Thus, through its "people's diplomacy" and with the help of the "Bandung spirit," Peking cultivated Afro-Asian support for its cause. A survey of the Communist Chinese press clearly suggests that throughout the years from 1954 to 1961, Peking's leaders had followed the events of the UN quite closely and with increasing interest. The frequent editorials on the UN seem to testify that Peking's leaders had continued to expect eventual participation in the UN on their own terms.

In fact, a transformation in the UN did take place between 1954 and 1961. The US was no longer in control of an automatic two-thirds majority in the General Assembly by 1956. Support for Peking's bid to take over the China seat from Taipei increased steadily year after year. However, to Peking's disappointment, before a UN of parliamentary diplomacy actually materialized, Peking's hope to enter into the world forum was shattered by the 1961 resolution that declared the question of Chinese representations an important one. In effect, Peking never benefited from the UN of parliamentary diplomacy, which was to take shape gradually after 1961. For Peking, the hope of using the UN from within was never realized.

The "Revolutionary" UN

In Chapter 9, Peking's search for a UN substitute and its effort to create a "revolutionary" UN was discussed. In a way, the revolutionary UN was the wishful thinking of Peking's leaders. Nonetheless, were it ever to materialize, it could easily be more useful to Peking than either the UN of the Charter or the UN of parliamentary diplomacy for the purpose of promoting the international revolutionary movement along the lines of Mao Tse-tung Thought. Peking would presumably be the leading actor in such an organization. In that sense, it could even serve Peking's national (as opposed to international) interests directly as did the Council for Mutual Economic Assistance (COMECON) for the USSR, for instance. Such speculations are no more than academic exercise now. But, the point is quite clear that Peking would prefer an anti-imperialist "revolutionary" UN over any other type of UN that it had conceptualized because its instrumental value would be greater than those of other types.

The UN of US-USSR Collusion

For Peking, the worst possible UN was perhaps one in which the US and the USSR conspired together to perpetuate their dominant position in the world at the expense of others, particularly the PRC. This was what Peking saw happening after 1964.

It is a foregone conclusion that this UN of US-USSR collusion can be of little help to Communist China. It may not pose another direct military threat to China's security as did the American-controlled UN in 1950; for it is highly unlikely that the UN will be involving itself in another police action along China's borders again.[7] But, as Peking sees it, the UN continues to undermine Peking's prestige by refusing to recognize the PRC, and by "meddling" in China's domestic affairs and accusing Peking of violating the fundamental rights and freedoms of the Tibetans.[8] It also prevents China's reunification by providing ground for the "two-Chinas" schemes, and obstructs China's rise to superpower status by endorsing the American-Soviet "conspiracy" to bolster the status quo.[9]

The Chinese leaders must, nevertheless, live with this UN of US-USSR collusion as long as it exists. In the meantime, Peking tries to use the UN for its own purposes as best it can. The UN of US-USSR collusion still plays two roles for Peking: (1) As a propaganda tool, it is now a symbol of both the "treacherous nature" of the US

"imperialist" and the "betrayal" of the Soviet "revisionist." The collaboration between these two superpowers, according to Peking, will
retard the success of the heroic struggle of the "revolutionary peoples
of the world" to establish a new world of lasting peace and justice.
(2) As a yardstick of Peking's international status, the UN has become
even more useful. More members of the UN have begun to make long
speeches on the Chinese question in the meetings of the UN organs each
year,[10] and they vote on several (rather than just one or two) resolutions,
each with different shades of friendship or hostility toward the Peking
regime.[11] This makes it possible for an observer to tell not only
whether or not a given member of the UN is in favor of seating Peking
in the UN, but also how much and why.

It must be emphasized, however, that the UN is by no means the
only such yardstick or even a sufficiently reliable one by itself. For
Peking, such uses of the UN are not very important. If Peking had its
way, it would want to see the UN of US-USSR collusion remolded, if not
destroyed.

In sum, there is little doubt that Peking tried to utilize the UN as
a tool for implementing its national policy. That it did not have much
success was perhaps a misfortune for the PRC, but Peking did not
change this expedient perspective on the UN.

14

IMPRINT
OF THE THOUGHT
AND PSYCHOLOGY
OF MAO TSE-TUNG

Still another aspect of continuity of Peking's UN policy is the imprint of the thought and psychology of Mao Tse-tung. In this Chapter, it will be shown (1) that, notwithstanding the changes and shifts, Peking's attitudes and approaches toward the UN (particularly "UN the actor") have consistently followed the patterns of relations between two opposites as prescribed by Mao's law of contradication; and (2) that, psychologically, Peking's language and behavior in respect to the UN have been characteristically those of a "Maoist," i.e., a party who feels wronged and is determined to carry on a resolute struggle against the alleged wrongdoer.

Mao Tse-tung Thought, as Franz Schurmann ably points out, is something unique and original.[1] Schurmann defines it in terms of an organizational ideology, i.e., "a systematic set of ideas with action consequences serving the purpose of creating and using organization." It is a practical (as opposed to pure) ideology derived from uniting the universal theory of Marxism-Leninism and concrete practice in China's revolution and construction. Its core concept is Mao's version of the law of contradiction, which we have already discussed in Chapter 1.

The "Maoist" psychology also can be described as a combination of two components: the feelings of indignation and the daring to struggle. Its indignation is aimed against social injustice, exploitation and oppression; its daring is propelled by a sense of class hatred and of satisfaction from defying the evil foes. Its most concrete expression is the so-called Yenan spirit.

That Mao Tse-tung and the "Maoist" psychology together constitute an aspect of continuity in Peking's UN policy should be understood in the light of their interdependence and their flexible nature. In a sense the two phenomena are two sides of a coin; they reinforce each other. The thought provides the philosophical foundation for the psychology; the psychology enlivens the thought.

Contrary to common assumptions, these two phenomena are not dogmatic, rigid and unchanging. Both are pragmatic, flexible, and changing in actual operation. Mao Tse-tung Thought has been credited by the Communist Chinese as a creative development of Marxism-Leninism. The "Maoist" psychology similarly stresses the need to introduce a new way of thinking about man, his nature, his hidden capability and his commitment. The emphasis is on creative, not automatic, application.

THE CREATIVE APPLICATION
OF MAO TSE-TUNG THOUGHT

The pattern of relations between the opposites in a contradiction, according to Mao Tse-tung, depends upon whether the contradition is antagonistic or non-antagonistic. Very briefly, antagonistic contradictions are to be handled by drawing a distinctive line between the enemy and the "people" and by carrying out a resolute struggle until the contradictions are resolved. Non-antagonistic contradictions, on the other hand, require the distinction between right and wrong and the transformation of the wrong into right by means of criticism, persuasion, re-education and unity.

In Chapter 1, it was deduced by theoretical analysis that, from Peking's point of view, the UN as an arena is neutral; it may be a contradiction in itself, but there is no inherent antagonistic contradiction between the PRC and UN the arena. It was also concluded that the UN as an actor may be either a partner or a foe of Peking, depending on which of the two opposing forces within the organization--the oppressing forces led by the UN (and the US) and the revolutionary forces led by (the USSR) and the PRC--happened to hold the upper hand in their struggle against each other. In effect, these theoretical propositions have been largely verified by the empirical analysis in Part II. It was found, in the survey of the period 1949-71, that Peking had consciously or unconsciously treated UN the arena differently from UN the actor, but always remained faithful to Mao Tse-tung Thought.

Specifically, the flexible application of Mao's law of contradiction in Peking's UN policy is demonstrated in at least two areas: (1) the general policy of classifying UN members into ideological categories; and (2) consistent objection to UN involvement in cases wherein Peking saw an opportunity for enhancing the international revolutionary movement.[2]

Ideological Categorization of UN Members

The practice of classifying the nations of the world (i.e., UN members) into categories and formulating appropriate policy principles in regard to each is clearly an application of Mao Tse-tung Thought in a flexible and creative way. First, between 1949 and 1953 or so, there were two categories: the oppressing imperialists and the revolutionary Socialists; Peking "leaned to one side," declaring that there was no such thing as a neutral in international politics. Beginning in 1954, there were three categories; in addition to the fraternal Socialist countries led by the Soviet Union and "US imperialism and its lackeys," there appeared a third group of "countries with different social systems" (the first intermediate zone) with which Peking proposed a policy of peaceful coexistence.

By 1963, each of the three categories of nations had split into two subcategories: the Soviet Union and its proxy, Yugoslavia, became the traitorous "revisionists"; India and a number of others became "reactionaries"; and, within the imperalist camp, a number of US allies such as France, Canada, West Germany were re-classified into a "second intermediate zone" with which Peking expanded trade and contacts. As a result, after 1963 Peking's categories of UN members looked like the following chart.

Pattern of Relations / Ideology	Foes/Hostility	Friends/Conciliation
Socialist Camp	USSR and Other Traitorous Revisionists	Fraternal Socialists
Countries with Different Social System	Reactionaries and Lackeys of US Imperialists	All Other Countries of Asia, Africa, Latin America (First Intermediate Zone)
Imperialist Camp	US Imperialists and Collaborators	US Allies who Disagree with US in Important Aspects (Second Intermediate Zone)

The composition of the categories or the categories themselves were adjusted as the world situation changed, but Peking's practice of ideological classification of nations and its adherence to the Marxist-Leninist line remained essentially the same.

That categorization of nations along ideological lines had direct bearing upon Peking's UN policy is testified to by Communist Chinese commentaries such as this:

> The US, assisted by the UK, France and the reactionary governments of other countries, has done many bad things endangering international peace and security in the UN. On the other hand, the Soviet Union and other peace-loving countries have consistently struggled for the maintenance of international peace and security. . . .

> [The aggressive activities of the US] have caused the UN to deviate from the course provided in the Charter and on the contrary, even on many occasions became the instrument of the US for conducting cold war and carrying out its policy of aggression. Therefore under the pressure of the US, the UN has betrayed the expectations of the people of the world and has reduced its own moral authority. . . . On the other hand, as the result of the effort of the Soviet Union and other peace-loving countries, the UN also has [to a certain extent] developed its normal functions and has produced some positive effect on international affairs. . . .[3]

Selective Objection to Peace-Keeping Operations of the UN

Another direct and convincing evidence of the imprint of Mao Tse-tung Thought was the way Peking had evaluated the actual operation of UN the actor. On both the question of the UN organs' power to take "action" to maintain international peace and security and the question of "domestic jurisdiction," Peking's main criterion was clearly based on Mao Tse-tung Thought.

According to Communist Chinese commentators, the November 3, 1950, Uniting for Peace Resolution was an American way of openly undermining the principle of unanimity of the Big Powers and impairing the function of the Security Council, "in an attempt to transform the UN

into an instrument of war."[4] That this Uniting for Peace Resolution
was looked upon as an anti-socialist measure is understandable; in
reality, anti-socialist purposes guided the sponsors of that Resolution.
What is more significant is that the condemnation of the PRC as an
"aggressor" was passed by the General Assembly on February 1, 1951,
i.e., within three months after the adoption of the Uniting for Peace
Resolution. There can be no mistake that Peking saw a direct link
between the two resolutions of the Assembly. On February 3, 1951,
a statement by Chou En-lai stated, inter alia, that

> Since there is now a representative of the Soviet Union in
> the Security Council to observe the Charter and uphold
> justice, the US resolution slandering China was directly
> submitted to the UN General Assembly in an outright, un-
> lawful bypassing of the Security Council and in violation
> of the principle of unanimity among the great powers.[5]

This insistence on the principle of unanimity of the great powers
and the objection to the transfer of "action" powers from the Security
Council to the General Assembly represented both a tacit admission
that the interests of the Communist nations were more important than
the strengthening of the UN, particularly the UN controlled by the US,
and an implied expectation that the Soviet Union would protect the
interests of the PRC in the UN. Both the admission and the expectations
were consistent with Mao Tse-tung Thought.

As to the question of "domestic jurisdiction," on the surface
Peking seems to have always insisted on the principle of non-interference in internal affairs (Article 2, paragraph 7 of the Charter).[6]
In reality, when UN actions were directed at correcting the behavior
of Peking's foes, that principle was conveniently forgotten. Thus, on
the one hand, the PRC denounced the UN's considerations of the question of the status of Taiwan (1950), the Korean question (since 1951),
the Hungarian question (1956), the Tibetan question (since 1959), the
Laotian question (1962) and the Vietnam question (since 1964), among
others. On the other hand, the UN resolutions in the case of the Suez
Canal Crisis (1956), the question of apartheid in South Africa (since
1967) and other colonial questions were lauded as measures taken
for international peace and security.

The question of Taiwan, which deals with the legal status of that
island, Peking claimed, was a matter of China's internal affairs. A
clear distinction was drawn between that question and the question of
"American aggression in China's territory Taiwan," which Peking
wanted the UN to consider.[7]

The arguments relating to all the other questions on which Peking contended that the UN had no legal jurisdiction were usually based on Article 2, paragraph 7 of the Charter. On the Korean question, there was an added argument:

> The UN has been reduced to a belligerent in the Korean War and has long since lost the competence and moral authority to deal fairly and reasonably with the Korean question.[8]

Yet, when the actions of the UN were directed at Peking's foes, the reasoning was reversed. The Assembly resolution calling for the withdrawal of the UK, France and Israel from Egyptian territory in the 1956 Suez Crisis was referred to that Assembly in accordance with the Uniting for Peace Resolution, but Peking voiced no objection to that. Instead, the Jen-min Jih-pao editorial of November 13, 1956, stated that it was "the first time that the UN has adopted resolutions against aggression in conformity with the Charter."[9] On the question of apartheid in South Africa, Peking's opinion was that it could not be considered a matter of internal affairs. As a Communist Chinese author put it:

> The acts of suppressing national liberation movements are not a question of a state's internal affairs. Such acts violate the fundamental UN Charter principles of national self-determination and respect for human rights and also threaten the peace and security of the world. Therefore, the General Assembly and the Security Council have the duty and the authority to handle this matter.[10]

Such a double standard is, nevertheless, consistent with the dictation of Mao Tse-tung Thought. The real question for Peking is not whether the Charter of the UN was actually followed or violated, but whether the action of the UN would contribute to or obstruct Peking's efforts in promoting the international revolutionary movement. In other words, UN the actor was judged, so to speak, by the "intrinsic merits" of its actions on the basis of Mao Tse-tung Thought.

THE DYNAMICS OF "MAOIST" PSYCHOLOGY

In Chapter 2, it was pointed out that Mao Tse-tung's personality is characterized by a predisposition to defy unjust pressure. Mao's life story has been one of intense hatred for social unjustice and daring protracted struggle. Concerning Mao's hatred, biographer Jerome Ch'en explained:

> Some attribute the intensity of Mao's hatred to the harsh treatment he suffered at the hands of his father, others

suggest that it was aroused by his early reading of such
novels as The Water Margin (Sui Hu). I think rather that its
origin is to be found in his reading of Darwin, Rousseau,
J. S. Mill and F. Paulsen, which broadened his vision and
encouraged him to break away from obsolete tradition. Revolutionary literature by anarchists and Marxists later suggested how the emancipation of his nation could be achieved.
His own experience and observation of injustice, poverty,
and incessant civil war further increased his indignation.
There can be no other rational explanation of his persistent
hatred. No one can sustain such hatred without continually
seeking a way to end it. Thus Mao's hatred sharpened his
vision and enable him to see beyond the thing he hated so
much to a new China, the China he wanted to create, which
would be independent, free, peaceful, united and above all,
strong and prosperous.[11]

It was suggested that in this profound feeling for the unfortunate and
his spirit of "daring to struggle" until the final victory lies the basis
of Mao's charisma. It was also proposed that as long as Mao remains
the "helmsman" of Peking, the PRC's international posture will be more
adamant than otherwise.

In fact, Mao's charisma and the psychological predisposition
that he personifies also help to explain Peking's words and deeds regarding the UN. Specifically, it is suggested that there are three
manifestations of the impact of "Maoist" psychology upon Peking's
UN policy throughout most of the two decades under investigation.
These manifestations can be characterized as (1) the acute indignation
of a wronged party; (2) the defiant daring of a determined revolutionary;
and (3) the chauvinistic fervor of a jealous self-appointed liberator.

The Acute Indignation of a Wronged Party

Anyone who has read Peking's yearly commentaries on the sessions of the UN General Assembly cannot fail to detect a sense of indignation in Peking's pronouncements. Peking's carefully phrased
sentence that keeps appearing in all of its editorials and commentaries
reads something like this:

Through the control it exercises over the UN, the US has
again excluded the PRC from this international body and
allowed the elements of the Chiang Kai-shek bandit gang to
usurp China's seat.

Year after year, this self-portrayal as a victim becomes for the reader
as devasting as it is unfailing. Perhaps the most pointed expression
of the acute sense of indignation over the UN's unfair treatment that
Peking felt was the December 4, 1964, editorial of Jen-min Jih-p̄ao
that was quoted in Chapter 9 (see pp. 132 and 133. That editorial not
only pointed out the fact that the UN had made an unjustifiable exception
of the PRC in dealing with the question of representation of a member
state who had experienced a revolution or a coup d'état; it also went
on to say that inviting the PRC to take a seat in the UN without first
correcting the wrongs against her would not be a satisfactory solution.
About nine months later, when Ch'en Yi pronounced Peking's conditions
for participation in the UN, Ch'en's candid and difficult conditions left
little doubt about Peking's righteous anger at the UN itself.

Indeed, Peking has real cause to be indignant. Not only has the
PRC been excluded on unfair grounds, it has also been officially branded
an outlaw by that body. Three Secretary-Generals of the UN have all
made the plea to let the PRC come into the world organization; their
efforts have been in vain. In spring 1966, during an interview with
the BBC of London, U Thant voiced his concern over the effect of the
UN's ostracism on Peking in these words:

> . . .I feel that countries and states, like individuals, have to
> undergo certain tensions, certain emotional upsets and even
> be subject to emotional breakdowns, or nervous breakdowns.
> From time to time, if you assess the statements of the Chinese
> leaders coming out from Peking, I get the impression that
> the Chinese leaders from time to time speak in a rather
> strange way, even at times, with hysteria, with a certain de-
> gree of arrogance. I think we have to understand their state
> of mind in the context of the circumstances in which China
> has been ostracized for so long. . . . [12]

Many respected American observers have also expressed their
sympathy for Peking's position vis-à-vis the UN. Inis L. Claude, Jr.,
for instance, pointed out that

> The Chinese Communist regime has been debarred from
> occupying China's seat in the UN on moral and political
> grounds, but it has nevertheless been treated as if it were
> the government of that state for the purpose of assessing
> responsibility for China's international misbehavior.[13]

Logically, should not the ROC government be responsible for all the
words and deeds of Peking since it claims to represent the whole of

China, including the mainland? But no one seems to find that question worth consideration. John Stoessinger also observed that an increasing number of UN members felt that the UN could hardly expect the PRC to observe the UN Charter if at the same time the UN denied the PRC her right to participate in UN proceedings.[14]

So intense was Peking's indignation at being wronged that the vibrations sometimes appear to have been felt across the world. Guy Wint wrote in 1960 of a joke that must not be very funny to Peking:

> There is an old State Department joke that the three coun-
> tries which are against China's admission to the UN are
> America, Russia, and China: America for obvious reasons,
> Russia because it does not want its dissensions with China
> to become apparent in the Security Council, and China be-
> cause it does not want to give up its grievances against
> America. . . .[15]

Sheldon Appleton explained this psychology of indignation in the con-text of Peking's expectations thusly:

> The Communist leaders in Peking seem to look upon a UN
> seat as a right befitting Communist China's new status as
> an equal of the great powers of the West. It is the confir-
> mation of this new status of equality, plus the sweetness of
> victory over the Nationalists and the US, which would be the
> principal benefits to Peking of a seat in the UN.[16]

Expecting "sweetness" in the beginning, Peking actually tasted only bitter. Its bellicose utterances are, therefore, not difficult to under-stand.

The Defiant Daring of a Determined Revoluntionary

Another impression that students of Peking's foreign policy acquire is Peking's bold and sometimes defiant response to pressure, be it from the US, the USSR or the UN. Mao thrives on struggle, daring and perseverance. The CPC under his leadership displayed the same operational features throughout the years of the Long March, Yenan, the war of resistance against Japan, the civil war with the KMT and, since 1949, the cold wars with the US and the USSR. It is certainly not by accident that leading figures in Peking, notably P'eng Teh-huai and his backers, who advocated a policy of conciliation with the USSR when the Kremlin was exerting pressure upon the PRC, sooner or later were purged from positions of power. One of Liu Shao-ch'i's alleged crimes was that he favored and formulated a policy of "three surrenders, one suppression" (i.e., surrendering to US imperialism, Soviet modern revisionism and reactionaries, and suppressing revolutionary movements in other countries).[17]

In a way, one may think of Mao's many strategic and tactical concepts as the elements that underwrite Peking's daring. For instance, the Jen-min Jih-pao editorial of January 10, 1965, condemned "the cult of the UN," and called the UN a "paper tiger."[18] It said, "President Sukarno has kicked the backside of this tiger. This is a great help in ending the blind faith to the UN." Both the terminology and the intent were clearly based on Mao's teaching that one should "despise the enemy strategically." One suspects that behind such public utterances, Peking's leaders, particularly Mao, might have felt an inkling of satisfaction for being the power to defy the UN in a manner that sovereign nations usually do not consider as apt.

The principle of strategically despising the enemy also seems to have its reserve application. That is, when Peking realizes that the PRC is really the biggest paper tiger in terms of real capabilities, or when it becomes clear that the PRC is isolated, Peking's practice seems to be to issue outlandish, sometimes almost derisive, self-claims that "China has friends all over the world," that "Mao Tse-tung Thought lights the whole world," or that "the international situation is excellent" and "China's great influence in the world is irresistible." What comes through, as an outside observer reads such phrases, are, as has been suggested in Chapter 2, signs of Peking's awareness of serious difficulties and frustrations, and its resolve to persist in defiant and bold courses of action. Perhaps this kind of self-deception is a form of self-administered psychological therapy; its net effect may well be a short-term improvement of the psychological health of the masses. But, one should not lose sight of the fact that Peking's "friends" usually refer to all those whom Peking claimed were travelling the "revolutionary" road like itself and not necessarily those who maintained cordial relations with Peking. Likewise, the "excellent international situation" usually meant the sprouting of rebellious activities on various spots on the world map, not peace and prosperity.

Although Mao never specifically referred to an analogy between his idea of a protracted war and the game of chess, a recent study by a young American "Go" (Wei-ch'i) enthusiast suggests that a protracted war is essentially like a "Go" game.[19] What counts in a chess game is the final victory. Peking's leaders, many of them veteran protracted war strategists, no doubt think in terms of the long term and are prepared for the necessary sacrifices. For them, time is on the side of the revolutionary who has the support of the masses. All they have to do is to struggle, struggle and struggle. "Dare to struggle, dare to win"--so a chapter of <u>Quotations from Chairman Mao Tse-tung</u> is captioned. Indeed, it is important that we consider and evaluate Peking's UN policy in terms of the long run and, in so doing, not forget the daring of Mao and his revolutionary comrades and pupils.

The Chauvinistic Fervor of a Jealous,
Self-Appointed Liberator

There is perhaps a combination of two psychological motivations that make Mao want to speak for the oppressed people and nations of the world. One is his sense of social justice (or hatred for injustice) wherever it occurs. The other is his aspiration to see China play a leadership role in modern world politics. Chapter 6 mentioned that, as early as 1952, Peking had called a Peace Conference of the Asian and Pacific Regions to stage its own political show. In subsequent periods, Peking's performance at Bandung and other international conferences involving the Afro-Asians, its contention with the Soviet Union for the leadership of the Socialist international movement and its call for the establishment of a "revolutionary" UN all displayed a chauvinist fervor as well as a love to appear on the world stage in the costume of the leading international spokesman of all the downtrodden.

In a sense, by portraying itself as a victim of the American-controlled UN, Peking probably hoped to gain acceptance by the newly emerging Afro-Asian nations who had themselves been victims of Western colonialism and imperialism. Appealing to the sympathy of these nations is undoubtedly a way of building up Mao's international following. Besides pointing out their common background as victims of colonialism, Peking also asserts the "international significance" of Mao Tse-tung Thought (including the CPC's experience in China's revolution and construction).

China's revolutionary model, Peking's leaders claim, is relevant to national liberation movements in Asia, Africa and Latin America. As early as 1951, Chou En-lai spoke proudly of "the influence of the success of the Chinese Revolution" on Asian liberation movements.[20] On the occasion of the Tenth National Day, Ch'en Yi expounded on how Chinese successes revolution and construction were "tremendous encouragement to all the oppressed nations and peoples of the world fighting for their liberation," and that "the Chinese people see their yesterday in all the oppressed nations. . . ."[21] When Japanese workers asked for an inscription in 1962, Mao wrote:

> The Japanese revolution will undoubtedly be victorious, pro-
> vided the universal truth of Marxism-Leninism is really in-
> tegrated with concrete practice of the Japanese revolu-
> tion.[22]

The inference to the Chinese model is subtle but unmistakably clear.

When the PRC conducted successful nuclear tests, Peking issued communiques emphasizing that such tests were blows at "the policy of
nuclear threat and nuclear blackmail" pursued by the US and the USSR.
Such communiques also invariably state that the PRC's successes are
"a very great encouragement and support to . . . the revolutionary
people of the world," as if the PRC has been conducting all those tests
on behalf of the oppressed people around the world.

In 1965, Snow's report of his interview with Mao was almost a
window looking into Mao's mind. Mao said that the Afro-Asians simply
could not afford to "wait for the Soviet Union to demonstrate the
superiority of the socialist system and then wait a century for parlia-
mentarianism to arise in the underdeveloped areas and peacefully
establish socialism." Implicitly, Mao was telling the world via Snow
that the Chinese model represented the only hope for the Afro-Asians.

However, by far the most chauvinistic and most naked proclamation of "the international significance" of the Chinese revolutionary
model was the November 6, 1967, joint editorial of Peking's three
leading media commemorating the 50th anniversary of the October
Revolution.[23] It claimed that "the center of world revolution has
since [the October Revolution] gradually moved to China and Mao
Tse-tung's Thought has come into being," succeeding its predecessors,
the French Revolution, Marxism and Leninism.

Thus, we see that "Maoist" psychology, like Mao Tse-tung Thought,
also left its imprint on Peking's UN policy. All three manifestations
of that psychology pertain to the language and behavior that Peking
has employed or performed at one time or another. They have one
thing in common: the drive of "Maoist" indignation and daring. That
drive determined, to a degree, Peking's foreign policies, including
UN policy.

This exposition began with a proposition that Peking has always had a UN policy that involves aspects of both continuity and change. That proposition has been verified, both theoretically and empirically, by the evidence presented in the preceding chapters.

In Part I, it was concluded that, despite apparent constitutional incompatibilities, the UN as an actor is not necessarily a foe of the PRC but may be a friend if its membership is favorably composed. It was also concluded that, as an arena, the UN offers many uses for a member possessing the features of the PRC and, therefore, it would be theoretically a sound move for the PRC to adapt to the UN.

Part II demonstrated that Peking's attitudes and approaches toward the UN changed from time to time in response to changing developments in the internal conditions of the PRC, in the UN itself and in the PRC's relevant international environment as perceived by the decision-makers of Peking. However, at no time did Peking forget that there was a UN to which it must adapt or with which it must contend.

Part III has shown that an unyielding legal position, an expedient political view and the imprint of the thought and psychology of Mao Tse-tung characterized Peking's policy toward the UN throughout the 22-year period under investigation.

In conclusion, two further observations seem pertinent. First, Peking's rigid legal position and flexible political calculations are reflective of the behavioral norms of the UN members. Any nation would have behaved as did the PRC under similar conditions. In that sense, Peking's UN policy has been normal and not deviant. It must be pointed out that Peking's attitude and approach toward the UN have always been countered by certain UN attitudes and approaches toward the PRC, which have had a great deal to do with the question of "China and the UN." In many ways, it can be said that the UN has been more anti-PRC than the PRC has been anti-UN. Peking tried to come into the UN, albeit on its own terms; but the UN did not really want Peking's participation, whatever the terms. If Peking's UN policy seemed hostile, it was not primarily because of Peking's initial choice; on

225

the contrary, it was a reaction to the UN's hostility toward the PRC.

Second, that Peking's UN policy has not been free from the imprint of the thought and psychology of Mao Tse-tung is, on the other hand, a testimonial of its deviant nature. This deviation may be a consequence of the peculiar, transitional nature of the PRC system.

The present political system of the PRC can be described, somewhat arbitrarily but not without justification, by paraphrasing Abraham Lincoln's famous quote: It is a system of the proletariat, by the Communist Party, for the people. In other words, in Communist China the traditional "Mandate of Heaven" has been replaced by a sort of mandate of the proletariat (the property-less class). The Confucian norms and values have been discarded in favor of a Marxist-Leninist Mao Tse-tung Thought. And the cadres of a conscious, dynamic organization--the CPC--have become the substitute for the gentry officials as the true elite. The transition between two systems of such fundamental and far-reaching differences certainly cannot be smoothly and completely accomplished within the time period of two decades, particularly when one realizes that the traditional Confucian system had dominated the Chinese scene for over 2,000 years. During the transition period, it is to be expected that the ruling elite of the new system would be unusually self-conscious and sensitive to their social status and constantly stress the need to follow a logically pre-scribed course of action, more likely than not an unconventional one. Such is the state of affairs of the PRC. Therefore, Peking's UN policy must be explained in that context.

This point is echoed and further inspired by Franz Schurmann in his monumental book, Ideology and Organization in Communist China. Schurmann advanced the theory that the trinity of ethos, status group and modal personality (respectively represented by Confucianism, the gentry and the pater familias) were the core elements of the tra-ditional Chinese social system. However, in present-day Communist China, that trinity has been replaced by another, of ideology, leader-ship organization and cadre (respectively represented by Mao Tse-tung Thought, the CPC and the revolutionary leader). As Schurmann ex-plains it, the traditional Chinese social system has disappeared along with the traditional trinity of authority and that, before a new social system is built up, an organization has been created to pull and hold the society together. A social system is held by an ethos, a belief system that expresses basic values and norms of that society; an organization, particularly a leading organization, is held together by an ideology that prescribes the values and goals of socio-political action and achievement. An ethos is loosely formed; an ideology is logical and integrative. The former is also conservative and static; the latter, progressive and dynamic. But all organization tends to routinization and the CPC is not an exception. To combat such tendencies, ideology then becomes the Party leaders' major instrument. In other words, the PRC's behavior, including its policy toward the UN, has been characteristically that of a transitional organization guided by an integrative and logical ideology. Hence, the imprint of the thought and psychology of Mao Tse-tung.

In October 1971, the UN will celebrate its 26th anniversary and the PRC, its 22nd. Both are young and just maturing. The continuing growth of the two systems seems to require that each tries to accommodate the other in its own future plan. The present difficult relationship between these two systems will change in the not too distant future.

APPENDIXES

APPENDIX A

VOTING RECORDS ON THE QUESTION OF CHINESE REPRESENTATION IN THE GENERAL ASSEMBLY, 1950-70

Year	Total UN Membership	Pro-PRC	Con-PRC	Abstentions	Absent
1950	59	16 (27%)	33 (56%)	10	0
1951	60	11 (18)	37 (62)	4	8
1952	60	7 (12)	42 (69)	11	0
1953	60	10 (17)	44 (73)	2	4
1954	60	11 (18)	43 (72)	6	0
1955	60	12 (20)	42 (70)	6	0
1956	79	24 (31)	47 (59)	8	0
1957	82	27 (33)	48 (59)	6	1
1958	81	28 (35)	44 (54)	9	0
1959	82	29 (35)	44 (54)	9	0
1960	99	34 (35)	42 (42)	22	1
1961	104	37 (36)	48 (46)	19	0
1962	110	42 (38)	56 (51)	12	0
1963	111	41 (37)	57 (51)	12	1
1964	114	GA Session Postponed			
1965	117	47 (40)	47 (40) .	20	3
1966	121	46 (38)	57 (47)	17	1
1967	122	45 (37)	58 (48)	17	2
1968	126	44 (35)	58 (46)	23	1
1969	126	48 (38)	56 (44)	21	1
1970	127	51 (40)	49 (39)	25	2

Sources: Yearbooks of the United Nations, 1950-67. UN Monthly Chronicle, 1967-70.

APPENDIX B

DIPLOMATIC RELATIONS OF THE
PRC AND THE ROC,
AUGUST 31, 1971

The following listings are based on similar lists in A. M. Halpern (ed.), POLICIES TOWARD CHINA: VIEWS FROM SIX CONTINENTS (New York: McGraw-Hill, 1965), pp. 495-502. Changes since March 1, 1965, have been corrected to reflect the actual situation as of June 30, 1971.

APPENDIX B-1

COUNTRIES MAINTAINING DIPLOMATIC RELATIONS
WITH THE PEOPLES' REPUBLIC OF CHINA
(AS OF AUGUST 31, 1971)

UN MEMBERS	RECOGNITION	DIPLOMATIC RELATIONS
1. Afghanistan	January 12, 1950	January 20, 1955
2. Albania	November 21, 1949	November 23, 1949
3. Algeria	July 3, 1962	July 3, 1962
4. Austria	May 26, 1971	May 28, 1971
5. Bulgaria	October 3, 1949	October 4, 1949
6. Burma	December 16, 1949	June 8, 1950
7. Cameroon	March 26, 1971	March 26, 1971
8. Canada	October 13, 1970	October 13, 1970
9. Ceylon	January 7, 1950	January 7, 1957
10. Chile	January 5, 1971	January 5,1971
11. Congo (Brazzaville)	February 18, 1964	February 22, 1964
12. Cuba	September 2, 1960	September 28, 1960
13. Czechoslovakia	October 5, 1949	October 6, 1949
14. Denmark	January 9, 1950	May 11, 1950
15. Equatorial Guinea	October 15, 1970	October 15, 1970
16. Ethiopia	November 24, 1970	November 24, 1970
17. Finland	January 13, 1950	October 28, 1950
18. France	January 27, 1964	January 27, 1964
19. Guinea	October 4, 1959	October 4, 1959
20. Hungary	October 4, 1949	October 6, 1949
21. India	December 30, 1949	April 1, 1950
22. Iran	August 16, 1971	August 16, 1971
23. Iraq	July 18, 1958	August 25, 1958

24.	Italy	November 6, 1970	November 6, 1970
25.	Kenya	December 14, 1963	December 14, 1963
26.	Kuwait	March 22, 1971	March 22, 1971
27.	Laos	June 28, 1962	June 28, 1962
28.	Mali	October 14, 1960	October 27, 1960
29.	Mauritania	July 19, 1965	July 19, 1965
30.	Mongolia	October 6, 1949	October 16, 1949
31.	Morocco	October 31, 1958	November 1, 1958
32.	Nepal	August 1, 1955	August 1, 1955
33.	Netherlands	March 27, 1950	November 19, 1954
34.	Nigeria	February 10, 1971	February 10, 1971
35.	Norway	January 7, 1950	October 5, 1954
36.	Pakistan	January 5, 1950	May 21, 1951
37.	Poland	October 5, 1949	October 7, 1949
38.	Rumania	October 3, 1949	October 5, 1949
39.	Sierra Leone	July 29, 1971	July 29, 1971
40.	Somalia	December 14, 1960	December 16, 1960
41.	South Yemen	January 31, 1968	January 31, 1968
42.	Sudan	November 29, 1958	December 1, 1958
43.	Sweden	January 14, 1950	May 9, 1950
44.	Syria	July 3, 1956	August 10, 1956
45.	Tanzania	December 9, 1961	December 9, 1961
46.	Turkey	August 4, 1971	August 4, 1971
47.	Uganda	October 18, 1962	October 18, 1962
48.	United Arab Republic	May 16, 1956	May 30, 1956
49.	United Kingdom	January 6, 1950	June 17, 1954
50.	USSR	October 2, 1949	October 3, 1949
51.	Byelorussia SSR	-	-
52.	Ukraine SSR	-	-
53.	Yemen	August 21, 1956	September 24, 1956
54.	Yugoslavia	October 5, 1949	January 10, 1955
55.	Zambia	October 25, 1964	October 29, 1964

NON-UN MEMBERS

56.	German Democratic Republic (East)	October 27, 1949	October 27, 1949
57.	Korea, Democratic People's Republic of (North)	October 5, 1949	October 6, 1949
58.	San Marino	May 6, 1971	May 6, 1971
59.	Switzerland	January 17, 1950	September 14, 1950

60. Vietnam, Democratic
    Republic of (North)   January 15, 1950   January 18, 1950

APPENDIX B-2

COUNTRIES MAINTAINING DIPLOMATIC
RELATIONS WITH THE REPUBLIC OF CHINA
(AS OF AUGUST 31, 1971)

UN MEMBERS

1. Argentina
2. Australia
3. Barbados
4. Belgium
5. Bolivia
6. Botswana
7. Brazil
8. Central African Republic
9. Chad
10. Colombia
11. Congo (Kinshasa)
12. Costa Rica
13. Cyprus
14. Dahomey
15. Dominican Republic
16. Ecuador
17. El Salvador
18. Gabon
19. Gambia
20. Greece
21. Guatemala
22. Haiti
23. Honduras
24. Ivory Coast
25. Jamaica
26. Japan
27. Jordan
28. Lebanon
29. Lesotho
30. Liberia
31. Libya
32. Luxembourg
33. Malagasy Republic

UN MEMBERS

34. Malawi
35. Maldive Islands
36. Malta
37. Mexico
38. New Zealand
39. Nicaragua
40. Niger
41. Panama
42. Paraguay
43. Peru
44. Philippines
45. Portugal
46. Rwanda
47. Saudi Arabia
48. Senegal
49. Spain
50. Swaziland
51. Thailand
52. Togo
53. United States
54. Upper Volta
55. Uruguay
56. Venezuela

NON-UN MEMBERS

57. Korea, Republic
    of (South)
58. Vatican State
59. Vietnam, Republic of

APPENDIX B-3

COUNTRIES MAINTAINING DIPLOMATIC
RELATIONS WITH NEITHER THE
PRC NOR THE ROC
(AS OF AUGUST 31, 1971)

Countries Recognizing the PRC

| UN MEMBERS | RECOGNITION | DIPLOMATIC RELATIONS | |
		Established	Suspended
1. Burundi	December 23, 1963	December 23, 1963	January 1965
2. Cambodia	July 18, 1958	July 23, 1958	March 20, 1970
3. Ghana	July 5, 1960	July 5, 1960	November 5, 1966
4. Indonesia	April 13, 1950	June 9, 1950	October 31, 1967
5. Israel	January 9, 1950		
6. Tunisia	January 10, 1964	January 10, 1964	September 26, 1967

Countries Recognizing the ROC

1. Iceland	-	-	-
2. Malaysia	-	-	-

Countries Recognizing Neither the PRC Nor the ROC

UN MEMBERS

1. Fiji
2. Guyana
3. Ireland
4. Mauritius
5. Singapore
6. Trinidad-Tobago

NON-UN MEMBERS

7. Andorra
8. Bahrein
9. Germany, Federal Republic of (West)
10. Liechtenstein
11. Monaco
12. Muscat & Oman
13. Nauru
14. Southern Rhodesia
15. Tonga
16. Western Samoa

LIST OF ABBREVIATIONS USED IN THE NOTES

AJIL	American Journal of International Law
APSR	American Political Science Review
AS	Asian Survey
CB	Current Background (American Consulate-General, Hong Kong)
CFYC	Cheng-fa Yen-chiu (Studies in Government and Law) (Peking)
CHAN WANG	Chan Wang (Look Fortnightly) (Hong Kong)
CQ	China Quarterly (London)
FCNP	Fei-ch'ing Nien-pao (Yearbook on Chinese Communism) (Taipei: Institute for the Study of Chinese Communist Problems)
FEER	Far Eastern Economic Review (Hong Kong)
GAOR	General Assembly Official Record
HC	Hung Ch'i (Red Flag) (Peking)
IO	International Organization
JMJP	Jen-min Jih-pao (People's Daily) (Peking)
JPRS	US Joint Publications Research Service
KCWTYC	Kuo-chi Wen-t'i Yen-chiu (Studies in International Problems) (Peking)
KTTH	Kung-tso T'ung-hsun (Bulletin of Activities) (Peking)
NCNA	New China News Agency
NYT	New York Times
NYTM	New York Times Magazine
PC	People's China (Peking)
PR	Peking Review (Peking)
SCCS	Shih-chieh Chih-shih (World Knowledge) (Peking)
SCCSNC	Shih-chieh Chih-shih Nien-chien (Yearbook of World Knowledge) (Peking: Shih-chieh Chih-shih Ch'u-pan-she)
SCMM	Selection from China Mainland Magazines (American Consulate-General, Hong Kong)
SCMP	Survey of China Mainland Press (American Consulate-General, Hong Kong)
SCOR	Security Council, Official Record
SELECTED WORKS	Selected Works of Mao Tse-tung (Peking: Foreign Languages Press, 1961-1965 4 vols.
TSU KUO	Tsu Kuo (China Monthly) (Hong Kong)
TWKHWCC	Chung-hua Jen-min Kung-ho-kuo Tui-wai Kuan-hsi Wen-chien-chi (Collection of Documents Relating to the Foreign Relations of the People's Republic of China) (Peking: Shih-chieh Chih-shih Ch'u-pan-she)
UN YEARBOOK	Yearbook of the United Nations

Notes to the Introduction

1.   George Modelski, A Theory of Foreign Policy (N.Y.: Praeger, 1962), pp. 6-7 Definition adopted with modification.

2.   See Carol A. Cosgrove and Kenneth J. Twitchett (eds.), The New International Actors: The UN and the EEC (N.Y.: Macmillan, 1970) Part III; and David A. Kay (ed.), The United Nations Political System (N.Y.: John Wiley, 1967), Part IV.

3.   Morton A. Kaplan, System and Process in International Politics (N.Y.: John Wiley, 1957), pp. 83-85.

4.   See Byron S. J. Weng, "Peking's Position on the Status of Taiwan," in Shao-ch'uan Leng and Hungdah Chiu (eds.), Communist China and Selected Problems of International Law. (Dobbs Ferry, N.Y.: Oceana Publications, Forthcoming).

5.   Franz Sherman, Ideology and Organization in Communist China (Berkely: University of California Press, 1966), p. 14.

PART I

Notes to the Introduction to Part I

1.   This sketch of a foreign policy system is based on George Modelski, A Theory of Foreign Policy (N.Y.: Praeger, 1962), with some modifications.

Notes to Chapter 1

1.   Full Texts of the 1945, 1954 and 1969 Constitutions of the CPC can be found in (1) Conrad Brandt, Benjamin Schwartz and John K. Fairbank, A Documentary History of Chinese Communism (N.Y.: Atheneum, 1966), pp. 422-39; (2) Theodore H. E. Chen (ed.), The Chinese Communist Regime: Documents and Commentary (N.Y.: Praeger, 1967), pp. 127-48; (3) PR, April 30, 1969 (No. 18), pp. 36-39.

2.   If we take the wording in the 1969 version seriously, Mao Tse-tung Thought is no longer just a practical (as opposed to pure) ideology, as Franz Schurmann defined it. It has become a new manifestation of the theory. Just like Leninism added to Marxism, so

Mao Tse-tung Thought adds to Marxism-Leninism. Schurmann,
nonetheless, is correct in observing that the word "Maoism" is non-
existent in the Chinese Communist vocabulary as yet. See Franz
Schurmann, Ideology and Organization in Communist China (Berkeley
and Los Angeles: University of California Press, 1966), p. 22.

3. Selected Works, I, pp. 311-12.

4. Ibid., p. 312.

5. Ibid., p. 313.

6. Ibid., pp. 321-22.

7. Mao Tse-tung, "On the Correct Handling of Contradictions
among the People" (Peking: China Pictorial, 1967), p. 1.

8. Ibid., p. 5.

9. For an excellent discussion on the application of the law of
contradiction in Peking's foreign policy, see Franklin W. Houn,
"The Principles and Operational Code of Communist China's International Conduct," Journal of Asian Studies, November 1967 (Vol.27,
No. 1), pp. 21-40.

10. Peking does not believe in the inevitability of a nuclear war,
only the inevitability of class wars in forms permitted by the existing
circumstances.

11. Houn, Supra, p. 23.

12. PR, July 7, 1961 (Nos. 26-27), p. 11.

13. PR, April 30, 1969 (No. 18), p. 33.

14. David Apter, The Politics of Modernization (Chicago: University of Chicago Press, 1965), pp. 28-38.

15. Ernst B. Haas, Collective Security and the Future International System (Denver, Colo.: The Social Science Foundation and
Graduate School of International Studies, University of Denver, 1968).
pp. 8-13.

16. Apter, Supra, note 14, pp. 31-32.

17. Ernst B. Haas, Tangle of Hopes (Englewood Cliffs, N.J.: Prentice-Hall, 1969), pp. 24-27.

Notes to Chapter 2

1. J. D. Simmonds, China's World (New York: Columbia University Press, 1970), Part 1.

2. Chung-kung Jen-ming Lu (Who's Who in Communist China) (Taipei: Institute of International Relations, 1967), pp. 569, 747.

3. A. Doak Barnett, China after Mao (Princeton, N.J.: Princeton University Press, 1967), Chapter III.

4. Donald W. Klein, "Peking's Leaders: A Study in Isolation," CQ, July-September 1961 (No. 7), pp. 35-43.

5. Edgar Snow, The Other Side of the River: Red China Today (N.Y.: Random House, 1962), p. 150.

6. Mao Tse-tung, "On the Ten Great Relationships," (April 1956), from a collection of statements by Mao, no title, n.d., pp. 19-28. English text in CB, October 21, 1969 (No. 892), pp. 21-34.

7. See, for instance, Lin Piao, "Long Live the Victory of the People's War!" PR, September 3, 1965 (Vol. 8, No. 36), pp. 9-30, and "Report to the Ninth National Congress of the Communist Party of China," PR, April 30, 1969 (No. 18), pp. 16-35.

8. For a useful chronology of Mao's political activities between 1919 and 1966, see Jerome Ch'en (ed.), Mao (Englewood Cliffs, N.J.: Prentice-Hall, 1969), p. 62.

9. The discussion on Lin Piao is largely based on a brief biography of Lin in China and U.S. Far East Policy, 1945-1966 (Washington: Congressional Quarterly Service, 1967), pp. 227-28; and Chung-kung Jen-ming Lu, Supra, note 2, pp. 232-34.

10. See P'eng Teh-huai (Hong Kong: Chih Luen Press, 1969, in Chinese), particularly, pp. 111, 120, 130-40.

11. Thomas W. Robinson, "Chou En-lai's Political Style: Comparisons with Mao Tse-tung and Lin Piao," AS, December 1970 (Vol. X, No. 12), P. 1111.

12. The discussion of Li'u and Teng is based on China and U.S. Far East Policy, Supra, note 9, pp. 229-32; and Chung-kung Jen-ming Lu, Supra, note 2, pp. 607-09, 642-43.

13. Tang Tsou, "The Cultural Revolution and the Chinese Political System," CQ, April-June 1969 (No. 38), pp. 63-91. See also, Chin Ssu-k'ai, "Looking at the Mao-liu Struggle from a Different Angle," Tsu Kuo, November 1, 1969 (No. 68), pp. 6-11.

14. See "Evidence of the Crime of the No. 1 Party Person in Authority Taking the Capitalist Road in Advocating the System of Capitalist Exploitation," PR, April 21, 1967 (No. 17), pp. 7-10; and Cheng Li-chia, "Down with the Capitulationism of China's Khrushchev!" PR, July 28, 1967 (No. 31), pp. 19-22.

15. See "Materials on Counterrevolutionary Revisionists (Part 3)," Tsu Kuo, April 1, 1969 (No. 61), pp. 37-38.

16. For instance, I Fan, "Liu Shao-ch'i's Plan for Forming Trusts," Tsu Kuo, October 1, 1968 (No. 55), pp. 20-22; Chin, Supra, note 13; and Quotations from Chairman Liu (Hong Kong: Chih Luen Press, 1967).

17. China and U.S. Far East Policy, Supra, note 9, p. 231.

18. Ibid., p. 232.

19. The discussion on Chou is based on China and U.S. Far East Policy, Supra, note 9, pp. 228-29; Chung-kung Jen-ming Lu, Supra, note 2, pp. 219-21; and Kai-yu Hsu, Chou En-lia: China's Gray Eminence (Garden City, N.Y.: Doubleday, 1968), note 20.

20. Kai-yu Hsu, Supra, p. xviii.

21. Ibid., p. 224.

22. Ibid., p. 225.

23. Joseph P. Lash, Dag Hammarskjold--Custodian of the Brushfire Peace (Garden City, N.Y.: Doubleday, 1961), pp. 61-65.

24. The discussion on Ch'en Yi is based on Chung-kung Jen-ming Lu, Supra, note 2, pp. 416-20; and Ch'en Yi Yen-lun Hsuan (Selected Speeches of Ch'en Yi) (Hong Kong: Chih Luen Press, 1967).

25. See Melvin Gurtov, "The Foreign Ministry and Foreign Affairs During the Cultural Revolution," CQ, October-December 1969 (No. 40), pp. 65-102.

26. See Tsu Kuo, July 1, 1969 (No. 64), p. 49.

27. See Ch'ien Ta-chin, "Ch'iao Kuan-hua and Ch'ai Ch'eng-wen," Tsu Kuo, February 1, 1970 (No. 71), p. 43.

28. See Donald W. Klein, "Peking's Evolving Ministry of Foreign Affairs," CQ, October-December 1960 (No. 4), pp. 28-39, especially p. 29.

29. See US Senate, Committee on Government Operations, Staffing Procedures and Problems in Communist China (Washington: Government Printing Office, 1963), pp. 26-32.

30. See US Senate, Committee on the Judiciary, Chinese and Russian Communists Compete for Foreign Support (Washington: Government Printing Office, 1964), pp. 1-15, which contains the testimony of Tung Chi-p'ing, a PRC staff member at the PRC's embassy in Burundi who defected to the West, in a Staff Conference of a subcommittee of the Senate Judiciary Committee; and US Senate, Committee on the Judiciary, Testimony of a Defector from Communist China (Washington: Government Printing Office, 1962), pp. 1-15, which contains the testimony of Chao Fu, stationed at the PRC embassy in Stockholm. Information obtained through Liao Ho-shu, Peking's Charge d'Affairs in the Netherlands before his defection in 1969 should prove even more revealing.

31. See Arthur Lall, "How Communist China Negotiates" (New York and London: Columbia University Press, 1968) Chapters 1 and 2; see also, US Senate, Committee on Government Operations, Peking's Approach to Negotiation: Selected Writings compiled by the Subcommittee on National Security and International Operations (Washington: Government Printing Office, 1969).

32. For example, see "Situation of World Revolution Is Excellent," PR, October 18, 1968 (No. 42), pp. 14-18. A quick check of the index to Peking Review (Nos. 26 and 52 yearly) is instructive enough.

Notes to Chapter 3

1. See John K. Fairbank (ed.), The Chinese World Order: Traditional China's Foreign Relations (Cambridge, Mass.: Harvard University Press, 1968).

2. See Chiang Kai-shek, China's Destiny (N.Y.: Macmillan, 1947), authorized translation by Wang Ch'ung-hui; and Mao Tse-tung, "On New Democracy," in Selected Works, II, pp. 339-84.

3. Richard H. Solomon, "Mao's Linking of Foreign Relations with China's Domestic Political Process," in Tang Tsou and Ping-ti Ho (eds.), China in Crisis, Vol. I: China's Heritage and the Communist Political System (Chicago: University of Chicago Press, 1968), pp. 570-78.

4. Ibid., p. 576.

5. PR, April 30, 1969 (No. 18), p. 33.

Notes to Chapter 4

1. Adopted from David O. Wilkinson, Comparative Foreign Relations: Framework and Methods (Belmont, Calif.: Dickenson Publishing Co., 1969), pp. 33-34.

2. Based on Ibid., Chapter 4.

3. Robert C. North, The Foreign Relations of China (Belmont, Calif.: Dickenson Publishing Co., 1969), p. 15.

4. See Morton H. Halperin, "Chinese Attitudes toward the Use and Control of Nuclear Weapons," and Frank E. Armbruster, "China's Conventional Military Capability," both in Tang Tsou and Ping-ti Ho (eds.), China in Crisis, Vol. II: China's Policies in Asia and America's Alternatives (Chicago: University of Chicago Press, 1968), pp. 135-60 and 161-97.

5. See North, Supra, note 3, Chapter 3; Donald S. Zagoria, "Communist China Is a Paper Dragon," NYTM, October 18, 1964, pp. 40ff.; Chalmers Johnson, "How Sharp Are the Dragon's Claws?" NYTM, February 28, 1965, pp. 22ff.; Morton H. Halperin, China and the Bomb (N.Y.: Praeger, 1965); and J. G. Godaire, "Communist China's Defense Establishment: Some Economic Implications," in US Congress, Joint Economic Committee, An Economic Profile of Mainland China, Vol. I (Washington: Government Printing Office, 1967), pp. 155-65.

6. See US Congress, Joint Economic Committee, Supra, Vols. I and II.

7. From "Talk with the American Correspondent Anna Louise Strong," Selected Works, IV, pp. 100-101.

8. See Morton H. Halperin and Dwight H. Perkins, Communist China and Arms Control (N.Y.: Praeger, 1965), Chapter XI; and Morton H. Halperin (ed.), Sino-Soviet Relations and Arms Control (Cambridge, Mass.: MIT Press, 1967), Chapters 2 and 7.

9. See Jack C. Plano and Robert E. Riggs, Forging World Order: The Politics of International Organization (N.Y.: Macmillan, 1967), Chapters 14-16.

10. Lin Piao, "Long Live the Victory of the People's War!" PR, September 3, 1965 (Vol. 8, No. 36), pp. 19, 22.

11. See Jan S. Prybyla, "Communist China's Strategy of Economic Development: 1961-1966," AS, October 1966 (Vol. 6, No. 10), pp. 589-603.

12. The Eight Principles are: (1) The Chinese government bases itself on the principles of equality and mutual benefit in providing aid to other countries. It never regards such aid as a kind of unilateral alms but as something mutual and helpful to economic co-operation. (2) In providing aid to other countries, the Chinese government strictly respects the sovereignty and independence of the recipient countries, and never attaches any conditions or asks for any privileges, (3) China provides economic aid in the form of interest-free or low-interest loans and extends the time limit for repayment, when necessary, so as to lighten, as far as possible, the burden on the recipient countries. (4) In providing aid to other countries, the purpose of the Chinese government is not to make the recipient countries dependent upon China but to help them embark, step by step, on the road of self-reliance and independent economic development. (5) The Chinese government tries its best to help the recipient country build projects that require less investment while yielding quicker results so that the recipient governments may increase their income and accumulate capital. (6) The Chinese government provides the best quality equipment and material of its own manufacture at international market prices. If the equipment and material provided by the Chinese government are not up to an agreed specification and quality, the Chinese government undertakes to replace them. (7) In giving any particular technical assistance, the Chinese government will see to it that the personnel of the recipient country fully master the techniques. (8) The experts and technical personnel dispatched by China to help in

construction in the recipient countries will have the same standard of living as the experts and technical personnel of the recipient country. The Chinese experts and technical personnel are not allowed to make any special demand or enjoy any special amenities.

13. See Robert P. Newman, Recognition of Communist China? A Study in Argument (N.Y.: Macmillan, 1961), Chapter 4.

14. Ibid., p. 112.

15. See, for instance, A New China Policy: Some Quaker Proposals-- A Report Prepared for the American Friends Service Committee (New Haven, Conn.: Yale University Press, 1965), pp. 31-41; and Robert Blum, The United States and China in World Affairs (N.Y.: McGraw-Hill, 1966), Chapter 11.

16. Webster's Seventh Collegiate Dictionary.

17. Quotations from Chairman Mao Tse-tung (Peking: Foreign Languages Press, 1966), Chapter viii. The quote is from "Be Concerned with the Well-Being of the Masses, Pay Attention to Methods of Work," Selected Works, I, p. 147.

18. For an excellent study on this grand scheme, see Tang Tsou and Morton H. Halperin, "Mao Tse-tung's Revolutionary Strategy and Peking's International Behavior," APSR, March 1965 (Vol. 59, No. 1), pp. 80-99. See also, Lin Piao, Supra, note 10 pp. 22-30.

19. See Selected Works, II, pp. 134-36.

20. "Comrade Mao Tse-tung pointed out long ago that war, this monster, 'will be finally eliminated by the progress of human society, and in the not too distant future too. But there is only one way to eliminate it and that is to oppose war with war, to oppose counter-revolutionary war with revolutionary war'." Lin Piao, Supra, note 10, p. 30.

21. Lin Piao, Supra, note 10, p. 19.

22. "Speech at the Moscow Meeting of Communist and Workers' Parties," in Quotations . . ., Supra, note 17, pp. 79-80 .

23. "Problems of Strategy in China's Revolutionary War," in Selected Works, I, p. 237.

24. Lin Piao, Supra, note 10, pp. 28-29.

25. Ibid., p. 24.

26. Robert Strausz-Hupe, et al., Protracted Conflict: A Challenging Study of Communist Strategy (N.Y.: Harper and Row, 1959), pp. 86-87.

27. David Muzingo, "Maoist Imprint on China's Foreign Policy," in Frank E. Armbruster, et al., China Briefing, (Chicago: University of Chicago Center For Policy Study, 1968), p. 43-52.

28. Alexander Dallin, The Soviet Union At The United Nations. New York: Praeger, 1962. Particularly Chapter XII.

PART II

Notes to Chapter 5

1. "On Coalition Government," in Selected Works, III, pp. 306-07.

2. See Stuart R. Schram, The Political Thought of Mao Tse-tung (N.Y.: Praeger, Second ed., 1969), pp. 390-91.

3. See Theodore Chen (ed.), The Chinese Communist Regime: Documents and Commentary (N.Y.: Praeger, 1967), pp. 33-34.

4. UN Doc. A/1123. Also, TWKHWCC, I, pp. 85086; Ajia Seikei Gakkai, (ed.), Chuka Jimmin Kyowkoku Gaiko Shiryo Soran (Collection of Diplomatic Documents of the Peoples Republic of China) (Tokyo: Hitotsubashi Shobo, 1960), p. 147.

5. UN Doc. A/1123; TWKHWCC, I, pp. 86-87.

6. TWKHWCC, I, p. 90; Ajai Seikei Gakkai, Supra, note 4, pp.147-48.

7. SCOR, 458th Meeting, December 29, 1949, p. 3.

8. SCOR, 459th Meeting, January 10, 1950, p. 3.

9. SCOR, 461st Meeting, January 13, 1950. In favor: USSR, Yougoslavia, India; against: China, Cuba, Ecuador, Egypt, France, US; abstension: Norway, UK. Provisional Rules of Prodecure of the Security Council, Rule 17: "Any representative on the Security

Council, to whose credentials objection has been made within the
Security Council, shall continue to sit with the same rights as other
representatives until the Security Council has decided the matter."

10. TWKHWCC, I, pp. 90-91; Ajia Seikei Gakkai, Supra, note 4,
p. 148.

11. TWKHWCC, I, p. 96; Ajia Seikei Gakkai, Supra, note 4, p. 149.

12. Two possibile counter-evidences have been pointed out by
some analysts. One was Peking's seizure of the American consular
compounds in Peking; the other was Peking's untimely recognition
of the Ho Chi-minh regime. Allegedly, the former led to the recall
of American official personnel from China, and the latter prevented
the French from recognizing the PRC and voting for its seating in the
Security Council. In this writer's evaluation, these two events hardly
prove that Peking was not interested in joining the UN. The former
was prompted by American intransigence as well as Peking's. [See
United States Relations with China, Department of State Publication,
No. 3573 (Washington: Government Printing Office, 1949), pp. 514-15].
The latter was the behavior normally to be expected. Besides, the
Security Council voted on the China question on January 13, 1950.
Peking seized the American Consulate compound and recognized the
Ho regime on January 14 and 19 respectively. If there were any
correlations between these events, it would seem that Peking retaliated
against the US and France for not supporting its bid for China's seat
in the UN. [See NTY, January 15, 1950, pp. 1, 4; Trygve Lie, In the
Cause of Peace (N.Y.: Macmillan, 1954), p. 266; and Tang Tsou,
America's Failure in China, 1941-50 (Chicago: University of Chicago
Press, 1963), pp. 518, 523-27].

13. See A. M. Halpern, "Communist China's Demands on the
World," in Morton A. Kaplan (ed.), The Revolution in World Politics
(N.Y.: John Wiley, 1962), p. 238.

14. See O. Edmund Clubb, Twentieth Century China (N.Y.:
Columbia University Press, 1964), Part I; Ssu-yu Teng and John K.
Fairbank, China's Response to the West: A Documentary Survey,
1839-1923 (Cambridge, Mass.: Harvard University Press, 1961).

15. See Franklin W. Houn, A Short History of Chinese Communism
(Englewood Cliffs, N.J.: Prentice-Hall, 1967).

16. A. Doak Barnett, "Profile of Red China," Foreign Policy
Reports, February 15, 1950. Reprinted in A. Doak Barnett,

Communist China: The Years 1949-1955 (N.Y.: Praeger, 1964), p. 8.

17. Ernst B. Haas, "Types of Collective Security: An Examination of Operational Concepts," APSR, March 1955 (Vol. 49, No. 1), pp. 40-62.

18. Legal Aspects of the Problem of Representation in the United Nations, memorandum transmitted to the President of the Security Council by the Secretary-General, March 8, 1950. UN Doc. S/1466.

19. General Assembly Resolution 490 (V), September 19, 1950.

20. UN Doc. A/AC.38/SR.18-24, 57-60.

21. UN Doc. A/AC.38/L.6.

22. UN Doc. A/AC.38/L.21.

23. SCOR, 460th Meeting, January 12, 1950, p. 6.

24. See NYT, January 6, 1950, pp. 1, 3 and 4.

25. See Byron S. J. Weng, "Russia, Communist China, and the United Nations," Vidya-Journal of the RCIE (Pittsburgh), Spring 1967 (No. 1), pp. 41-47.

26. See Howard L. Boorman, "The Sino-Soviet Alliance: A New Dimension in World Politics," Journal of International Affairs 1957 No. 2, pp. 122-31.

27. See Douglas M. Johnston and Hungdah Chiu (eds.), Agreements of the People's Republic of China, 1949-1967: A Calendar (Cambridge, Mass.: Harvard University Press, 1968), Appendix, Table 2.

28. The five were USSR, Yugoslavia, India, UK and Norway. France and Egypt were then expected to extend their recognition of the PRC.

29. See UN Yearbook, 1950, p. 968.

30. See Byron S. J. Weng, "Peking's Position on the Status of Taiwan," in Shao-ch'uan Leng and Hungdah Chiu (eds.), Communist China and Selected Problems of International Law. (Dobbs Ferry, N.Y.: Oceana Publications Forthcoming).

31. Full text in Theodore McNelly (ed.), Sources in Modern East Asian History and Politics (N.Y.: Appleton-Century-Crofts, 1967), pp. 65-72.

32. Article II, The Treaty of Shimonoseki, April 17, 1895.

33. Edgar Snow, Red Star Over China (N.Y.: Grove Press, 1961), p. 96.

34. Conrad Brandt, et al., A Documentary History of Chinese Communism (N.Y.: Atheneum, 1966), p. 244.

35. Selected Works, II, p. 27.

36. See United States Relations with China, with Special Reference to the Period 1944-1949, (The White Paper), Department of State Publication No. 3573 (Washington: Government Printing Office, 1949), p. 309.

37. Ibid., p. 404.

38. Hua-shang Pao, I-chiu- ssu-chiu-nien Shou-ts'e (1949 Handbook) (Hong Kong: Hua-shang Pao-she, 1949), p. 2.

39. See A. Doak Barnett, China on the Eve of Communist Takeover (N.Y.: Praeger, 1963), p. 310; and Allen S. Whiting, China Crosses the Yalu: The Decision to Enter the Korean War (N.Y.: Macmillan, 1960), p. 21.

40. See William A. Williams (ed.), The Shaping of American Diplomacy, Vol. II (Chicago: Rand McNally, 1956), pp. 1108-1111.

41. American Foreign Policy, 1950-1955, Basic Documents, Vol. II (Washington: Government Printing Office, 1957), pp. 2448-49.

42. Ibid., pp. 2456-58.

43. Ibid., p. 2468.

44. See China Handbook 1951 (Taipei: China Publishing Co.), 1951, p. 115.

45. See Chinese People's Institute of Foreign Affairs (ed.), Oppose U.S. Occupation of Taiwan and "Two Chinas" Plot (Peking: Foreign Languages Press, 1958), pp. 5-8.

Notes to Chapter 6

1. UN General Assembly Resolution 396 (V), December 14, 1950.

2. The Agrarian Reform Law of the PRC was promulgated by the Central People's Government on June 30, 1950, five days after the North Korean troops crossed the 38th Parallel.

3. About the PRC's role in the Korean War, Allen S. Whiting has concluded in his excellent study, China Crosses the Yalu: The Decision to Enter the Korean War (N.Y.: Macmillan, 1960), inter alia, that the PRC "had a strong interest in the attack of June 1950, but lacked direct responsibility for its initiation or outcome," (p. 46) and that "contrary to some belief, the Chinese Communist leadership did not enter the Korean War either full of self-assertive confidence or for primarily expansionist goals." (p. 159).

4. SCOR, 488th Meeting, August 17, 1950, p. 8.

5. Whiting, Supra, note 3, p. 92.

6. See SCOR, 501st Meeting, September 12, 1950, pp. 14-15; Annual Report of the Secretary-General on the Work of the Organization, July 1, 1950-June 30, 1951, pp. 75-78.

7. See SCOR, 483rd Meeting, August 4, 1950, p. 4; 496th Meeting, September 5, 1950, pp. 20-21. UN Doc. S/1703.

8. NYT, September 9, 1950, p. 1.

9. Martin Lichterman, "Korea; Problems in Limited War," in Gordon B. Turner and Richard B. Challener (eds.) National Security in the Nuclear Age, (N.Y.: Praeger, 1960), p. 34.

10. PC, October 16, 1950 (Vol. 2, No. 10), p. 9. See also Trygve Lie, In the Cause of Peace (N.Y.: Macmillan, 1954), pp. 350ff.

11. K. M. Panikkar, In Two Chinas, Memories of a Diplomat (London: Allen and Unwin, 1955), pp. 109-10.

12. Whiting, Supra, note 3, pp. 118, 122.

13. UN Doc. A/1923.

14. UN Doc. A/1950.

15. Text of the cable in <u>Important Documents Concerning the Question of Taiwan</u> (Peking: Foreign Languages Press, 1955), pp. 18-20. Also UN Doc. S/1583.

16. Text in <u>Ibid.</u>, pp. 21-22. UN Doc. S/1715.

17. See <u>UN Yearbook</u>, 1950, p. 289. For text of the cable see UN Doc. S/1795.

18. Provisional Rules of Procedure of the Security Council, Article 39: "The Security Council may invite members of the Secretariat or other persons, whom it considers competent for the purpose, to supply it with information or to give other assistance in examining matters within its competence." See UN Doc. S/96/Rev. 4 (July 29, 1952).

19. See <u>China Accuses! Speeches of the Special Representative of the Central People's Government of the People's Republic of China at the United Nations</u> (Peking: Foreign Languages Press, 1951), pp. 5-6.

20. <u>Ibid.</u>, pp. 44-45; UN Doc. S/1921.

21. <u>UN Yearbook</u>, 1950, pp. 293-94.

22. Text in <u>Important Documents</u> . . ., <u>Supra</u>, note 15, pp. 23-25 and UN Doc. A/C.1/590.

23. See <u>China Accuses!</u> . . ., <u>Supra</u>, note 19, pp. 89-92.

24. Text in Important Documents . . ., <u>Supra</u>, note 15, pp. 71-108. Also UN Doc. A/C.1/661.

25. See UN Doc. A/C.1/643.

26. See Report of the First Committee, February 9, 1951, UN Doc. A/1773, paragraph 10-12.

27. See <u>UN Yearbook</u>, 1950, pp. 297-298.

28. See U.N. Document A/C.1/590.

29. See <u>China Accuses!</u> . . ., <u>Supra</u>, note 19, pp. 16-17.

30. See <u>UN Yearbook</u>, 1950, p. 262.

31. PC, November 1, 1952 (No. 21), Supplement.

Notes to Chapter 7

1. See China and U.S. Far East Policy, 1945-66 (Washington: Congressional Quarterly Service, 1967), pp. 64-65.

2. Alice L. Hsieh, Communist China's Strategy in the Nuclear
Era (Englewood Cliffs, N.J.: Prentice-Hall, 1962, xix-xx.

3. Ibid., p. xx.

4. See UN Department of Public Information, How the United
Nations Met the Challenge of Korea, UN Publication Sales No. 1953.
1, 24; and "Korean Armistice Agreement and Other Documents,"
Supplement to PC, August 1, 1953 (No. 15) for texts of relevant documents.

5. Tang Tsou and Morton H. Halperin, "Mao Tse-tung's Revolutionary Strategy and Peking's International Behavior," APSR, March
1965 (Vol. 59, No. 1), pp. 80-99. There is a recent re-emphasis on this
strategy. See also Mao Tse-tung, "Problems of Strategy in Guerrilla
War Against Japan," PR, August 27, 1965 (Vol. 8, No. 35), pp. 8-22; and
Lin Piao, "Long Live the Victory of the People's War," PR, September
3, 1965 (Vol. 8, No. 36), pp. 9-30.

6. Tsou and Halperin, Supra, note p. 5, 84.

7. Robert P. Newman, Recognition of Communist China? A
Study in Argument (N.Y.: Macmillan, 1961), 109.

8. See Urban Whitaker, "China Lobby's New Gambit, "Nation,
October 7, 1961 (Vol. 193, No. 11), pp. 225-28; F. X. Boyle, "The Truth
About Communist China," Fact, November-December 1964 (Vol. 1,
Issue 6), pp. 33-41, for helpful clarification on this point.

9. For full text of this Constitution, see Theodore Chen (ed.),
The Chinese Communist Regime: Documents and Commentary (N.Y.:
Praeger, 1967), pp. 75-92.

10. Full text in Ch'en, Supra, note 9, pp. 127-48.

11. The "Five Principles" are: (1) Mutual respect for each
other's territorial integrity and sovereignty; (2) Non-aggression;
(3) Non-interference in each other's internal affairs; (4) Equality and

mutual advantage; and (5) Peaceful coexistence and economic co-operation.

12. For instance, in the preamble to the Sino-Afghanistan Treaty of Friendship and Mutual Non-Aggression, August 26, 1960, the two parties concluded the treaty "in accordance with the fundamental principles of the United Nations Charter," PR, May 13, 1960 (Vol. 3, No. 20), p. 18.

13. George McT. Kahin, The Asian-African Conference (Ithaca: Cornell University Press, 1956), 14ff. See also Richard Wright, The Color Curtain (Cleveland and N.Y.: World Publishing Co., 1956), p. 173.

14. China and the Asian-African Conference: Documents (Peking: Foreign Languages Press, 1955), pp. 22-24.

15. SCMP, November 17, 1956 (No. 1412), 22-24.

16. The Korean Armistice Agreement, Article 4, Para. 60.

17. Arthur H. Dean, "What It's Like to Negotiate with the Chinese," NYTM, October 30, 1966, pp. 44ff.

18. Kenneth T. Young, Negotiating with the Chinese Communists: The United States' Experience, 1953-1967. (N.Y.: McGraw-Hill, 1968), pp. 24-34.

19. See Congressional Quarterly Service, Supra, note 1, p. 68.

20. Ibid., P. 229; Edgar Snow, The Other Side of the River: Red China Today (N.Y.: Random House, 1962), pp. 94-95.

21. Young, Supra, Note 18, pp. 37-38.

22. See Congressional Quarterly Serivee, Supra, note 1, p. 69.

23. "Report on the Work of the Government Delivered at the First Session of the First National People's Congress, September 23, 1954." See Oppose U.S. Occupation of Taiwan and "Two Chinas" Plot (Peking: Foreign Languages Press, 1958), pp. 11-12.

24. See Joseph P. Lash, Dag Hammarskjold--Custodian of the Brushfire Peace (Garden City N.Y.: Doubleday, 1961), pp.61-65. See also Richard I. Miller, Dag Hammarskjold and Crisis Diplomacy (Dobbs Ferry; N.Y.: Oceana Publications, 1961), Chapter 2.

25. See Congressional Quarterly Service, Supra, note 1, p. 74.

26. See Lash, Supra, note 24, pp. 61-65.

27. PR, May 16, 1955 (No. 10), Supplement; NYT, April 24, 1955; Young, Supra, note 18, p. 44.

28. See Young, Supra, note 18, pp. 44-59.

29. See Gregory Clark, In Fear of China (Melborne: Landsdowne Press, 1967), pp. 22-26, 62-71; Hsieh, Supra, note 2, pp. 17-19.

30. Peking's official position on Taiwan can be assessed from four collections of documents published by its Foreign Languages Press: (1) Important Documents Concerning the Question of Taiwan, 1955; (2) Oppose U.S. Occupation of Taiwan and "Two Chinas" Plot, 1958; (3) Oppose U.S. Military Provocations in the Taiwan Strait Area, September 1958; and (4) Oppose the New U.S. Plots to Create "Two Chinas," 1960-61.

31. Important Documents . . . , Supra, note 30, p. 123.

32. Ibid., pp. 121-24.

33. See Harold Hinton, Communist China In World Politics (Boston: Houghton Mifflin, 1966), Chap. 10.

34. Important Documents . . . , Supra, note 30, pp. 127-33.

35. Ibid., pp. 150-60; PC, November 1, 1954 (No. 21), Supplement.

36. Oppose U.S. Occupation . . . , Supra, note 30, 18-27.

37. Ibid., pp. 28-30.

38. Ibid., pp. 31-34; UN Doc. S/3358.

39. Important Documents . . . , Supra, note 30, pp. 183-84.

40. UN Treaty Series, Vol. 248, pp. 214ff.

41. Ibid., 117. See also O. Edmund Clubb, "Sino-American Relations and the Future of Formosa," Political Science Quarterly, March 1965 (Vol. 80, No. 1), pp. 1-21.

42. Sanmin Morning News (Chicago), July 7, 1964. Reportedly, Chang Shih-chao appeared in Hong Kong again in 1964 and met General Chang Fa-kuei several times. But the latter denied the said report.

43. See Peter P.C. Cheng, "The Formosa Tango: A Formosan View," Agents Survey, November, 1967, VII, 11. p. 794; Lewis Gilbert, "Peking and Tibet", Mancall, ed. Formosa Today (New York: Praeger 1964), p. 117-118.

Notes to Chapter 8

1. SCMP, August 28, 1958 (No. 1842), pp. 39-40.

2. A. G. Mezerir (ed.), China Representation in the United Nations (N.Y.: International Review Service, 1965), p. 68.

3. NCNA, October 10, 1959. See SCMP, October 15, 1959. (No. 2117), p. 24.

4. SCMP, October 29, 1959 (No. 2126), pp. 33-34.

5. Ibid., p. 34.

6. Ibid., p. 41.

7. SC MP, October 25, 1960 (No. 2364), p. 40.

8. Alice L. Hsieh, Communist China's Strategy in the Nuclear Era (Englewood Cliffs, N.H.: Prentice-Hall, 1962).

9. SCMP, Sept. 5, 1957 (No. 1604), p. 34; JMJP, August 30, 1957.

10. SCMP, October 10, 1957 (No. 1628), pp. 40-41.

11. Ibid.

12. CB, November 13, 1957 (No. 480), p. 15.

13. Mao Chu-hsi Tsai Su-lien Ti Yen-lun (Chairman Mao's Speeches in the Soviet Union) (Peking, 1957), pp. 14-15.

14. See "A Comment on the Soviet Government's Statement of August 3," Aug. 15, 1963. English text in William E. Griffith, The Sino-Soviet Rift (Cambridge, Mass.: MIT Press, 1964), 340-53, particularly, p. 351.

15. See Gregory Clark, In Fear of China (Melborne: Landsdowne Press, 1967), pp. 90-105.

16. See FCNP, 1967, pp. 647-58.

17. Peter Tang, Communist China Today, Vol. 1 (N.Y.: Praeger, 1957), pp. 502-03.

18. U Thant, "A Burmese View of World Tensions," Annals of the American Academy of Political and Social Science, July 1958 (No. 318), pp. 34-42; Urban Whitaker reached a similar conclusion after intensive interviews with 96 UN delegations during 1960. See "Last Chance on China," The Progressive, October, 1961 (Vol. 25, No. 10), pp. 9-12.

19. Richard D. Baum, "'Red and Expert' the Politico-Ideological Foundations of China's Great Leap Forward," AS, September 1964 (Vol. 4, No. 9), pp. 1048-57.

20. "Speech at the Supreme State Conference (January 28, 1958)" Tsu Kuo, December 1969 (No. 69), pp. 38-39; "Talks to Small Group Leaders at the Enlarged Meeting of the Military Commission," Ibid., pp. 39-42. See also Tien-chien Hwang, Fei-wei Cheng-ch'uan Shi-pa-nien (Eighteen Years of Communist Chinese Rule) (Taipei: Cheng-chung, 1967), pp. 23-40.

21. FCNP, 1967, p. 578.

22. Congressional Quarterly Service, China and U.S. Far East Policy, 1945-1966 (Washington: 1967), p. 82.

23. Ibid., 86

24. Chinese People's Institute of Foreign Affairs (ed.), Oppose U.S. Occupation of Taiwan and "Two Chinas" Plot (Peking: Foreign Languages Press, 1958), pp. 54-58.

25. PR, July 8, 1958 (Vol. 1, No. 18), pp. 21-22.

26. Hsieh, Supra, note 8, pp. 119-30.

27. For a discussion on the effects of the Three Red Banners, see Joseph Alsop, "On China's Descending Spiral," CQ, July-September 1962(No. 11), 21-37; and comments on the article by Alexander Eckstein, et al., in Ibid., October-December, 1962 (No. 12), pp. 19-56.

28. See George P. Jan, "Failure of the Chinese Commune Experiment," in George Jan (ed.), Government of Communist China (San Francisco: Chandler, 1966), pp. 453-74.

29. See, e.g., Robert F. Emery, "Recent Economic Developments in Communist China," AS, June 1966 (Vol. 6, No. 6), pp. 303-09.

30. See "Memorandum by P'eng Teh-haui," Tsu Kuo, March 1, 1968 (No. 48), pp. 42-44.

31. "Mao Tse-tung's Talks at the Central Work Conference (October 25, 1966)," Tsu Kuo, March 1968 (No. 48), p. 41.

32. "P'eng Teh-huai's Confessions," Tsu Kuo, May 1968 (No. 50), pp. 40-41. See also, P'eng Teh-huai (Hong Kong: Chih Luen Press, 1969), Parts 4 and 5.

33. "Documents on Mao Tse-tung and P'eng Teh-huai at the Lu-shan Conference," Tsu Kuo, May 1, 1968 (No. 50), p. 35.

34. "Speech at the Lu-shan Conference (July 23, 1959)," Tsu Kuo, December 1969 (No. 69): pp. 42-43; English text in Chinese Law and Government, Winter, 1968-69 (Vol. 1, No. 4), pp. 27-43.

35. (See "Memorandum by P'eng Teh-huai, Supra, note 30.)

36. See FCNP, 1967, p. 568; J. D. Simmonds, "P'eng Teh-huai: A Chronological Reexamination," CQ, January-March 1969 (No. 37), pp. 120-38.

37. "Speech at the Tenth Plenary Session of the Eighth Central Committee (September 24, 1962)," Tsu Kuo, January 1970 (No. 70), p. 46; English translation in Chinese Law and Government, Winter, 1968-69 (Vol. 1, No. 4), pp. 85-93.

38. See "A Comment on the Soviet Government's Statement of August 3, " Supra, note 14.

39. 1,390 experts were withdrawn, and 343 contracts concerning technical aid, and 257 projects of scientific and technical co-operation were cancelled.

40. K. S. Karol, China, The Other Communism (N.Y.: Hill and Wang, 1967); translated from the French by Tom Baistow, pp. 376-78; see also David Floyd, Mao Against Khrushchev: A Short History of the Sino-Soviet Conflict (N.Y.: Praeger, 1963), pp. 284-85, 313-30.

41. Kenneth T. Young, Negotiating with the Chinese Communists: The United States' Experience, 1953-1967 (N.Y.: McGraw-Hill, 1968), p. 184.

42. Ibid., pp. 190-93.

43. "P'eng Teh-huai's Message to the People of Taiwan," PR, October 7, 1958 (Vol. 1, No. 32), p. 1 and Supplement.

44. Congressional Quarterly Service, Supra, note 22, p. 90.

45. Young, Supra, note 41, p. 161.

46. For the Soviet view on the UNEF and UNOGIL, see Alexander Dallin, The Soviet Union at the United Nations (N.Y.: Praeger, 1962), Chapter X; and Lincoln P. Bloomfield, et al., International Military Forces (Boston: Little, Brown, 1964), Chapter 4.

47. The Soviet position on the ONUC reflects her concern over the division of power between the Security Council and the General Assembly. See John G. Stoessinger, "Financing Peacekeeping Operations," in John G. Stoessinger and Alan F. Westin (eds.), Power and Order (N. Y.: Harcourt, Brace and World, 1964), pp. 140-78.

48. See Kuo Chi, "What Is the So-called 'UN Permanent Forces'?" SCCS, May 10, 1965 (No. 9), pp. 26-27.

49. Arthur Schlesinger, Jr., A Thousand Days (New York: Houghton Mifflin. 1965), p. 483.

50. Mezerik, Supra, note 2, p. 76.

51. SCMP, December 29, 1961 (No. 2648), pp. 34-36.

52. Ibid.

Notes to Chapter 9

1. Inis L. Claude, Jr., Swords into Plowshares: The Problems and Progress of International Organization (N.Y.: Random House, 3rd ed., 1964), Chapter 14.

2. See Sydney D. Bailey, "The Troika and the Future of the UN," International Conciliation, May 1962 (No. 538).

3. KTTH, April 25, 1961 (No. 17). English translation in J. Chester Cheng, et al. (eds.), The Politics of the Chinese Red Army: A Translation of the Bulletin of Activities of the PLA (Palo Alto, Calif.: The Hoover Institute on War, Revolution, and Peace, 1966), p. 480

4. See George Modelski, International Conference on the Settlement of the Laotian Question, 1961-1962 (Canberra: Department of International Relations Australian National University, 1962); and Arthur Lall, How Communist China Negotiates (N.Y.: Columbia University Press, 1968), Chapter VI.

5. Edgar Snow gave the following account of the secret negotiations:

> A Hong Kong newspaper owned by Chiang Ching-kuo, the Cheng Pao, has published a number of stories which imply the existence of negotiations. On July 29, 1962, Chiang's paper carried a report that Mao had recommended to the Politburo that better terms be offered to Taiwan. That report implied that Peking might 'continue' the disrupted Kuomintang-Communist negotiations which had been conducted with General Li Tsung-jen. . . . One implication of the Hong Kong story is that Chiang Ching-kuo might seek to use General Li by recognizing him as the legal president in order to prevent Chen Cheng from taking power. . . .

> Terms of a settlement rumored to have been discussed, but totally lacking any official confirmation (and, naturally, denied by Taiwan at this stage of the game), include: (1) Taiwan to be permanently recognized as an autonomous region within the Chinese state; (2) Nationalist armed forces to withdraw from the offshore islands but remain on Taiwan and the Pescadores; (3) the Nationalist president to become a vice-chairman of the People's Republic and concurrently deputy commander in chief of the armed forces of the Republic; (4) the Kuomintang to be reorganized to include the Kuomintang Revolutionary Committee, now in Peking, and to form a coalition Taiwan regime represented in the mainland National Congress and Cabinet; (5) the People's Republic to assume all diplomatic representation abroad; (6) Taiwan to control its defense forces for ten years but gradually to reduce them to provincial status; (7) for a specified

period (ten years? twenty years?) Peking would send no
armed forces to Taiwan but would provide training and
supplies for the existing forces. The Other Side of the
River: Red China Today (N.Y.: Random House, 1, pp.
765-66.

Similarly, Dennis Bloodworth reported in the London Observer of
August 12, 1962, via a dispatch from Singapore, that a "secret agreement" had actually been reached between the Chiang family and the
communists in Peking. The terms of agreement included: (1) neither
side would make a serious attack on the other during Chiang Kai-shek's
lifetime; (2) after Chiang's death, Taiwan would be allowed an autonomous status under Peking "similar to that held by Tibet", (3) during
the subsequent decade or so, there would be a referendum to determine
whether Formosa would be independent or part of China proper. See
Lewis Gilbert, "Peking and Taipei," in Mark Mancall (ed.), Formosa
Today (N.Y.: Praeger, 1964), pp. 117-18. See also Peter P. C. Cheng,
"The Formosa Tangle: A Formosan's View," AS November 1967
(Vol. 7, No. 11), pp. 791-806.

6. See, for instance, William Clifford, "Free China's Dirt Farm
Diplomacy," The Lion, October 1967 (Vol. 50, No. 4), pp. 30-32.

7. An Indian observer writing in late 1964 correctly detected
Communist China's disinterest in the UN. See K. V. Narain, "Peking's
Game at the UN," Atlas, November 1964 (Vol. 8, No. 4), pp. 239-40.
Professor Levi Werner thought otherwise. See "China and the United
Nations," Current History, September 1964 (Vol. 47, No. 277), pp.
149-55, 180.

8. It is true that Peking had hinted in the World Peace Council
as early as 1950 at the desirability of a "more effective means" than
the UN to meet "the world's hopes for peace." But those words would
seem to imply frustration rather than serious contemplation.

9. PR, December 27, 1963 (Vol. 6, No. 52), pp. 14-16.

10. See Jan S. Prybyla, "Communist China's Strategy of Economic
Development: 1961-1966," AS, October 1966 (Vol. 6, No. 10), pp.
589-603.

11. See Harry Hamm, China: Empire of the 700 Million (Garden
City, N.Y.: Doubleday, 1966), translated from German by Victor
Anderson, Chapter 23.

12. In 1963, representatives of the PRC took part in the Afro-Asian Solidarity Conference held in Tanganyika from February 7 to 10; Liu Shao-ch'i toured four Southeast Asian nations in April; the Chinese athletic team trampled a mediocre team from Russia at the first Games of the New Emerging Forces (GANEFO 1) in November; and, in December, Chou En-lai, Ch'en Yi and an impressive entourage of more than 50 were on a seven-week visit in ten African countries, spreading the idea of a "third force" consisting of countries from Asia, Africa and Latin America.

13. See Milton Kovner, "Communist China's Foreign Aid to Less-Developed Countries," in US Congress, Joint Economic Committee, An Economic Profile of Mainland China (Washington, D.C.: Government Printing Office, 1967), Vol. 2, p. 612.

14. See Robert L. Price, "International Trade of Communist China," in Ibid, p. 584.

15. See W. A. C. Adie, "Chou En-lai on Safari," CQ, April-June 1964 (No. 18), pp. 174-94; and Afro-Asian Solidarity Against Imperialism: A Collection of Documents, Speeches and Press Interviews from the Visits of Chinese Leaders to Thirteen African and Asian Countries (Peking: Foreign Languages Press, 1964).

16. See PR, October 16, 1964 (Vol. 7, No. 42), pp. 1ff.

17. SCMP, December 9, 1964 (No. 3353), pp. 28-31; PR, December 11, 1964 (Vol. 7, No. 50), pp. 11-13.

18. See "Indonesian Withdrawal from the United Nations," Current Notes on International Affairs (Canberra), January 1965 (Vol. 36, No. 1), pp. 40-44; and UN Monthly Chronicle, February 1965 (Vol. 2, No. 2), pp. 5-6.

19. PR, January 15, 1965 (Vol. 8, No. 3), p. 4.

20. Ibid.

21. Ibid., pp. 5-6.

22. Ibid., pp. 6-9.

23. PR, January 29, 1965 (Vol. 8, No. 5), pp. 5-6.

24. Edgar Snow, "Interview with Mao," The New Republic, February 27, 1965 (Vol. 152, No. 9), pp. 19-23.

25. Ibid.

26. The Economist (London), June 26, 1965 (Vol. 215, No. 6357), p. 1492.

27. Kuang-ming Jih-pao (Kuang-ming Daily) (Peking), June 29, 1965, p. 1.

28. PR, October 29, 1965 (Vol. 8, No. 44), pp. 5-6.

29. PR, October 8, 1965 (Vol. 8, No. 41), p. 10.

30. PR, October 22, 1965 (Vol. 8, No. 43), pp. 7ff., for a Chinese account of the "September 30 Movement." For five months, Peking tolerated the purge of the PKI and the massacre of overseas Chinese in Indonesia in the hope that Sukarno might regain an upperhand. But Sukarno was forced to give up power on March 11, 1966. Afterward, Chinese attacks on the Indonesian "right wing" became very sharp.

31. See Herbert L. Matthews, "Three Continents Plus Cuba," NYT, February 7, 1966, p. 28; and PR, February 25, 1966 (Vol. 9, No. 9), pp. 13-25.

32. See PR, March 11, 1966 (Vol. 9, No. 11), pp. 7-11.

33. Snow "Interview with Mao," Supra, note 22, pp. 19-23.

34. The Economist (London), June 26, 1965 (Vol. 215, No. 6457), pp. 1492-93.

35. Liu Shao-ch'i paid a visit to Pakistan in late March 1966, and regained some Pakistani ties to the PRC. See PR, April 1, 1966 (Vol. 9, No. 14), pp. 3-6.

36. See NYT, April 10, 1966, p. 17; and PR, April 8, 1966 (Vol. 9, No. 15), p. 16.

37. Herbert L. Matthews, Supra, note 29, p. 28.

38. PR, January 1, 1966 (Vol. 9, No. 1), pp. 13-14.

39. Both Ch'en Yi and Chou En-lai made public pronouncements expressing such demands upon the UN in late 1965. Among Peking's leading personalities, these two men have been generally considered

as relatively more knowledgeable about the outside world and more
realistic in their approach. The fact that such demands were made on
the eve of the Great Proletarian Cultural Revolution suggests the possibility that they might have been under domestic pressure to do so.
According to Taiwan sources, in February 1967, when the Red Guards
turned their spearhead on Ch'en Yi, Ch'en wrote a sarcastic and bitter
but frank and bold "confession," entitled "A Foreign Minister Like
Me." Among other things, he said.

> I am. . .head of the foreign affairs system. I say you can
> cut off my head, and my blood can smear the ground, but I
> will not give up my leadership. . . . If we diplomats should
> hang boards with Chairman Mao's quotations on our necks and
> wave the little Red Book, wouldn't we look like priests?. . .
> In my opinion the wall posters criticizing Chairman Mao may
> not be all wrong. . . . Lin Piao is also of no importance. He
> used to be under my command. Is it possible for only those
> two to lead the Cultural Revolution? . . . You should study well
> President Liu Shao-ch'i's Thought. He is my teacher, my
> master, my King. . . . Criminal charges against him are
> sometimes concocted. . . .

See Chinese Information Service, "Missing Ambassadors A Mystery--
Peiping's Foreign Affairs Drift on Without Direction," Report on
Mainland China (New York) No. 18 January 27, 1969), p. 8. Hong Kong's
account of Ch'en's self-criticism does not include such passages.
See Tsu Kuo, July 1970 (No. 76), pp. 33-35. According to the Hong
Kong account, Ch'en submitted his confession on January 24 rather
than in February. It is not known whether Ch'en actually made more
than one confession.

40. The full text of this important press conference is in PR,
October 8, 1965 (Vol. 8, No. 41), pp. 7-14. Also see an earlier speech
by Chou En-lai in PR, January 29, 1965 (Vol. 8, No. 5), pp. 5ff.

41. Myres S. McDougal and Richard M. Goodman, "Chinese
Participation in the United Nations," AJIL, October 1966 (Vol. 60,
No. 4), pp. 671-727, particularly, p. 703.

42. See Hungdah Chiu and R. R. Edwards, "Communist China's
Attitude Toward the United Nations: A Legal Analysis," AJIL,
January 1968 (Vol. 62, No. 1), p. 23.

43. For Peking's reaction to Indonesian withdrawal from the UN,
see PR, January 15, 1965 (Vol. 8, No. 3), pp. 5ff. For Peking's

reaction to Cambodian withdrawal from the UN special committee on decolonization, see PR, October 1, 1965 (Vol. 8, No. 40), pp. 15-16.

44. PR, December 11, 1964 (Vol. 7, No. 50), pp. 11-13.

45. China and U.S. Far East Policy, 1945-66 (Washington: Congressional Quarterly Service, 1967), p. 162.

46. Soviet invasion in Hungary, 1956; in Czechoslavakia, 1968; and American intervention in the Dominican Republic in 1965 come to mind as examples.

47. See PR, December 27, 1963 (Vol. 6, No. 52), pp. 14-16. In 1961, Peking also argued that "revision of the Charter needs the PRC," but that the question of Chinese representation and the question of broadening the membership of the two Councils "are of entirely different nature: one procedural, one substantial." McDougal and Goodman seem to be mistaken in asserting that Peking had made the seating of the PRC a pre-condition to enlargement of the two Councils. Cf. Chou Keng-sheng, "China's Legitimate Rights in the United Nations Must Be Restored," JMJP, December 5, 1961. English translation in SCMP (No. 2637), pp. 38ff. and McDougal and Goodman, Supra, note 39, p. 710, note 197.

48. In the China-Pakistan Joint Communique of March 7, 1965, the reorganization of the UN was advocated with these words. See PR, March 12, 1965 (Vol. 8, No. 11), p. 10. A similar statement appeared in the China-Burmese Joint Communique. See PR, August 6, 1965 (Vol. 8, No. 32), p. 30.

49. See PR, January 15, 1965 (Vol. 8, No. 3), pp. 6-7.

50. According to Peking's spokesman, the splitting of Germany represents a situation different from that of the Chinese. While the former was divided on the basis of international agreements growing out of World War II, the latter has been entirely a domestic affair, albeit foreign intervention. See Shao Chin-fu, "The Absurd Theory of 'Two Chinas' and Principles of International Law," in Oppose the New U.S. Plots to Create "Two Chinas" (Peking: Foreign Languages Press, 1960-61), pp. 82-85. In fact, Peking has long been ready to recognize "two Germanys." This was one of the three principles that Chou En-lai and Marshall Montgomery agreed upon in 1961 in order to ease tension in the international situation. See JMJP, September 23, 1961, p. 1.

Notes on Chapter 10

1. The term "Cultural Revolution" was first proposed formally by Liu Shao-ch'i in his 1956 political report to the Eight Party Congress. See Chin Szu-k'ai, "The 1966 Great Proletarian Cultural Revolution Movement in Communist China," Tsu Kuo, March 1967 (No. 36), p. 3. See also Edward Friedman, "Cultural Limits of the Cultural Revolution," AS, March 1969 (Vol. 9, No. 3), p. 188.

2. "The May 16, 1966, Circular," PR, May 19, 1967 (Vol. 10, No. 21), p. 6.

3. See Chao Ch'ung, "An Account of the Great Proletarian Cultural Revolution," Part 7, Tsu Kuo, July 1968 (No. 52), pp. 15-21; Part 8, Tsu Kuo, August 1968 (No. 53), pp. 10-15.

4. Excerpts in Tsu Kuo, March 1968 (No. 48), pp. 44, 46.

5. Text in PR, May 19, 1967 (Vol. 10, No. 21), pp. 6-9.

6. See PR, July 29, 1966 (Vol. 9, No. 31), pp. 3-7.

7. See Liu's "Self-Criticism" in Tsu Kuo, September 1969 (No. 66), p. 34.

8. PR, January 1, 1966 (Vol. 9, No. 1), pp. 8-9.

9. See Michael B. Yahuda, "Chinese Foreign Policy After 1963: The Maoist Phases," CQ, October-December 1968 (No. 36), pp. 93-113. Yahuda sees a widening of the gap between Peking's aspirational and operational policies, rather than an isolationist tendency.

10. See PR, March 25, 1966 (Vol. 9, No. 13), pp. 5-6; April 8, 1966 (Vol. 9, No. 15), pp. 19ff.; and NYT, March 24, 1966, p. 14.

11. See PR, January 7, 1966 (Vol. 9, No. 2), pp. 5-9; May 13, 1966 (Vol. 9, No. 20), p. 5; China and U.S. Far East Policy, 1945-66 (Washington,: Congressional Quarterly Service, 1967), pp. 187, 216; and Yun Ho, "Communist China's Foreign Relations, 1966," Tsu Kuo, February 1967 (No. 35), pp. 17-30.

12. Dayton Daily News, February 18, 1966, p. 6.

13. See Melvin Gurtov, "The Foreign Ministry and Foreign Affairs During the Cultural Revolution," CQ, October-December 1969 (No. 40), pp. 61-102.

14. See NYT, March 2, 1966, p. 1; March 8, 1966, p. 5; March 10, 1966, p. 1.

15. PR, January 1, 1966 (Vol. 9, No. 1), pp. 13-16.

16. PR, February 4, 1966 (Vol. 9, No. 6), pp. 9-10.

17. Congressional Quarterly Service, Supra, note 11, p. 185.

18. Text in PR, August 11, 1967 (Vol. 10, No. 33), p. 5.

19. Text in PR, August 12, 1966 (Vol. 9, No. 33), pp. 6-11; see also "The Communique of the 11th Plenary Session of the 8th Central Committee of the CPC," PR, August 19, 1966 (Vol. 9, No. 34), pp. 4-8.

20. See "Collection of Mao Tse-tung's Directives During the Cultural Revolution, Part 2," Tsu Kuo, October 1, 1969 (No. 67), pp. 36ff, particularly Document No. 9.

21. See Chao, Supra, note 3, Part 23, Tsu Kuo, December 1969 (No. 69), pp. 23-32; Part 24, Tsu Kuo, January 1970 (No. 70), pp. 33-39.

22. Text in Tsu Kuo, July 1970 (No. 76), pp. 33-35.

23. The "three-in-one combination" refers to provisional organs of power consisting of leading members of revolutionary mass organizations, leading members of local PLA units and revolutionary leading cadres of Party and government organizations. See PR, February 10, 1967 (Vol. 10, No. 7), pp. 16, 19.

24. Chu Chuan-fu, "An Account of the 'Revolutionary Committees'," Chan Wang, October 1, 1968 (No. 160), pp. 18-21.

25. See Gurtov, Supra, note 13, pp. 85-89.

26. NCNA, September 24, 1967. See Chan Wang, October 16, 1967 (No. 137), p. 22.

27. PR, September 8, 1967 (Vol. 10, No. 37), pp. 7-8.

28. PR, November 1, 1968 (Vol. 11, No. 44), Supplement.

29. PR, August 19, 1966 (Vol. 9, No. 34), pp. 4-8.

30. PR, January 1, 1967 (Vol. 10, No. 1), pp. 8-15.

31. PR, November 10, 1967 (Vol. 10, No. 46), p. 16.

32.   Yun Ho, "Foreign Relations of Communist China, 1967,"
Tsu Kuo, March 1968 (No. 48), pp. 33-40; April 1968 (No. 49), pp. 30-
42. See also Wang Jo-min, "New Direction of Communist China's
Foreign Policy," Chan Wang, January 1, 1969 (No. 166), pp. 5-6; Hung
Tung-ch'ing, "Communist China's New Internal and External Movement
and Direction," Chan Wang, June 16, 1969 (No. 177), pp. 12-15.

33. PR, April 28, 1967 (Vol. 10, No. 18), p. 37.

34. NCNA, Press Communiques, May 9, 1966; October 27, 1966;
December 28, 1966; June 17, 1967; December 28, 1968; October 4,
1969; and April 25, 1970.

35. See PR, November 18, 1966 (Vol. 9, No. 47), p. 34; December
16, 1966 (Vol. 9, No. 51), p. 37.

36. Christian Science Monitor, March 30, 1967, p. 11. See also
PR, March 24, 1967 (Vol. 10, No. 13), pp. 21ff.

37. PR, August 12, 1966 (Vol. 9, No. 33), p. 5; August 30, 1968
(Vol. 11, No. 35), pp. 30-31; October 18, 1968 (Vol. 11, No. 42), p. 30;
and November 22, 1968 (Vol. 11, No. 47), p. 4.

38. PR, March 3, 1967 (Vol. 10, No. 10), p. 30.

39. PR, September 15, 1967 (Vol. 10, No. 38), pp. 32-34; March
7, 1969 (Vol. 12, No. 10), p. 16.

40. PR, December 8, 1967 (Vol. 10, No. 50), pp. 38-39.

41. PR, July 5, 1968 (Vol. 11, No. 27), pp. 29-30.

42. According to CQ, by the end of September 1967, Peking had
been involved in quarrels of varying magnitude with 32 countries.
See "Quarterly Chronicle and Documentation," CQ, October-December
1967 (No. 32), p. 221.

43. PR, December 9, 1966 (Vol. 9, No. 50), pp. 26-27.

44. Ibid.

45. PR, July 14, 1967 (Vol. 10, No. 29), p. 36.

46. PR, December 8, 1967 (Vol. 10, No. 50), pp. 20-21.

47. See "Communique of the Second Plenary Session of the Ninth Central Committee of the CPC," PR, September 6, 1970 (Vol. 13, No. 37), pp. 5-7.

48. See Wang Hsiang, "China's State Council Steps Up Its Own Organizational Construction," Chan Wang, February 1, 1971 (No. 216), pp. 12-13.

49. See Chin Ti, "Communist China's Party Affairs in 1970," Tsu Kuo, May 1971 (No. 86), pp. 2-9.

50. PR, November 1, 1968 (Vol. 11, No. 44), Supplement.

51. Chang Man, "The Suspension and Resumption of the 'Red Flag' Magazine," Tsu Kuo, September 1968 (No. 54), pp. 2-7.

52. PR, April 28, 1969, Special Issue, p. 20.

53. Chiang I-shan, "The 'Three-Support' and 'Two Military' Tasks of PLA in the Present Stage," Tsu Kuo, August 1969 (No. 65), pp. 2-10.

54. See Chin Ti, "Communist China's Party Affairs in 1969," Tsu Kuo, May 1970 (No. 74), pp. 2-13. For analyses of central personnel changes in the CPC since the GPCR and their implications, see Ting Wong, "Personnel Problems in CPC Central Committee," Part 1, Tsu Kuo, December 1968 (No. 57), pp. 26-30; Part 2, Tsu Kuo, January 1969 (No. 58), pp. 9-22; "The Vicissitudes of Members of CPC 8th Central Committee," Tsu Kuo, June 1969 (No. 63), pp. 45-49; and Donald W. Klein and Lois B. Hager, "The Ninth Central Committee," CQ, January-March 1971 (No. 45), pp. 37-56.

55. Richard Baum, "Years of the Mango," AS, January 1969 (Vol. IX, No. 1), p. 7.

56. See Yu Heng, "Huang Yung-sheng as 'T'an Chen-lin in Kwangtung'," Tsu Kuo, September 1968 (No. 54), pp. 25-26, 52; Huo Huei-sheng, "Mao Tse-tung Has Already Fallen From the Center of Power," Chan Wang, November 1, 1969 (No. 186), pp. 12-14; and Huo Huei-sheng, "The Present Situation Regarding the Power Struggle in Communist China," Chan Wang, February 1, 1970 (No. 192), pp. 5-7.

57. See Fan P'eng-tao, "The Political Line of New 'Persons in Authority' in Communist China," Tsu Kuo, April 1970 (No. 73), p. 24; cf. PR, September 19, 1969 (Vol. 12, No. 38), p. 4; and October 3, 1969 (Vol. 12, No. 40), p. 41.

58. Daniel Tretiak, "Is China Preparing to 'Turn Out'?: Changes in Chinese Levels of Attention to the International Environment," AS, March 1971 (Vol. XI, No. 3), pp. 226-27.

59. See "Quarterly Chronicle and Documentation," CQ, April-June 1969 (No. 38), pp. 191-95; July-September 1969 (No. 39), pp. 160-63.

60. See "A Sinister Counter-Revolutionary Conference in Moscow: A Despicable Plot, Editorial by Albanian Paper Zeri i Popullit," PR, June 13, 1969 (Vol. 12, No. 24), pp. 14-18.

61. PR, July 4, 1969 (Vol. 12, No. 27), pp. 22-23.

62. See PR, November 29, 1968 (Vol. 11, No. 48), pp. 30-31; "A Symposium on the Sino-American Talks," Chan Wang, January 16, 1969 (No. 167), pp. 7-13; and Yun Ho, "Foreign Relations of Communist China, 1968," Part 1, Tsu Kuo, May, 1969 (No. 62), pp. 14-29; Part 2, Tsu Kuo, June, 1969 (No. 63), pp. 26-37.

63. PR, February 21, 1969 (Vol. 12, No. 8), p. 4. See also Yun Ho, "Foreign Relations of Communist China, 1969," Tsu Kuo, January, 1970 (No. 70), pp. 14-28.

64. "Quarterly Chronicle and Documentation," CQ, October-December 1969 (No. 40), p. 181.

65. "US Imperialism Extremely Unpopular for Pushing Anti-China Policy in United Nations," PR, November 29, 1968 (Vol. 11, No. 48), pp. 26-28.

66. Ibid., p. 28.

Notes on Chapter 11

1. The term "B.C." as used here was coined by a "Western observer" according to Newsweek, November 30, 1970, p. 41.

2. See Yun Ho, "Foreign Relations of Communist China, 1969," Tsu Kuo, January 1970 (No. 70), p. 26; also NYT, September 1 1969, p. 1.

3. "US Imperialism Becomes Ever More Isolated in Manipulating UN to Oppose China," PR, November 21, 1969 (Vol. 12, No. 47), pp. 23-24.

4. See "Communique of the Second Plenary Session of the Ninth Central Committee of the Communist Party of China," PR, September 11, 1970 (Vol. 13, No. 37), pp. 5-7; and Chin Ti, "Communist China's Party Affairs in 1970," Tsu Kuo, May 1970 (No. 86), pp. 2-3.

5. See "Joint Communique of Government of People's Republic of China and Government of Canada Concerning Establishment of Diplomatic Relations Between China and Canada," PR, October 16, 1970 (Vol. 13, No. 42), p. 12. In this formula, "The Chinese government reaffirms that Taiwan is an inalienable part of the territory of the People's Republic of China. The Canadian government takes note of this position of the Chinese government."

6. See Joint Communiques between the PRC and the Republic of Equatorial Guinea, October 15, 1970, PR, October 23, 1970 (Vol. 13, No. 43), p. 10; the Imperial Ethiopian Government, November 24, 1970, PR, December 11, 1970 (Vol. 13, No. 50), p. 7; the Federal Republic of Nigeria, February 10, 1971, PR, February 19, 1971 (Vol. 14, No. 8), p. 5; Kuwait, March 22, 1971, PR, April 2, 1971 (Vol. 14, No. 14), p. 16; the Federal Republic of Cameroon, March 26, 1971, PR, April 9, 1971 (Vol. 14, No. 15), p. 9; the Republic of San Marino, May 6, 1971, PR, May 14, 1971 (Vol. 14, No. 20), p. 7; and the Republic of Austria, May 26, 1971, PR, June 4, 1971,(Vol. 14, No. 23), p. 11. There were two exceptions, however. In the cases of Italy and Chile, the Canadian formula was repeated. See PR, November 13, 1970 (Vol. 13, No. 46), p. 6; and PR January 8, 1971 (Vol. 14, No. 2), p. 3.

7. See Huo Hui-sheng, "Changes in Communist Chinese Diplomacy and Taipei," Chan Wang, November 16, 1970 (No. 211), pp. 7-8.

8. PR, November 6, 1970 (Vol. 13, No. 45), pp. 21-22.

9. Ibid., pp. 19-20.

10. PR, November 27, 1970 (Vol. 13. No. 48), pp. 20-22.

11. The following nations are likely to switch their votes in favor of the PRC in 1971 if the "important question" resolution is brought up in the General Assembly again: Botswana, Central African Republic, Ireland, Luxembourg, Austria, Canada, Italy, Iceland, Bolivia, Malta, Senegal and the United Kingdom.

12. John M. Hightower in an AP dispatch. See Dayton Daily News April 15, 1971, p. 11.

13. Henry Tanner in NYT, May 30, 1971, p. 15.

14. See, Chin Ti, supra, note 4; and Chung Hua-min, "Communist China in 1970," Tsu Kuo, January 1971 (No. 82), pp. 2-4.

15. Harry Harding, "China: Toward Revolutionary Pragmatism," AS, January 1971 (Vol. 11, No. 1), p. 52.

16. See Ch'en Kuo, "Position of the Mao Faction Continues to Decline," Chan Wang, March 1, 1971 (No. 218), pp. 7-8.

17. Time, July 26, 1971, pp. 14-15.

18. In the Joint Editorial of Renmin Ribao, Hongqi and Jiefangjun Bao commemorating the 50th anniversary of the CPC, there is one passage that reads: "In contradistinction to the type of person who claims to be a "humble little commoner" but is actually a big careerist, we should sincerely learn from the masses while tirelessly educating them in Mao Tse-tung Thought, overcome erroneous tendencies and raise the political consciousness of the people." See PR, July 2, 1971 (Vol. 14, No. 27), p. 20. According to the ROC's Chinese Information Service, during the course of the GPCR, Mao's wife, Chiang Ching, told her followers on several occasions that "Comrade Po-ta always says that he is a humble little commoner (Hsiao Hsiao Lao Pai Hsing)." It does seem Ch'en Po-ta is in trouble. He has not been seen in public since August, 1970. See Chinese Information Service (New York), Background on China, July 16, 1971 (B. 71-36), p. 1; and Ch'en Kuo, Supra, note 16, p. 7.

19. See Chin Ti, Supra, note 4; Wang Hsiang, "Why Have There Been No Changes in the CPC's Provincial Leaders?" Chan Wang, April 1, 1971, (No. 220), pp. 15-16; and Huo Hui-sheng, "Speculations on Trends in Sino-American Detente," Chan Wang, May 16, 1971 (No. 223), p. 5.

20. See Edgar Snow, "A Conversation with Mao Tse-tung," Life, April 30, 1971, pp. 46-48.

21. See Harding, Supra, note 15, pp. 53.

22. The PRC became a space power with the launching of two spacecrafts on April 24, 1970, and March 3, 1971. See Chiang I-shan, "Military Affairs of Communist China, 1970," Tsu Kuo, January 1971 (No. 82), pp. 5-14.

23. See Fan Peng-tao, "The Political Line of New 'Persons in Authority' in Communist China," Tsu Kuo, April 1970 (No. 73), pp. 23-27.

24. PR, October 24, 1969 (Vol. 12, No. 43), pp. 8-9.

25. "Quarterly Chronicle and Documentation," CQ, January-March 1970 (No. 41), p. 181.

26. See NYT, July 19, 1971, p. 7.

27. See "Brief Introduction to Communist China's Present Diplomatic Envoys," Chan Wang, May 16, 1971 (No. 223), pp. 17-18;

28. They are incorporated in the March 1, 1971, Joint Communique on China-Japan Trade Memorandum as follows:

> The Chinese side will not have trade exchanges with factories, firms and enterprises belonging to any of the following categories:
> First, factories and firms helping the Chiang Kai-shek gang stage a come-back to the mainland or helping the Pak Jung Hi clique intrude into the Democratic People's Republic of Korea;
> Second, factories and firms with large investment in Taiwan or South Korea;
> Third, enterprises supplying arms and ammunition to US imperialism for aggression against Vietnam or Laos or Cambodia; and
> Fourth, US-Japan joint enterprises or subsidiaries of US companies in Japan.

See PR, March 12, 1971 (Vol. 14, No. 11), p. 25.

29. Richard M. Nixon, "Asia After Vietnam," Foreign Affairs, October 1967 (Vol. 46, No. 1), p. 121.

30. NYT, February 19, 1969, p. 1.

31. Among them, Senators Jacob Javits and George McGovern. The list would also include Arthur Goldberg, Charles Yost, and later a 50-member Presidential Commission led by Henry Cabot Lodge.

32. NYT, July 22, 1969, p. 1.

33. NYT, July 26, 1969, pp. 1, 8.

34. NYT, December 20, 1969, p. 1.

35. NYT, February 19, 1970, p. 1.

36. NYT, November 13, 1970, p. 1.

37. NYT, February 26, 1971, pp. 1, 13.

38. NYT, March 16, 1971, p. 2.

39. See Snow, Supra, note 20.

40. Newsweek, May 10, 1971, p. 43.

41. Newsweek, April 26, 1971, p. 16.

42. "Text of Chou En-lai's Conversations with American Reporter Snow," Chan Wang, January 1, 1971 (No. 214), pp. 7-8.

43. Snow, Supra, note 20.

44. Newsweek, April 26, 1971, p. 16.

45. Snow, Supra, note 20.

46. Newsweek, April 26, 1971, p. 17.

47. NYT, June 11, 1971, p. 8.

48. NYT, April 21, 1971, p. 1.

49. NYT, May 6, 1971, p. 12.

50. NYT, July 1, 1971, pp. 1, 22.

PART III

Notes on Chapter 12

1. See Byron S. J. Weng, "Some Conditions of Peking's Participation in International Organizations," in Jerome A. Cohen (ed.),

China and International Law: Cases (Cambridge, Mass.: Harvard
University Press, forthcoming).

2. See Byron S. J. Weng, "Peking's Position on the Status of
Taiwan," in Shao-ch'uan Leng and Hungdah Chiu (eds.), Communist
China and Selected Problems of International Law (Dobbs Ferry, N.Y.:
Oceana Publications, forthcoming).

3. See, e.g., Mei Ju-au, "Po-ch'u Ch'in lueh-che ti Fa-lu Wai-i"
("Strip the Aggressor's Legal Cloak"), JMJP, January 31, 1955; and
"President Chiang Kai-shek's speech on the Fifth Anniversary of the
Recovery of Taiwan, October 25, 1950." In Selected Speeches and
Messages of President Chiang Kai-shek, 1949-52 (Taipei: Office of
Government Spokesman, 1952), pp. 64-69.

4. See Mei, Supra, note 2; and Hirano Yoshitaro, "Ts'ung Kuo-
chi-fa Po-ch'ih 'I-Chung I-T'ai' Miow-lun" ("Refuting the Absurd
Theory of 'One-China, One-Taiwan' by International Law"), Ta Kung
Pao (Hong Kong), May 30, 1964.

5. See, e.g., Lim Keh-hiok, "Taiwan ti Kuo-chi-fa shang Ti-wei"
("Taiwan's Status in International Law"), Taiwan Chinglien (Taiwan
Youth), January 25, 1967 (No. 74), pp. 29-31, and March 25, 1967 (No.
76), pp. 24-30; Lung-chu Chen and Harold Lasswell, Formosa, China
and the United Nations: Formosa in the World Community (N.Y.: St.
Martins Press, 1967), pp. 126-40; Ely Mauer, "Legal Problems Regarding Formosa and the Offshore Islands," Department of State Bulletin, December 22, 1958 (Vol. 39, No. 1017), pp. 1005-11; and Georg
Schwarzenberger, "Title to Territory: Response to a Challenge,"
in Leo Gross (ed.), International Law in the Twentieth Century (N.Y.:
Appleton-Century-Crofts, 1969), p. 293.

6. Frank P. Morello, The International Legal Status of Formosa
(The Hague: Martinus Nijhoff, 1966), particularly, pp. 90-92.

7. See, e.g., D. P. O'Connell, "The Status of Formosa and the
Chinese Recognition Problem," AJIL, April 1956 (Vol. 50, No. 2),
pp. 405-16; T'ang Wu, Chung-kuo Yu Kuo-chi-fa (China and International
Law), Vol. 2 (Taipei: Chung-hua Wen-hua Ch'u-pan Shihyeh Wei-yuan-
hui [Committee on Chinese Cultural Publications Affairs] 1957), p.
436; and Hungdah Chiu, Hsien-tai Kuo-chi-fa Wen-t'i (Selected Problems
of Modern International Law) (Taipei: New Century Publishing Co.,
1966), pp. 97-111.

8. Chester Bowles, "The 'China Problem' Reconsidered,"

Foreign Affairs, April 1960 (Vol. 38, No. 3), pp. 476-86.

9. In any such negotiations, the interests of the native Formosan inhabitants are not likely to be represented. See Edgar Snow, The Other Side of the River: Red China Today (N.Y.: Random House, 1962), pp. 765-66; Lewis Gilbert, "Peking and Taipei," in Mark Mancall (ed.), Formosa Today (N.Y.: Praeger, 1964), pp. 112-20; and Peter P. C. Cheng, "The Formosa Tangle: A Formosan's View," AS, November 1967 (Vol. 7, No. 11), p. 791-806.

10. See Chen and Lasswell, Supra, note 4, pp. 150-55.

11. There has been a Formosan Declaration of Independence drafted by P'eng Ming-min, a former professor at the National Taiwan University and a noted authority on the international law of civil aviation. See Douglas Mendel, The Politics of Formosan Nationalism (Berkeley and Los Angeles: University of Calif. Press, 1970), particularly Chapter 7 and Appendix.

12. Quincy Wright seems to favor this method. See J. P. Jain, "The Legal Status of Formosa, A Study of British, Chinese and Indian Views," AJIL, January 1963 (Vol. 57, No. 1), p. 29.

13. This was recommended by the Roosa Committee of the UNA-USA in October 1966, China, the United Nations and United States Policy (UNA-USA, 1966), p. 11. Regarding this alternative solution, Thomas Weiss made the following observation:

> The character of the two regimes involved is at the heart of the issue. If the Peking government were not communist, the United States, in justice, good conscience and good politics, could have allowed Taiwan to fall to the mainland regime in 1950. . . . On the other hand, if there were a representative government on Taiwan--one in which the mainlanders did not have the dominant voice-- that government would not cherish a claim to the mainland and the United States could then support Taiwan's independence without having to uphold the one-China fiction.

Thomas J. Weiss, "Taiwan and U.S. Policy," Orbis, Winter 1969 (Vol. 12, No. 4), p. 1179.

14. John K. Fairbank suggests this "in-between" formula as a bridge toward an eventual "one-China, one-Taiwan" solution. China:

The People's Middle Kingdom and the U.S.A. (Cambridge, Mass.:
The Belknap Press of the Harvard University Press, 1967), pp. 78-79;
see also "A Brief Account of the U.S. 'Two Chinas' Plot," in Chinese
People's Institute of Foreign Affairs (ed.), Oppose the New U.S. Plots
to Create "Two Chinas" (Peking: Foreign Languages Press, 1962),
p. 106.

15. The most significant and controversial advocate of this
alternative is the Conlon Report of 1959. See U.S. Congress, Senate,
Committee of Foreign Relations, United States Foreign Policy: Asia
(Studies prepared by Conlon Associates, Ltd., Washington: Government
Printing Office, 1959), pp. 119ff. Peking seems to have intentionally
ignored this report. But Taipei gave it special attention. A group of
ROC scholars attacked the report with the following words:

> . . . if the United States is only interested in a piece of
> real estate and treats its occupants like dirt, then even
> with the help of high-sounding words (i.e., promising in-
> dependence to Taiwanese), skillful maneuvers (i.e., holding
> discussion with Japan, Burma and India), she would not be
> able to escape the stern judgment of history and would
> stand condemned as having committed the following
> crimes: (1) Creating puppets, (2) Betraying her ally, and
> (3) Committing aggression in disguise. . . .

Lin Yutang, et al., "An Analysis of the Conlon Report: Its Fallacies
and Contradictions as Viewed by Asians," Chinese Culture (Taipei),
December 1966, p. 99. Other American commentators supporting
the one-China, one-Taiwan solution include Chester Bowles, Supra,
note 7; George Kerr, Formosa Betrayed (Boston: Houghton Mifflin,
1965), pp. 451ff.; Douglas Mendel, Jr., "An Open Letter to Ambassador
Arthur Goldberg," Independent Formosa (Tokyo), April 1967 (Vol. 4,
No. 2), pp. 11-12; John D. Gardner, "Where U.S. Opposes Self-Determination," Independent Formosa (Tokyo), Spring 1969 (Vol. 8, No. 1),
p. 10; John C. Vincent and Mary Lou Shields, "John Carter Vincent
Interviewed," Independent Formosa (Tokyo), Fall 1968 (Vol. 7, No. 3),
pp. 3-4; Harold Lasswell, Supra, note 4; Thomas J. Weiss, Supra,
note 12; David Wurfel, "Taiwanese Nationalism: Problem for United
States Policy," in R. K. Sakai (ed.), Studies on Asia (Lincoln, Neb.:
University of Nebraska Press, 1963), pp. 101ff.

16. In 1950, Trygve Lie suggested a five-year UN trusteeship
over Formosa to be followed by a plebiscite. See In the Cause of
Peace (N.Y.: Macmillan, 1954), pp. 264-65. A similar proposal was
urged by Sir John Kotelawala, Ceylon's Premier at the time of the

Bandung Conference, NYT, Apr. 22, 1955, p. 1; and by Adlai E. Stevenson, "Putting First Things First," Foreign Affairs, January 1960 (Vol.38, No. 2), pp. 191-208. Even Li Tsung-jen, former Acting President of the ROC, suggested a temporary UN "custodianship" over Taiwan in 1961. See "Memorandum on the Chinese Question," appended in Chang Hsin-hai, America and China: A New Approach to Asia (N.Y.: Simon and Schuster, 1966), pp. 260-61.

17. Oppose U.S. Occupation of Taiwan and "Two Chinas" Plot (Peking: Foreign Languages Press, 1958), pp. 5-6.

18. FCNP, 1967, pp. 606-07.

19. See William L. Tung, The Political Institutions of Modern China (The Hague: Martinus Nijhoff, 1964), p. 274.

20. See Theodore H. E. Chen (ed.), The Chinese Communist Regime: Documents and Commentary (N.Y.: Praeger, 1967), p. 35.

21. See Franklin W. Houn, "Communist China's New Constitution," in George P. Jan (ed.), Government of Communist China (San Francisco: Chandler, 1966), p. 215.

22. Chung-hua Jen-min Kung-ho-kuo Fa-kuei Hui-pien (Collection of Laws and Regulations of the People's Republic of China), Vol. 1 (Peking: Fa-lu Ch'u-pan-she [The Law Press], 1956), pp. 553-56.

23. For details, see Chapter 11.

24. Peking Review did report in the "Round the World" column: "At the June 11 rally, Chairman Kazafi announced Libya's full diplomatic recognition of the People's Republic of China and that it would establish diplomatic relations with China." See PR, June 18, 1971 (Vol. 14, No. 25), p. 21.

25. See Myres S. McDougal and Richard M. Goodman, "Chinese Participation in the United Nations," AJIL, October 1966 (Vol. 60, No. 4), pp. 671-76.

26. Prior to 1955, the two superpowers, the US and the USSR, engaged in what John G. Stoessinger has called "competitive exclusion" in regard to UN membership. In 1955, an agreement on a large "package" deal ended that and ushered in a period of rapid expansion, underscoring the concept of universality. See John G. Stoessinger, The United Nations and the Superpowers: United States-Soviet

Interaction at the United Nations (N.Y.: Random House, 1965), p. 22.
Note also Inis L. Claude, Jr., Swords into Plowshares: The Problems
and Progress of International Organization (N.Y.: Random House,
third edition, 1964, Chapter 5), p. 108:

> "If the UN is to be directed toward its originally stated
> objectives, it needs to add new members, making a rational
> approach to universality; if it is to become an anti-Soviet
> coalition combined with peripheral members who will
> serve reliably to bless and legitimize coalition policy, it
> needs to divest itself of many of its present members,
> making a rational approach to selectivity."

27. See the Roosa Report, Supra, note 12, pp. 35-36.

28. Chou Keng-sheng, "China's Legitimate Rights in the United
Nations Must Be Restored," JMJP, December 5, 1961. English translation in Oppose the New US Plots . . . . Supra, Note 13, p. 59.

29. Ibid.

30. Ibid., p. 55.

31. Ibid., p. 60.

32. Ibid., p. 65.

33. Ibid., pp. 70-71.

34. Ibid., p. 72.

NOTES ON CHAPTER 13

1. Alexander Dallin, The Soviet Union at the United Nations
(N.Y.: Praeger, 1962), p. 192. Also Philip E. Mosely, "The Soviet
Union and the United Nations," IO, Summer 1965 (Vol. 19, No. 3),
pp. 666-77.

2. See Lincoln P. Bloomfield, The United Nations and US
Foreign Policy: A New Look at the National Interest (Boston: Little,
Brown, 1967, Rev. Ed.), pp. 239-45; and Inis L. Claude, Jr., The
Changing United Nations (N.Y.: Random House, 1967), Chap. 4.

3. See David A. Kay, "Instruments of Influence in the UN

Political Process," in David A. Kay (ed.), The United Nations Political
System (N.Y.: John Wiley, 1967), pp. 92-107.

4. Indonesia withdrew from the UN in January 1965, but resumed
full participation on September 28, 1966. Official announcement explained that Indonesia's temporary absence was "based not upon a
withdrawal from the UN, but upon a cessation of cooperation." See
UN Monthly Chronicle, October 1966 (Vol. 3, No. 9), p. 11. South
Africa has rejected almost 100 resolutions of the General Assembly,
refused admittance to the state for UN investigatory commissions,
and insisted that its stand on South West Africa's status and the
apartheid system are matters of her "domestic jurisdiction." Attempts
by the Commonwealth of Nations to force a liberalization of her social
policies resulted in South Africa's withdrawal from the Commonwealth.
But South Africa has not withdrawn from the UN. Colin de B. Webb
contends that the UN membership is what saves South Africa from
complete isolation. See "The Foreign Policy of the Union of South
Africa," in Joseph E. Black and Kenneth W. Thompson (eds.), Foreign
Policies in a World of Change (N.Y.: Harper and Row, 1963), pp. 425-49.

5. Of all the "sovereign" entities who are not members of the
UN, only Western Samoa and Nauru are known to have voluntarily declined membership without legal restriction (Switzerland's neutrality)
or political difficulties (the divided Germany, Korea, and Vietnam);
Vatican officials expressed an interest in membership in the UN recently. See AP dispatch, Dayton Daily News, November 12, 1967,
p. 3-C.

6. Selected Works, III, pp. 306-07.

7. "The Korean campaign, a fading memory after a decade of
swift change, may be dismissed as a confusing exception to all the
rules, unique and unrepeatable . . ." Andrew Boyd, United Nations:
Piety, Myth, and Truth (Baltimore: Pelican Books, 1964), p. 47.

8. See PR, October 8, 1965 (Vol. 8, No. 41), p. 8; December
24, 1965 (Vol. 8, No. 52), p. 16.

9. See PR, December 9, 1966 (Vol. 9, No. 50), pp. 26-27;
December 8, 1967 (Vol. 10, No. 50), pp. 20-21.

10. UN membership has increased to 126 as of December 21,
1969. Most members have spoken on the question of China's representation in general debate or in the debate on this specific agenda
item or both.

11. In 1967, e.g., the General Assembly took five roll-call votes in relation to the question of Chinese representation. The results showed that some members voted in favor of Peking's position in some resolutions and opposed in others. See UN Monthly Chronicle, December 1967 (Vol. 4, No. 11), pp. 28-35; NYT, November 29, 1967, pp. 1, 4.

NOTES ON CHAPTER 14

1. Franz Schurmann, Ideology and Organization in Communist China (Berkeley and Los Angeles: University of Calif. Press, 1966), pp. 18, 29-30.

2. International organizations themselves also are categorized in accordance with their ideological orientations and given different treatments. See Byron S. J. Weng, "Some Conditions of Peking's Participation in International Organizations," in Jerome A. Cohen (ed.), China and International Law: Cases (Cambridge, Mass.: Havard Univ. Press, forthcoming).

3. Wan Chia-chun, What is the United Nations (Peking, 1956), pp. 40-41. Quoted in Hungdah Chiu and R. R. Edwards, "Communist China's Attitude Toward the United Nations: A Legal Analysis," AJIL, January 1968 (Vol. 62, No. 1), note 2, p. 48.

4. Chiu and Edwards, Supra, note 2, p. 45.

5. TWKHWCC, II, pp. 7, 9.

6. "Nothing contained in the present Charter shall authorize the UN to intervene in matters which are essentially within the domestic jurisdiction of any state or shall require the Members to submit such matters to settlement under the present Charter; but this principle shall not prejudice the application of enforcement measures under Chapter VII." (UN Charter, Art. 2, Para. 7).

7. See, e.g., "Chinese Foreign Ministry Statement on Sino-American Talks," PC, February 1, 1956, Supplement.

8. Note on the Korean Question Delivered by the Ministry of Foreign Affairs of Communist China to the British Charge d 'Affaires in Peking on March 4, 1959. See PR, March 10, 1959 (Vol. 2, No. 10), p. 21.

9. SCMP, November 16, 1956 (No. 1412), p. 22.

10. Kuo Ch'un, The United Nations (Peking, 1956), p. 15. Quoted in Chiu and Edwards, Supra, note 2, p. 48, note 77.

11. Jerome Ch'en, Mao and the Chinese Revolution (N.Y.: Oxford University Press, 1965), p. 6.

12. Quotation is from an interview with Erskin Childers and Robert McKenzie, May 1, 1966. See UN Monthly Chronicle, May 1966 (Vol. 3, No. 5), pp. 60-61.

13. Inis L. Claude, Jr., Swords into Plowshares: The Problems and Progress of International Organization (N.Y.: Random House, second ed., 1959), p. 106.

14. John Stoessinger, The United Nations and the Superpowers: United States-Soviet Interaction at the United Nations (N.Y.: Random House, 1965), pp. 30-32.

15. Guy Wint, "The First Decade: China and Asia," CQ, January-March 1960 (No. 1), p. 66.

16. Sheldon Appleton, "Red China and the UN," Current History, September 1962 (Vol. 41, No. 241), p. 143.

17. Reportedly, K'ang Sheng said in a speech on September 1, 1967, that the "three surrenders, one extinction" charge was mistaken, since it is the Central Committee that lays down foreign policy guidelines. Hung Wei Pao, September 15, 1967. See Melvin Gurtov, "The Foreign Ministry and Foreign Affairs during the Cultural Revolution," CQ, October-December 1969 (No. 40), p. 91.

18. PR, January 15, 1965 (Vol. 8, No. 3), pp. 6-9.

19. Scott A. Boorman, The Protracted Game: A Wei Ch'i Interpretation of Maoist Revolutionary Strategy (N.Y.: Oxford University Press, 1969).

20. Chou En-lai. "Political Report to the Third Session of the First National Committee of the CPPCC," NCNA, November 2, 1951. See also A. M. Halpern, "The Foreign Policy Uses of Chinese Revolutionary Model," CQ, July-September, 1961 (No. 7), pp. 1-16.

21. Ch'en Yi, "Ten years of Struggle for World Peace and Human Progress," in Ten Glorious Years (Peking: Foreign Languages Press, 1960). Quoted in Halpern, Supra, note 26, p. 10.

22. Based on a one-sheet reprint of Mao's inscription produced in Peking.

23. PR, November 10, 1967 (Vol. 10, No. 46), pp. 9-16.

BIBLOGRAPHY

MAINLAND CHINA SOURCES

A. General Reference Works

1. Hui-huang Ti Shih-nien (Glorious Ten Years), Peking: Jen-min Jih-pao Ch'u-pan She, 1959, 2 vols.

2. I-chiu-ssu-chiu Nien Shou-ts'e (1949 Handbook), Hong Kong: Hua-shang Pao-she, 1949.

3. Jen-min Shou-ts'e (People's Handbook), Shanghai, Tientsin, Peking: Ta-kung Pao, 1950-53, since 1955.

4. Shih-chieh Chih-shih Nien-chien (World Knowledge Yearbook, 1957, 1958), Peking: Shih-chieh Chih-shih Ch'u-pan She, 1957, 1958.

5. Wei-ta Ti Shih-nien: Chung-hua Jen-min Kung-ho Kuo Ching-chi ho Wen-hua Chien-she ti T'ung-chi (Ten Great Years: Statistics of the Economic and Cultural Achievements of the People's Republic of China), Peking: Kuo-Chia T'ung Chu (National Statistics Bureau), 1959.

B. Official Government and Party Documents

Kuo-wu Yuan (The State Council):

1. Chung-hua Jen-min Kung-ho-kuo K'ai-kuo Wen-hsien (Collection of Documents on the Founding of the People's Republic of China), Hong Kong: Hsin Min-chu Ch'u-pan She, 1949.

2. Chung-hua Jen-min Kung-ho-kuo T'iao-Yueh Chi (Treaties of the People's Republic of China), Peking: Fa-lu Ch'u-pan She, since 1957

3. Chung-hua Jen-min Kung-ho-kuo Tui-wai Kuan-hsi Wen-chien Chi (Documents of Foreign Affairs of the People's Republic of China), Peking: Shih-chieh Chih-shih Ch'u-pan She, since 1957.

4. China Accuses! Speeches of the Special Representative of the Central People's Government of the People's Republic of China at the United Nations, Peking: Foreign Languages Press, 1951.

5. Important Documents Concerning the Question of Taiwan, Peking: Foreign Languages Press, 1955.

6. Kuan-yu Kuo-chi Kung-ch'an-chu-i Yun-tung Tsung Lu-hsien Ti Chien-i Ho Yu-kuan Wen-chien (A Proposal Concerning the General Line of the International Communist Movement and Related Documents), Peking: Jen-min Ch'u-pan She, 1963.

7. Kuo Chi T'iao Yueh Chi (Collection of International Treaties), Peking: Shih-chieh Chih-shih She, 1950-52.

8. Tai-wan Wen t'i Wen-chein (Collected Documents on the Taiwan Question), Peking: Jen-min Ch'u-pan She, 1955.

Ch'uan-kuo Jen-min Tai-piao Ta-hui (National People's Congress):

1. Chung-hua Jen-min Kung-ho-kuo Ch'uan-kuo Jen-min Tai-piao Ta-hui Ch'ang-wu Wei-yuan-hui Kung-pao (Official Gazette of the Standing Committee of the National People's Congress of the People's Republic of China), Peking, Irregular.

2. Chung-hua Jen-min Kung-ho-kuo Ti-i-chieh Ch'uan-kuo Jen-min Tai-piao Ta-hui Ti-i-tz'u Hui-i Wen-chien (Documents of the First Session of the First National People's Congress of the People's Republic of China), Peking: Jen-min Ch'u-pan She, 1955.

3. Chung-hua Jen-min Kung-ho-kuo Ti-i-chieh Ch'uan-kuo Jen-min Tai-piao Ta-hui Ti-erh-tz'u Hui-i Wen-chien (Documents of the Second Session of the First National People's Congress of the People's Republic of China), Peking: Jen-min Ch'u-pan She, 1956.

4. Chung-hua Jen-min Kung-ho-kuo Ti-i-chieh Ch'uan-kuo Jen-min Tai-piao Ta-hui Ti-san-tz'u Hui-i Wen-chien (Documents of the Third Session of the First National People's Congress of the People's Republic of China), Peking: Jen-min Ch'u-pan She, 1956.

5. Chung-hua Jen-min Kung-ho-kuo Ti-i-chieh Ch'uan-kuo Jen-min Tai-piao Ta-hui Ti-ssu-tz'u Hui-i-k'an (Compedium of Documents of the Fourth Session of the First National People's Congress of the People's Republic of China), Peking: Jen-min Ch'u-pan She, 1957.

6. Second Session of the Second National People's Congress of the People's Republic of China (Documents), Peking: Foreign Languages Press, 1960.

Chung-kuo Kung-ch'an Tang (Communist Party of China):

1. Chung-kuo Kung-ch'an-Tang Ch'uan-kuo Tai-piao Hui-i Wen-chien (Documents of the National Conference of the Chinese Communist Party), Peking: Jen-min Ch'u-pan She, 1955.

2. Chung-kuo Kung-ch'an-tang Ti-pa-chieh Chung-yang Wei-yuan-hui Ti-liu-tz'u Ch-uan-t'i Hui-i Wen-chien (Documents of the Sixth Plenary Session of the Eighth Central Committee of the Communist Party of China), Peking: Jen-min Ch'u-pan She, 1958.

3. Chung-kuo Kung-ch'an-tang Ti-pa-chieh Chung-yang Wei-yuan-hui Ti-pa-tz'u Ch'uan-t'i Hui-i Wen-chien (Documents of the Eighth Plenary Session of the Eighth Central Committee of the Communist Party of China), Peking: Jen-min Ch'u-pan She, 1959.

4. Chung-kuo Kung-ch'an-tang Ti-pa-chieh Chung-yang Wei-yuan-hui Ti-chiu-t'zu Ch'uan-t'i Hui-i Kung-pao (Communique of the Ninth Plenary Session of the Eighth Central Committee of the Communist Party of China), Hong Kong: Sheng-huo Tu-shu Hsin-chih San-lien Shu-tien, 1961.

5. Circular of the Central Committee of the Communist Party of China, Peking: Foreign Languages Press, 1966.

6. Communique of the Eleventh Plenary Session of the Eighth Central Committee of the Communist Party of China, Peking: Foreign Languages Press, 1966.

7. Communique of the Enlarged 12th Plenary Session of the Eighth Central Committee of the Communist Party of China, Peking: Foreign Language Press, 1968.

8. "Communique of the Second Plenary Session of the Ninth Central Committee of the Communist Party of China." Peking Review, Vol. 13, No. 37, September 11, 1970, pp. 5-7.

9. Decision of the Central Committee of the Chinese Communist Party Concerning the Great Proletarian Cultural Revolution, Peking: Foreign Languages Press, 1966.

10. "Documents of the Ninth National Congress of the Communist Party of China." Peking Review, Vol. 12, No. 18, April 30, 1969. A Special Issue.

11. Eighth National Congress of the Communist Party of China, Peking: Foreign Languages Press, 1956, 3 vols.

12. The Great Proletarian Cultural Revolution in China, Books 1-10, Peking: Foreign Languages Press, 1966-67.

13. Second Session of the Eighth National Congress of the Communist Party of China, Peking: Foreign Languages Press, 1958.

C. Semi-Official Publications

1. Afro-Asian Solidarity Against Imperialism: A Collection of Documents, Speeches and Press Interviews from the Visits of Chinese Leaders to Thirteen African and Asian Countries, Peking: Foreign Languages Press, 1964.

2. Apologists of Neo-Colonialism, Peking: Foreign Languages Press, 1963.

3. China and the Asian-African Conference (Documents), Peking: Foreign Languages Press, 1955.

4. Chinese-African People's Friendship Association, The Chinese People Resolutely Support the Just Struggle of the African People, Peking: Foreign Languages Press, 1961.

5. Chinese People's Institute of Foreign Affairs, Oppose the New U.S. Plots to Create "Two Chinas," Peking: Foreign Languages Press, 1960-61.

6. _____, Oppose U. S. Military Provocations in the Taiwan Strait Area, Peking, Foreign Languages Press, 1958.

7. _____, Oppose U. S. Occupation of Taiwan and "Two Chinas" Plot, Peking: Foreign Languages Press, 1958.

8. _____, A Victory for the Five Principles of Peaceful Co-existence: Important Documents on the Settlement of the Sino-Burmese Boundary Question Through Friendly Negotiations and on the Development of Friendly Relations Between China and Burma, Peking: Foreign Languages Press, 1960.

9. Chung-kuo Jen-min K'ang-mei Yuan-ch'ao Tsung-hui, Hsuan-ch'uan Pu (Chinese People's Resist-America Aid-Korea Campaign

Committee, Propaganda Department), Wei-ta Ti K'ang-mei-yuan-ch'ao
Yun-tung (The Great Resist-America Aid-Korea Campaign), Peking:
Jen-min Ch'u-pan She, 1954.

10. Chung-kuo Jen-min Pao-wei Shih-chieh Ho-p'ing Fan-tui
Mei-kuo Ch'in-lueh Wei-yuan Hui (Chinese People's Committee for
World Peace and Against American Aggression), Ch'ao-hsien T'ing-
chan T'an-p'an Wen T'i (Cease-fire and Armistice Negotiations in
Korea), Peking: Shih-chieh Chih-shih Ch'u-pan She, 1951-52.

11. Mao Tse-tung, "People of the World, Unite and Defeat the
U.S. Aggressors and all Their Running Dogs!" Peking Review, May
23, 1970. Special Issue.

12. _____, Quotations from Chairman Mao Tse-tung, Peking:
Foreign Languages Press, 1966.

13. _____, Selected Military Writings, Peking: Foreign
Language Press, 1963.

14. _____, Selected Works of Mao Tse-tung, Peking: Foreign
Languages Press, 1961-65, 4 vols.

15. Peaceful Coexistence--Two Diametrically Opposed Policies,
Peking: Foreign Languages Press, 1963.

16. People of the World, Unite and Defeat the U.S. Aggressors
And All Their Lackeys, Peking: Foreign Languages Press, 1967.

17. People of the World, Unite! For TheComplete, Thorough,
Total and Resolute Prohibition and Destruction of Nuclear Weapons!
Peking: Foreign Languages Press, 1963.

18. Selected Documents on Sino-Indian Relations (December
1961-May 1962), Peking: Foreign Languages Press, 1962.

19. Sino-Indian Boundary Question, Peking: Foreign Languages
Press, 1962.

20. Sino-Soviet Alliance--Mighty Bulwark of World Peace,
Peking: Foreign Languages Press, 1960.

21. Statements by Mao Tse-tung Calling on the People of the
World to Unite to Oppose the Aggressive and Bellicose Policies of U.S.
Imperialism and Defend World Peace, Peking: Foreign Languages
Press, 1964.

22. Ti-erh-chien Ya-fei Jen-min T'uan-chien Ta-hui Wen-chien Hui-pien (Collected Documents of the Second Asian-African People's Solidarity Conference), Peking: Shih-chieh Chih-shih Ch'u-pan She, 1960.

23. Two Different Lines on the Question of War and Peace, Peking: Foreign Languages Press, 1963.

24. Two Tactics, One Aim: An Exposure of the Peace Tricks of U.S. Imperialism, Peking: Foreign Languages Press, 1960.

25. Ya-fei Hui-i Wen-chien Hsuan-chi (Selected Documents of the Asian-African Conference), Peking: Shih-chieh Chih-shih She, 1955.

D. Books and Pamphlets

1. Chan-wang Liu-shih Nien-tai (Prospects of the 1960's), Hong Kong: Shan-lien Shu-tien, 1960.

2. Chen, Po-ta, et al., Lun Liang-chung Shih-chieh Kuan (On the Two World Views), Hong Kong: San-lien Shu-tien, 1960.

3. Cheng-feng Wen-hsien (Documents on the Rectification Campaign), Hong Kong: Hsin Min-chu Ch'u-pan She, 1949 Enlarged Edition.

4. Ch'ing, Ju-chi, Mei-kuo Ch'in-lueh Shih (History of American Aggression in Taiwan), Peking: Chung-kuo Ch'ing-nien Ch'u-pan She, 1955.

5. Hsien-tai Kuo-chi Fa Shang Ti Chi-pen Yuan-tse Ho Wen-t'i, Kuo-chi Fa Len-wen (Essential Principles and Problems of Modern International Law, Essays on International Law), Vol. 1, Peking: Fa-lu Ch'u-pan She, 1956.

6. Hsien-tai Ying-mei Kuo-chi Fa Ti Ssu-hsiang Tung-hsiang (Trends in the Thought of Modern Anglo-American International Law), Peking: Fa-lu Ch'u-pan She, 1963.

7. Li, Ping, Jen-shih Wuo-men Ti Shih-chieh (Recognizing Our World), Peking: Kung-jen Ch'u-pan She, 1952.

8. Liao, Kai-lung, From Yenan to Peking: The Chinese People's War of National Liberation, Peking: Foreign Languages Press, 1954.

9. Lien-ho-kuo Wang Na-li Ch'u? (Whither the United Nations?), Hong Kong: San-lien Shu-tien, 1965.

10. Lin, Huan-p'ing, Chen-yang Jen-shih Che-ke Shih-chieh (How to Recognize This World), Hong Kong: Hsin Shao-nien Ch'u-pan She, 1950.

11. Lun "Chih Lao-Hu" Chuan-chi (A Special Collection of Essays on "The Paper Tiger"), Hong Kong: San-lien Shu-tien, 1958.

12. Pa Mei-ti-kuo-chu-i Kan-ch'u Ya-chou Ch'u (Drive the American Imperialists Out of Asia), Hong Kong: San-lien Shu-tien, 1960.

13. Strong, Anna Louise, Letters from China, Peking: New World Press, 1963, 3 vols.

14. Tang-ch'ien Ku-chi Hsing-shih (Contemporary International Situation), Hong Kong: San-lien Shu-tien, 1967.

15. Wan, Chia-chun, Shen-mo Shih Lien-ho-kuo? (What is the United Nations?), Peking: 1957.

16. Wu, Yu-chang, et al., The Great Turning Point, Peking: Foreign Languages Press, 1962.

E. Select Periodicals and Articles

Periodicals:

1. Cheng-fa Yen-chiu (Studies in Government and Law), Quarterly.

2. Chieh-fang-chun Pao (Liberation Army News), Daily since 1958.

3. China Reconstructs, Monthly.

4. Hsueh-hsi (Study), Semi-monthly.

5. Hung-ch'i (Red Flag), Semi-monthly.

6. Jen-min Jih-pao (People's Daily).

7. Kuang-Ming Jih-pao (Kuang-ming Daily).

8. Kung-tso T'ung-hsun (Bulletin of Activities), Irregular. For English translations, see Chester J. Cheng, et al., (eds.), The Politics of the Chinese Red Army: A Translation of the Bulletin of Activities of the People's Liberation Army, Palo Alto, Calif.: The Hoover Institute on War, Revolution, and Peace, 1966.

9. Kuo-chi Wen-t'i Yen-chiu (Studies on International Problems), Monthly.

10. Kuo-chi Wen-t'i Yi-ts'ung (Translation Digest of International Affairs), Irregular.

11. Peking Review, Weekly.

12. People's China, Semi-monthly.

13. Shih-chieh Chih-shih (World Knowledge), Weekly, September 1934-41, Semi-monthly, since September 1945.

Articles:

1. "The Big Character Poster Supporting Ch'en Yi by 91 Officials of the Foreign Ministry," Chan Wang (Look Fortnightly) (Hong Kong), No. 155, July 16, 1968, pp. 24-26.

2. "Chou En-lai is 'China's Second Khrushchev'," Tsu Kuo (China Monthly) (Hong Kong), No. 46, January 1968, pp. 46-47.

3. Chou, Keng-sheng, "China's Legitimate Rights in the United Nations Must Be Restored," Jen-min Jih-pao (People's Daily) (Peking), December 5, 1961.

4. Hsu, Meng-shan, "Resolutely Oppose the 'One China and One Taiwan' Scheme" Jen-min Joh-pao (People's Daily) (Peking), May 24, 1964.

5. Lin, Piao, "Long Live the Victory of the People's War!" Peking Review, Vol. 8, No. 36, September 3, 1965.

6. Shao, Chin-fu, "The Absurd Theory of 'Two Chinas' and Principles of International Law," Kuo-chi Wen-t'i Yen-chiu (Studies in International Problems) (Peking), 1959, No. 2,

7. Tung, Pi-wu, "The Tenth Anniversary of the United Nations," People's China (Peking), July 16, 1955, No. 14, pp. 6-8.

8. Yang, Hsin and Ch'en Chien, "Exposing and Criticizing the Fallacious Reasoning of Imperialists on Questions Concerning National Sovereignty," Cheng-fa Yen-chiu (Studies in Government and Law) (Peking), 1964, No. 4, pp. 6-11.

SOURCES OF NON-MAINLAND
CHINA ORIGINS

A. General Reference Works

1. Ajia Seikei Gakkai (Society for Asian Political and Economic Studies), Chugoku Seiji Keizai Soran (Political and Economic Views on Present Day China), Tokyo: Nikkan Rodo Tsushinsha, 1964.

2. _____ , Chuka Jimmin Kyowakoku Gaiko Shiryo Soran (Collection of Diplomatic Documents of the People's Republic of China), Tokyo: Hitosubashi Shobo, 1960.

3. Ambekar, G. V. and V. D. Divekar (eds.), Documents on China's Relations with South and South East Asia (1949-62), Bombay: Allied Publishers Private Ltd,. 1964.

4. Balcomb, John (ed.), " The United Nations," Worldmark Encyclopedia of the Nations, Vol. 1. New York: Worldmark Press, 3rd ed., 1967.

5. Brandt, Conrad, Benjamin Schwartz, and John K. Fairbank, A Documentary History of Chinese Communism, New York: Atheneum, 1966.

6. Chen, Theodore H. E. (ed.), The Chinese Communist Regime: Documents and Commentary, New York: Praeger, 1967.

7. China Yearbook, Taipei: China Publishing Co., since 1951.

8. Fei-Ch'ing Yen-chiu Tse-chih She (Institute for the Study of Chinese Communist Problems), 1967 Fei-ch'ng Nien-pao: Shih-ch'i-nien Lai Fei-ch'ng Tsung-lan (1967 Yearbook on Chinese Communism: A Summary of Chinese Communist Situation from 1949 to 1966), Taipei: Fei-Ch'ing Yen-chiu Tsa-chih She, 1967.

9. _____ , 1968 Fei-Ch'ing Nien-pao (1968 Yearbook on Chinese Communism), Taipei, Fei-ch'ing Yen-chiu Tsa-chih She, 1968.

10. Hu, Chang-tu (ed.), China: Its People, Its Society, Its Culture, New Haven, Conn.: Human Relations Area Files, 1960.

11. Huang, Tien-chien, Fei Wei Cheng-Ch'uan Shih-pa Nien (Eighteen Years of the Chinese Communist Regime), Taipei: Cheng-chung Shutien, 1967.

12. Japan, Gaimusho, Ajiakyoku (Japan, Ministry of Foreign Affairs, Bureau of Asian Affairs), Chukyo Juyo Bunken Chu--Taiheiyo Senso Shuryoji Yori 1952 Nen Made (Collection of Important Chinese Communist Documents--From the Time of the Conclusion of the Pacific War to 1952), Tokyo, 1952.

13. _____, Chukyo No Gaiko Shiryo (Diplomatic Documents of Communist China), Tokyo: Nihon Kokusai Mondai Kenkujo, since 1961.

14. Johnston, Douglas M. and Hungdah Chiu (eds.), Agreements of the People's Republic of China, 1949-1967: A Calendar, Cambridge, Massachusetts: Harvard University Press, 1968.

15. Kuo-fan Yen-chiu Yuan, Ti-ch'ing Yen-chiu Lun-wen Pien-ts'uan Wei-yuan-hui (National War College, Editorial Committee on Studies on Enemy Situations) Ti-ch'ing Yen-chiu Lun-wen Chi (Collection of Studies on Enemy Situations), Taipei: Kuo-fang Yen-chiu Yuan, 1961, 4 vols.

16. Tew, Eyvind S. (ed.), Yearbook of International Organizations, Brussels: Union of International Associations, 11th (1966-67) ed.

B. UN Documents

1. International Court of Justice, Conditions of Admission of a State to Membership in the United Nations, Advisory Opinion of May 28, 1948. International Document Service, 1948.

2. General Assembly, Official Records.

3. Secretariat, Legal Aspects of Problems of Representation in the United Nations, Memorandum of March 8, 1950. UN Doc. S/1466.

4. Security Council, Official Records.

5. United Nations Bulletin.

6. United Nations Documents Index.

7. United Nations Monthly Chronicle.

8. United Nations Review.

9. Yearbook of the United Nations.

C. Government Documents--
the Republic of China

1. Hsing-cheng Yuan, Hsin-wen Chu (Executive Yuan, Government Information Office), Chung-kuo Yu Lien-ho-kuo (China and the United Nations), Taipei, 1961.

2. _____, Yu-kuan Tang-ch'ien Chung-yao Wen-t'i Chih Chi-pen Ts'an-k'ao Tzu-liao (Basic Reference Materials Concerning the Important Questions of Today), Taipei, 1961.

3. Overseas Chinese Publication Service, The Two Faces of China, 1961.

4. Permanent Mission of the Republic of China to the United Nations, Appeasement, Another Setback; Statement by Dr. Wei Tao-ming to the 21st Session of the General Assembly, November 18, 1966.

5. _____, China Fights for Peace and Freedom, February, 1951.

6. _____, The Representation of China in the United Nations at the Twenty-second Session of the General Assembly, n.d.

7. _____, Should Peking Be Permitted in the United Nations? Ambassador Liu Chieh's address to the Conference on the United Nations and China sponsored by the University of Pennsylvania, April 16, 1966.

8. _____, Statements on the Representation of China in the United Nations, by H. E. Dr. Wei Tao-ming at the 22nd Session of the General Assembly, November 20, 1967.

9. _____, UN Membership for Mao? Issues and Answers, November 15, 1966.

10. _____, Whither the United Nations? Address by H. E. Mr. Shen Chang-huan to the 19th Session of the General Assembly on December 21, 1964.

11. Selected Speeches and Messages of President Chiang Kai-shek, Taipei: Government Information Office, 1952.

12. Wai-chiao Pu (Ministry of Foreign Affairs), Chung-wai T'iao-yueh Chi-pien 1927-57 (Treaties Between the Republic of China and Foreign States, 1927-57), Taipei, 1958.

13. _____, Wai-chiao Pu Kung-pao (Gazette of the Ministry of Foreign Affairs), Nanking, Chungking, Taipei: Wai-chiao Pu Ch'ing-pao Ssu, May, since 1928.

D. Government Documents--
United States of America

1. Department of State, A Background Reading List of Psychological Operations With Special Emphasis on Communist China, External Research Paper 153. Washington, 1964.

2. _____, Bloc Policy Towards Underdeveloped Countries; Selective List of Publications on Soviet and Communist Chinese Policy Towards Representative Underdeveloped Countries, External Research Paper 144. Washington, 1963.

3. _____, "Legal Problems Regarding Formosa and the Offshore Islands," by Ely Maurer, Department of State Bulletin, Vol. 39, No. 1017, December 22, 1958, pp. 1005-11.

4. _____, External Research Division, Reported Agreements Between the USSR and Communist China, Washington, 1956. (Mimeographed)

5. _____, The Thought of Mao Tse-tung; A Selected List of References to the Published Works and Statements Attributed to Mao Tse-tung and to the Literature of the Chinese Communist Leader, External Research Paper 138, Washington, 1962.

6. _____, United States Relations with China, With Special Reference on the Period 1944-49 (The White Paper), Department of State Publication 3573, Washington: Government Printing Office, 1949.

7. _____, Bureau of Intelligence and Research, Chinese Communist World Outlook: A Handbook of Chinese Communist Statements, the Public Record of a Militant Ideology. Department of State Publication 7379, Washington: Government Printing Office, 1962.

8. House of Representatives, Committee on Foreign Affairs, Expressions by the House of Representatives, the Senate, and the Committee on Foreign Affairs that the Chinese Communists Are Not Entitled to and Should Not Be Recognized to Represent China in the United Nations, 86th Congress, 1st Session, 1959.

9. _____, The Future United States in Asia and in the Pacific; Hearings before the Subcommittee on Asian and Pacific Affairs, 90th Congress, 2nd Session, February-April 1968, Washington: Government Printing Office, 1968.

10. _____, Sino-Soviet Conflict: Report on Sino-Soviet Conflict and Its Implications by the Subcommittee on the Far East and the Pacific, together with Hearings, 89th Congress, 1st Session. March 1965, Washington: Government Printing Office, 1965.

11. _____, United States Policy Toward Asia; Hearings before the Subcommittee on the Far East and the Pacific, 89th Congress, 2nd Session, January-March 1966, 2 Parts, Washington: Government Printing Office, 1966.

12. _____, Committee on Un-American Activities, Intellectual Freedom--Red China Style; Hearings, 87th Congress, 2nd Session, May 24 and 25, 1962, Washington: Government Printing Office, 1962.

13. _____, Senate, Committee on Armed Services and Committee on Foreign Relations, Military Situation in the Far East; Hearings, 82nd Congress, 1st Session, 1951, Washington: Government Printing Office, 1951, 5 Parts.

14. _____, Committee on Foreign Relations, Study of United States Foreign Policy: Summary of Views of Retired Foreign Service Officers, 86th Congress, 1st Session, Washington: Government Printing Office, 1959.

15. _____, The United States and the Korean Problem; Documents Compiled for the Committee, 83rd Congress, 1st Session, Washington: Government Printing Office, 1953.

16. _____, United States Foreign Policy: Asia; Studies prepared by Conlon Associates, Ltd., No. 5, 86th Congress, 1st Session, Washington: Government Printing Office, 1959.

17. _____, U.S. Policy with Respect to Mainland China; Hearings, 89th Congress, 2nd Session, March 1966, Washington: Government Printing Office, 1966.

18. _____, Peking's Approach to Negotiations; Selected Writings compiled by the Subcommittee on National Security and International Operations, 91st Congress, 1st Session, Washington: Government Printing Office, 1969.

19. Senate, Committee on Government Operations, Staffing Procedures and Problems in Communist China; A Study submitted by Subcommittee on National Security, Staffing and Operations, Washington: Government Printing Office, 1963.

20. _____, Committee on the Judiciary, Chinese and Russian Communist Compete for Foreign Support; Testimony of Tung Chi-p'ing, August 20, 1964, before a Staff Conference of the Subcommittee . . ., 88th Congress, 2nd Session, Washington: Government Printing Office, 1964.

21. _____, Institute of Pacific Relations; Report of the Subcommittee on Internal Security, 82nd Congress, 1st Session, Washington: Government Printing Office, 1952.

22. _____, Institute of Pacific Relations; Hearings before the Subcommittee on Internal Security, 82nd Congress, 1st Session, Washington: Government Printing Office, 1959, 15 Parts.

23. _____, Testimony of a Defector from Communist China; Hearings before the Subcommittee to Investigate the Administration of the Internal Security Act and other Internal Security Laws, November 29, 1962, 87th Congress, 2nd Session, Washington: Government Printing Office, 1962.

24. _____, Testimony of Frances Yuan and Col. Ve Shen Hsiang; Hearings before the Subcommittee . . ., 87th Congress, 2nd Session, Washington: Government Printing Office, 1963.

25. U.S. Congress, Joint Committee on Atomic Energy, Scope, Magnitude, and Implications of the United States Antiballistic Missile Program; Hearings before the Subcommittee on Military Applications,

90th Congress, 1st Session, November 6 and 7, 1967, Washington: Government Printing Office, 1968.

26. _____, Joint Economic Committee, An Economic Profile of Mainland China; Studies prepared for the Joint Economic Committee, 90th Congress, 1st Session, Washington: Government Printing Office, 1967, 2 vols.

27. _____, Mainland China in the World Economy; Hearings, Report together with Supplemental Views, 90th Congress, 1st Session, April 1967, Washington: Government Printing Office, 1967.

E. Books, Dissertations, Pamphlets

1. A New China Policy: Some Quaker Proposals--A Report Prepared for the American Friends Service Committee, New Haven, Connecticut: Yale University Press, 1965.

2. Adams, Mervyn W., Communist China and the United Nations--A Study of China's Developing Attitudes Towards the UN Role in International Peace and Security, MA Thesis, Columbia University, 1964.

3. Adams, Ruth (ed.), Contemporary China, N.Y.: Vintage Books, 1966.

4. Akra, A. Neylan, Some Aspects of the Problem of Chinese Participation in the United Nations, Ph. D. Dissertation, University of Pittsburgh, 1965.

5. Appadorai, A., The Bandung Conference, New Delhi: Indian Council of World Affairs, 1955.

6. _____, Appleton, Sheldon, The Eternal Triangle ? Communist China, the US and the UN, East Lansing: Michigan State University Press, 1961.

7. _____, The Question of Representation of China in the United Nations, Ph. D. Dissertation, University of Minnesota, 1961.

8. Armbruster, Frank E., et al., China Briefing, Chicago: University of Chicago Center for Policy Study, 1968.

9. Ballantine, Joseph W., Formosa, A Problem for U.S. Foreign Policy, The Brookings Institute, 1952.

10. Barnett, A. Doak, Cadres, Bureaucracy, and Political Power in Communist China, N.Y.: Columbia University Press, 1967.

11. _____, China after Mao, with selected documents, Princeton, N.J.: Princeton University Press, 1967.

12. _____, China on the Eve of Communist Takeover, N.Y.: Praeger, 1963.

13. _____, Communist China and Asia, N.Y.: Vintage Books, 1960.

14. _____, Communist China in Perspective, N.Y.: Praeger, 1962.

15. _____, Communist China: The Years 1949-55, N.Y.: Praeger, 1964.

16. _____, Communist Strategies in Asia, N.Y.: Praeger, 1963.

17. _____, "The United States and Communist China," in The American Assembly, The United States and the Far East, N.Y.: Columbia University Graduate School of Business, 1956, pp. 105-71.

18. Bloomfield, Lincoln P., The United Nations and U.S. Foreign Policy: A New Look at the National Interest, Boston: Little, Brown, 1967, Rev. ed.

19. Blum, Robert (ed. A. Doak Barnett), The United States and China in World Affairs, N.Y.: McGraw-Hill, 1966.

20. Boorman, Howard L., et al., The Moscow-Peking Axis, N.Y.: Harper, 1957.

21. Bouscaren, Anthony T., compiler, The Case for Free China, N.Y.: Twin Circle Publishing Co., 1967.

22. Boyd, R. G., Communist China's Foreign Policy, N.Y.: Praeger, 1962.

23. Brook, David, The United Nations and the China Dilemma, N.Y.: Vantage Press, 1956.

24. Brown, Benjamin and Fred Green, Chinese Representation:

A Case Study in United Nations Political Affairs, N.Y.: Woodrow
Wilson Foundation, 1955.

25. Buchan, Alstar (ed.), China and the Peace of Asia, 1965,
N.Y.: Praeger, 1966.

26. Buss, Claude, People's Republic of China, Princeton, N.J.:
Van Nostrand, 1962.

27. Chang, Hsin-hai, America and China: A New Approach to
China, N.Y.: Simon and Schuster, 1966.

28. Chen, Chiu-shan, American Recognition and Non-Recognition Policies in China: A Legal, Historical and Political Analysis,
Ph.D. Dissertation, Southern Illinois University, 1963.

29. Chen, Lung-chu and Harold D. Lasswell, Formosa, China
and the United Nations: Formosa in the World Community, N.Y.:
St. Martin's Press, 1967.

30. Chen, Ti-chiang, The International Law of Recognition,
N.Y.: Praeger, 1951.

31. Chin, Ssu-k'ai, Ten Years of Communist China's Foreign
Policy, in Tsu-kuo Chou-k'an She (China Monthly) (ed.) Chung Kung
Shih Nien (Ten Years of Communist China), Hong Kong: Yu-lein
Ch'u-pan She (Union Research Institute), 1960, pp. 322-69.

32. China and U.S. Far East Policy, 1945-66, Washington:
Congressional Quarterly Service, 1967.

33. China Institute of International Affairs, China and the
United Nations, N.Y.: Manhattan Publishing Co., 1959.

34. Chiu, Sin-ming, Some Basic Conceptions and Rules of
Conduct of Chinese Communism, Air Force Personnel and Training
Research Center, Texas, 1955.

35. Chow, Ching-wen, Ten Years of Storm, N.Y.: Holt, Rinehart
and Winston, 1960.

36. Clark, Gerald, Impatient Giant: Red China Today, N.Y.:
David McKay, 1959.

37. Clark, Gregory, In Fear of China, Melborne: Landsdowne
Press, 1967.

38. Claude, Inis L. Jr., The Changing United Nations, N.Y.: Random House, 1967.

39. _____, Swords into Plowshares: The Problems and Progress of International Organization, N.Y.: Random House, third ed., 1964.

40. Clubb, Oliver Edmund, Twentieth Century China, N.Y.: Columbia University Press, 1964.

41. Cooley, John K., East Wind over Africa: Red China's African Offensive, N.Y.: Walker, 1965.

42. Council of Foreign Relations, American Policy Towards China, A Report on the Views of Leading Citizens in 23 Cities, N.Y.: Council of Foreign Relations, 1950.

43. Dallin, Alexander, The Soviet Union at the United Nations, N.Y.: Praeger, 1962.

44. Davies, John P. Jr., Foreign and Other Affairs, N.Y.: W. W. Norton & Co., 1964.

45. Davies, Forrest and R.A. Hunter, The Red China Lobby, N.Y.: Fleet Publishing Corp., 1963

46. Dorrill, William F., Problems of Leadership and Succession in Communist China, Santa Monica, Calif.: Rand Corp., 1965

47. Dutt, Vidya Prakash, China's Foreign Policy, 1958-62, N.Y.: Asia Publishing House, 1964.

48. Eckstein, Alexander, China (People's Republic of China, 1949-   ) Commerce, N.Y.: McGraw-Hill, 1966

49. Elegant, Robert S., The Centre of the World: Communism and the Mind of China, London: Methuen, 1963.

50. Faribank, John K., China: The People's Middle Kingdom and the U.S.A., Cambridge, Mass.: The Belknap Press of Harvard University Press, 1967.

51. _____, The United States and China, Cambridge, Massachusetts: Harvard University Press, 1958.

52. Falk, Richard A., The Authority of the UN over Non-Members, Princeton, N.J.: Princeton University Press, 1965.

53. Fitzgerald, C. P., The Chinese View of Their Place in the World, London: Oxford University Press, 1964.

54. Floyd, David, Mao Against Khrushchev: A Short History of the Sino-Soviet Conflict, N.Y.: Praeger, 1963.

55. Friedman, Edward, "Peking and Washington: Is Taiwan the Obstacle ?" in Bruce Douglass and Ross Terrill (eds.), China and Ourselves: Explorations and Revisions by a New Generation, Boston: Beacon Press, 1969, pp. 155-73.

56. Geoffroy-Dechaume, Francois, China Looks at the World, N.Y.: Random House, 1967.

57. Gittings, John, The Role of the Chinese Army, New York: Oxford University Press, 1967.

58. _____, (ed.), The Sino-Soviet Dispute 1956-63, London: Oxford University Press, 1964.

59. Greene, Felix, Awakened China: The Country Americans Don't Know, Doubleday, 1961.

60. _____, A Curtain of Ignorance: How the American Public Has Been Misinformed about China, Garden City, N.Y.: Doubleday, 1964.

61. Grew, Joseph C., Invasion Alert: Red China Drives on the U.N., Baltimore: Maran Publishers, 1956.

62. Griffith, Samuel B. (Gen.), Mao Tse-Tung on Guerrilla Warfare, N.Y.: Praeger, 1961.

63. _____, Peking and Peoples' Wars: An Analysis of Statements by Official Spokesmen of the CCP on the Subject of Revolutionary Strategy, N.Y.: Praeger, 1966.

64. Griffith, William E., Albania and the Sino-Soviet Rift, Cambridge, Mass.: MIT Press, 1963.

65. Gross, Ernest A., "Sino-American Relations," in Christian Responsibility on a Changing Planet, N.Y.: National Council of Churches of Christ in the U.S.A., 1959.

66. Grzybowski, K., The Socialist Commonwealth of Nations, New Haven, Connecticut: Yale University Press, 1964.

67. Gurtov, Melvin, The First Vietnam Crisis: Chinese Communist Strategy and United States Involvement, 1953-54, N.Y.: Columbia University Press, 1967.

68. Haas, Ernst B., Collective Security and the Future International System, Denver, Colorado: The Social Science Foundation and Graduate School of International Studies, University of Denver, 1968.

69. Halperin, Morton H., China and Nuclear Proliferation, Chicago: University of Chicago Center for Policy Study, 1966.

70. _____, China and the Bomb, N.Y.: Praeger, 1965.

71. _____, Is China Turning In? Cambridge, Mass.: Harvard University Center for International Affairs, 1965.

72. _____, Sino-Soviet Relations and Arms Control, Cambridge, Mass.: MIT Press, 1967.

73. _____, and Dwight H. Perkins, Communist China and Arms Control, N.Y.: Praeger, 1965.

74. Halpern, A. M., "Communist China's Demands on the World," in Morton A. Kaplan (ed.), The Revolution in World Politics, N.Y.: John Wiley, 1962.

75. _____, (ed.), Policies Toward China: Views from Six Continents, N.Y.: McGraw-Hill, 1965.

76. Hamm, Harry, Albania-China's Beachhead in Europe, N.Y.: Praeger, 1963.

77. _____, China: Empire of the 700 Million, Garden City, N.Y.: Doubleday, 1966.

78. Hamrell, Sven, The Soviet Bloc, China and Africa, Uppsala: Scandinavian Institute of African Studies, 1964.

79. Henderson, H.W., Why Communist China Should Not Be Admitted to the UN, Frinds of Free China Association, 1956.

80. Hensman, C. R., China--Yellow Peril? Red Hope?, London: SCM Press, 1968.

81. Hevi, Emmanuel John, An African Student in China, N.Y.: Praeger, 1963.

82. _____, The Dragon's Embrace, N.Y.: Praeger, 1966.

83. Higgins, Rosalyn, The Development of International Law Through the Political Organs of the UN, London: Oxford University Press, 1963.

84. Hinton, Harold C., Communist China in World Politics, Boston: Houghton Mifflin, 1966.

85. Hornbeck, Stanley Kuhl, A Brief Study of Some Facts and Many Not-Facts Regarding China and United States "China Policy," N.Y.: American-Asian Educational Exchange, 1961.

86. Houn, Franklin W., A Short History of Chinese Communism, Englewood Cliffs, N.J.: Prentice-Hall, 1967.

87. Hsieh, Alice L., Communist China's Strategy in the Nuclear Era, Englewood Cliffs, N.J.: Prentice-Hall, 1962.

88. _____, The Sino-Soviet Nuclear Dialogue: 1963, Santa Monica, Calif.: Rand Corp., 1964.

89. Hsu, Kai-yu, Chou En-Lai: China's Gray Eminence, Garden City, N.Y.: Doubleday, 1968.

90. Hudson, G. F. et al., The Sino-Soviet Dispute, N.Y.: Praeger, 1961.

91. Hunter, Edward, The Blackbook on Red China, N.Y.: The Bookmailer, 1958.

92. Indian Federation of United Nations Associations, Chinese Aggression; Some Facts United Nations Associations Should Know, Delhi, 1963.

93. _____, The Fate of Panch Sheel: A Review of Sino-Indian Relations, 1948-63, Delhi, 1963.

94. Jacobs, Daniel N. (ed.), Chinese Communism, Selected Documents, N.Y.: Harper & Row, 1963.

95. Jan, George P. (ed.), Government of Communist China, San Francisco: Chandler, 1966.

96. Kahin, George McT., The Asian-African Conference, Ithaca, N.Y.: Cornell University Press, 1956.

97. Karol, K. S., China, the Other Communism, Tr., Tom Baistow, N.Y.: Hill and Wang, 1967.

98. Kay, David A. (ed.), The United Nations Political System, N.Y.: John Wiley, 1967.

99. Kerr, George H., Formosa Betrayed, Boston: Houghton Mifflin, 1965.

100. Koen, Ross K., The China Lobby in American Politics, N.Y.: The Macmillan, 1960.

101. Kubek, Anthony, How the Far East Was Lost: American Policy and the Creation of Communist China, 1941-49, Chicago: H. Regnery Co., 1963.

102. Kuo, Pin-chia, China: New Age and New Outlook, N.Y.: Knopf, 1956.

103. Lall, Arthur, How Communist China Negotiates, N.Y.: Columbia University Press, 1968.

104. Lash, Joseph P., Dag Hammarskjold--Custodian of the Brushfire Peace, Garden City, N.Y.: Doubleday, 1961.

105. Lauterpacht, Hersh, Recognition in International Law, Cambridge: Cambridge University Press, 1947.

106. Levi, Werner, Modern China's Foreign Policy, Minneapolis: University of Minnesota Press, 1953.

107. Lewis, John Wilson, Chinese Communist Party Leadership and the Succession to Mao Tse-Tung: An Appraisal of Tensions, Washington: External Research Staff, Bureau of Intelligence and Research, U.S. Department of State, 1964.

108. _____, Leadership in Communist China, Ithaca, N.Y.: Cornell University Press, 1963.

109. _____, (ed.), Major Doctrine of Communist China, N.Y.: W.W. Norton, 1964.

110. Li, Wen-pai, Chung-kung Wai-chiao Te Chien-t'ao (An Evaluation of Communist China's Foreign Policy), Hong Kong: Chih Luen Press, 1967.

111. Lie, Trygve, In the Cause of Peace, N.Y.: Macmillan, 1954.

112. Lindsay, Michael, China and the Cold War, Melbourne: Melbourne University Press, 1955.

113. Lyons, Daniel S. G., The Two Chinas, N.Y.: Twin Circle Publishing Co., 1968.

114. _____ and Stephen Pan, Voice of Peking, N.Y.: Twin Circle Publishing Co., 1967.

115. Mancall, Mark, (ed.), Formosa Today, N.Y.: Praegar, 1964.

116. McClelland, Charles A. (ed.), The United Nations: The Continuing Debate, San Francisco: Chandler Publishing Co., 1960.

117. Mendel, Douglas, The Politics of Formosan Nationalism, Berkeley and Los Angeles: University of California Press, 1970.

118. Mezerik, A. G. (ed.), China Representation in the United Nations, N.Y.: International Review Service, 1965.

119. Mishra, Vaidyanath, Peking's World Network: Survey of China Lobby in Five Continents, New Delhi, Perspective Publications, 1965.

120. Modelski, George, International Conference on the Settlement of the Laotian Question, 1961-62, Camberra: Department of International Relations, Australian National University, 1962.

121. _____ (ed.), Seato: Six Studies, Melbourne: F. W. Cheshire, 1962.

122. Morello, Frank P., The International Legal Status of Formosa, The Hague: Martinus Nijhoff, 1966.

123. Morgenthau, Hans J., "The China Policy of the United States," in Hans J. Morgenthau, (ed.), The Restoration of American Politics, Chicago: University of Chicago Press, 1962, pp. 395-64.

124. _____, "The Formosa Resolution of 1955," in Hans J. Morgenthau, (ed.) The Impasse of American Foreign Policy, Chicago: University of Chicago Press, 1962, pp. 278-82.

125. Neuhauser, Charles, Third World Politics: China and the Afro-Asian People's Solidarity Organization, 1957-67, Cambridge, Mass.: East Asian Research Center, Havard University, 1968.

126. Newman, Robert P., Recognition of Communist China? A Study in Argument, N.Y.: Macmillan, 1961.

127. Nomad, Max, Political Heretics, From Plato to Mao Tse-tung, Ann Arbor: University of Michigan Press, 1963.

128. North, Robert C., The Foreign Relations of China, Belmont, Calif.: Dickenson Publishing Co., 1969.

129. _____, Kuomintang and Chinese Communist Elites, Palo Alto, Calif.: Stanford University Press, 1952.

130. _____, Moscow and Chinese Communists, Palo Alto, Calif.: Stanford University Press, 1963.

131. Paige, G. D., The Korean Decision (June 24-30, 1950), New York: Free Press, 1968.

132. Paloczi-Horvath, George, Mao Tse-tung, Emperor of Blue Ants, N.Y.: Doubleday, 1963.

133. Pan, Stephen and Raymond J. de Jaegher, Peking's Red Guard, N.Y.: Twin Circle Publishing Co., 1968.

134. Panikkar, K. M., In Two Chinas, Memoirs of a Diplomat, London: Allen and Unwin, 1955.

135. Passin, H., China's Cultural Diplomacy, N.Y.: Praeger, 1963.

136. Pentory, D. (ed.), China, The Emerging Giant, San Francisco Chandler, 1962.

137. Petrov, Vladimir, What China Policy?, Hamden, Conn.: Shoe String Press, 1961.

138. Rankin, Karl Lott, China Assignment, Seattle: University of Washington Press, 1964.

139. Reischauer, Edwin O., Beyond Vietnam: The United States and Asia, N.Y.: Vintage Books, 1967.

140. _____, Wanted: An Asian Policy, N.Y.: Alfred A. Knopf, 1955.

141. Rejai, M. (ed.), Mao Tse-tung on Revolution and War, Garden City, N.Y.: Doubleday, 1969.

142. Riggs, Fred W., Formosa under Chinese Nationalist Rule, N.Y.: Macmillan, 1952.

143. Rubenstein, Alvin S., The Soviets in International Organisations, Princeton N.J.: Princeton University Press, 1964.

144. Scalapino, Robert A., "The Foreign Policy of the People's Republic of China," in Joseph E. Black and Kenneth W. Thompson (eds.), Foreign Policies in a World of Change, N.Y.: Harper & Row, 1963, pp. 549-88.

145. _____, On the Trail of Chou En-lai in Africa, Santa Monica, Calif.: Rand Corp. Research memo., 1964.

146. Schram, Stuart, Mao Tse-tung, Paris: Editions Armand Colin, 1963.

147. _____, The Political Thought of Mao Tse-tung, N.Y.: Praeger, Second ed., 1969.

148. Schurmann, Franz, Ideology and Organization in Communist China, Berkeley and Los Angeles: University of California Press, 1966.

149. _____ and Orville Schell (eds.), Communist China: Revolutionary Reconstruction and International Confrontation, 1949 to the Present, N.Y.: Vintage Books, 1967.

150. Schwartz, B., Communism and China: Ideology in Flux, Cambridge, Mass.: Harvard University Press, 1968.

151. Singh, Lalita Prasad, The Politics of Economic Cooperation in Asia: A Study of Asian International Organizations, University of Missouri Press, 1967.

152. Singh, Nagendra, Termination of Membership of International Organizations, N.Y.: Praeger, 1958.

153. Snow, Edgar, The Other Side of the River: Red China Today, N.Y.: Random House, 1962.

154. _____, Red Star over China, N.Y.: Grove Press, 1961.

155. Spanier, John W., The Truman-Macarthur Controversy and the Korean War, Cambridge, Mass.: Belknap Press, 1959.

156. Steel, A. T., The American People and China, N.Y: McGraw-Hill, 1966.

157. Steiner, H. Arthur, The International Position of Communist China: Political and Ideological Directions of Foreign Policy, N.Y.: American Institute of Pacific Relations, 1958.

158. Stewart, Walter E., "The Soviet Policy Towards Chinese Representation in the United Nations Organization," MA Thesis, N.Y. University, Graduate School of Arts and Science, 1954.

159. Stoessinger, John G., The United Nations and the Super-powers: United States-Soviet Interaction at the United Nations, N.Y.: Random House, 1965.

160. Stone, I. F., The Hidden History of the Korean War, N.Y: Monthly Review Press, 1952.

161. Stuart, John Leighton, Fifty Years in China, N.Y.: Random House, 1954.

162. Sutton, Joseph L., "China: A New Power in Europe," in Stephen D. Kertesz (ed.), East Central Europe and the World: Developments in the Post-Stalin Era, Notre Dame, Indiana: University of Notre Dame Press, 1962, pp. 264-77.

163. Swisher, Earl, Chinese Representation in the U.S., Boulder, Colorado: University of Colorado Press, 1967.

164. Szczepanik, E. F. (ed.), Symposium on Economic and Social Problems of the Far East, Hong Kong: Hong Kong University Press, 1962.

165. Tang, Peter S. H., Communist China as a Developmental Model for Underdeveloped Countries, Washington: Research Institute of the Sino-Soviet Bloc, 1960.

166. T'ang, Wu, Chung-kuo Yu Kuo-chi Fa (China and International Law), Taipei: Chung-hua Ch'u-pan Shih-yeh Wei-yuan-huei (China Culture Publishing Foundation), 1957.

167. Taylor, George E., "Sino-Soviet Trade and Aid," in David M. Abshire and Richard V. Allen (eds.), National Security: Political, Military and Economic Strategies in the Decade Ahead, N.Y.: Praeger, for the Hoover Institution on War, Revolution, and Peace, 1963.

168. Tondel, Lyman M. Jr. (ed.), The International Position of Communist China, Dobbs Ferry, N.Y.: Oceana Publications, 1965.

169. Tsou, Tang, America's Failure in China, 1941-50, Chicago: University of Chicago Press, 1963.

170. _____, Embroilment over Quemoy: Mao, Chiang, and Dulles, Salt Lake City: University of Utah Press, 1959.

171. _____, and Ping-ti Ho (eds.), China in Crisis, Vol. I, China's Heritage and the Communist Political System; Vol. II, China's Policies in Asia and America's Alternatives, Chicago: University of Chicago Press, 1968.

172. Tung, William L., International Organization under the United Nations System, N.Y.: Thomas Y. Crowell, 1969.

173. _____, The Political Institutions of Modern China, The Hague: Martinus Nijhoff, 1964.

174. United Nations Association of the United States of America, National Policy Panel, China, The United Nations and United States Policy, An Analysis of the Issues and Principal Alternatives with Recommendations for U.S. Policy, United Nations Association of the United States of America, October 1966.

175. _____, China, the United Nations and United States Policy, An Updating of the Issues with Recommendations for U.S. Policy, UNA-USA, September 1967.

176. Van Ness, Peter, Revolution and Chinese Foreign Policy: Peking's Support for Wars of National Liberation, Berkeley: University of California Press, 1970.

177. Vatcher, William H. Jr., Panmunjom: The Story of the Korean Military Armistice Negotiations, N.Y.: Praeger, 1958.

178. Vinacke, Harold Monk, United States Policy Toward China, Cincinnati: Center for the Study of U.S. Foreign Policy, University of Cincinnati, 1961.

179. Walker, Richard L., The China Danger, Chicago: American Bar Association, 1966.

180. _____, The Continuing Struggle, N.Y.: Atheneum Press, 1958.

181. Walton, C. L., The China Recognition Problem, MA Thesis, Ohio State University, 1959.

182. Warner, Denis Ashton, Hurricane from China, Macmillan, 1961.

183. Wei, Henry, Mao Tse-tung's "Lean-to-One-Side" Policy, Air Force Personnel and Training Research Center, 1955.

184. White, Theodore H. and Annalee Jacoby, Thunder out of China, N.Y.: William Sloan Assoc., 1946.

185. Whiting, Allen S., China Crosses the Yalu: The Decision to Enter the Korean War, N.Y.: Macmillan, 1960.

186. _____, "Foreign Policy of Communist China," in R. C. Macridis (ed.), Foreign Policy in World Politics, Englewood Cliffs, N.J.: Prentice-Hall, 3rd ed., 1967, pp. 314-37.

187. _____, "The United States and Taiwan," in the American Assembly, The United States and the Far East, N.Y.: Columbia University Graduate School of Business, 1956.

188. Wightman, David, Toward Economic Cooperation in Asia: The UN Ecafe, New Haven, Conn.: Yale University Press, 1963.

189. Wint, Guy, Common Sense about China, London: Victor Gollancz, Ltd., 1960.

190. Wright, Richard, The Color Curtain, Cleveland and N.Y.: World Publishing Co., 1956.

191. Wurfel, David, "Taiwanese Nationalism: Problem for United States Policy," in R. K. Sakai (ed.), Studies on Asia, Lincoln, Neb.: University of Nebraska Press, 1963.

192. Young, Kenneth, Diplomacy and Power in Washington-Peking Dealings, Chicago: University of Chicago Policy Study Center, 1967.

193. _____, Negotiating with the Chinese Communist: The United States' Experience, 1953-67, N.Y.: McGraw-Hill, 1968.

194. Yu, Frederick T. C., "Communications and Politics in Communist China," in Lucian Pye (ed.), Communications and Political Development, Princeton, N.J.: Princeton University Press, 1963.

195. Zagoria, Donald S., The Sino-Soviet Conflict, 1956-61, N.Y.: Atheneum, 1964.

F. Select Periodicals

1. Analysis of Current Chinese Communist Problems, Taipei: Institute of International Relations, Monthly.

2. Asian Recorder, New Delhi, Weekly.

3. Asian Survey, Berkeley, Calif.: University of California., Institute of International Studies, Monthly.

4. Chan Wang (Look Fortnight), Hong Kong: Chan Wang Tsa-chih She.

5. Chin-jih Ta-lu (Mainland Today), Taipei: Chin-jhi Ta-lu Editorial Committee, Semi-monthly.

6. China News Analysis, Hong Kong, Weekly.

7. China Notes, N.Y.: National Council of Churches of Christ, Far Eastern Office, Quarterly.

8. China Quarterly, London: Contemporary China Institute, School of Oriental and African Studies, London University.

9. Chinese Communist Affairs, Taipei: Institute of Political Research, Quarterly.

10. Chinese Culture, Taipei: Institute of Chinese Culture, Quarterly.

11. Current Scene, Hong Kong: Green Pagoda Press, Irregular.

12. Far Eastern Economic Review, Hong Kong, Weekly.

13. Harvard University, Regional Research Seminars, Papers on China, Cambridge, Mass.: Harvard University Press.

14. Independent Formosa, Tokyo: United Young Formosans for Independence, Quarterly.

15. Issues and Studies, Taipei: Institute of International Relations, Monthly.

16. Journal of Asian Studies, Ann Arbor, Mich.: Association of Asian Studies, Quarterly.

17. Pacific Affairs, Vancouver, B.C.: Institute of Pacific Relations, Quarterly.

18. Problems of Communism, Washington, D.C.: United States Information Agency, Bi-monthly.

19. Taiwan Chinglian (Taiwan Youth), Tokyo: United Young Formosans for Independence, Monthly.

20. Tsu Kuo (China Monthly), Hong Kong: Union Research Institute.

21. U.S. Consulate-General, Hong Kong, Current Background, Approx. Weekly.

22. U.S. Consulate-General, Hong Kong, Selections from China Mainland Magazines, Approx. Weekly.

23. U.S. Consulate-General, Hong Kong, Survey of China Mainland Press, Approx. Daily.

24. U.S. Joint Publication Research Service, Communist China Digest, Washington, D.C., Irregular.

G. Select Articles

1. Adie, W. A. C., "Some Chinese Attitudes," International Affairs (London), Vol. 42, No. 2, April 1966, pp. 241-52.

2. Allen, Peter J., "Does Stalin Really Want Red China in the United Nations?" The Reporter, Vol. 3, No. 5, August 29, 1950, pp. 26-27.

3. Appleton, S., "The United Nations 'China Tangle'," Pacific Affairs, Summer 1962, pp. 160-67.

4. Ascoli, Max, Charles Wertenbaker and Philip Horton, "The China Lobby," The Reporter, Vol. 6, No. 8, April 15, 1952, pp. 5-24; Vol. 6, No. 9, April 29, 1952.

5. "Assembly Decision," United Nations Monthly Chronicles, Vol. 3, December 1966, pp. 36-43.

6. "Assembly Decision: Representation of China," United Nations Monthly Chronicles, Vol. 2, December 1965, pp. 52-57.

7. Bailey, Sidney, "China and the United Nations--Time for Reappraisal," The Progressive, Vol. 25, March 1961, pp. 24-25.

8. _____, "Peking and the United Nations Charter Amendment," The World Today, Vol. 20, No. 5, May 1964, pp. 208-15.

9. Bloomfield, L. P., "China, the U.S., and the United Nations," International Organization, Vol. 20, Autumn 1966, pp. 653-76.

10. Boorman, Howard L., "Mao Tse-tung: The Lacquered Image," China Quarterly, No. 16, November-December 1963, pp. 1-55.

11. _____, "Sources of Chinese Communist Conduct," Virginia Quarterly Review, Vol. 42, No. 4, Autumn 1966, pp. 512-26.

12. Bowles, Chester, "The 'China Problem' Reconsidered," Foreign Affairs, Vol. 38, No. 3, April 1960, pp. 476-86.

13. Boyer, W. W. and N. Akra, "U.S. and the Admission of Communist China," Political Science Quarterly, Vol. 76, September 1961, pp. 332-53.

14. Boyle, F. X., "The Truth about Communist China," Fact, Vol. 1, Issue 6, November-December 1964, pp. 33-41.

15. Brecht, Arnold, "Fairness in Foreign Policy: The Chinese Issue," Social Research, Vol. 28, Spring 1961, pp. 95-104.

16. Briggs, H. W., "Chinese Representation in the United Nations," International Organization, Vol. 6, May 1952, pp. 192-209.

17. Brook, D., "The Problem of China's Representation in the United Nations: A Study," Journal of East Asiatic Studies, Vol. 5, No. 1, January 1956, pp. 43-68.

18. Brook-Shepherd, Gordon, "The Chinese Puzzle at the United Nations," The Reporter, Vol. 24, June 22, 1961, pp. 32-34.

19. Chai, Winberg, "China and the United Nations: Problems of Representation and Alternatives," Asian Survey, Vol. X, No. 5, 1970, pp. 397-409.

20. Chen, Chih-shih, "The So-called Chinese Representation Question," Tung-fang Cha-chih (Eastern Miscellany) (Taipei), Vol. 1, No. 4, October, 1967, pp. 21-27.

21. Chen, Shao-hsien, "'The Question of Chinese Representation at the United Nations," Wen-t'i Yu Yen-chiu (Issues and Studies) (Taipei), November 1964.

22. Cheng, Peter P. C., "The Formosa Tangle: A Formosan's View," Asian Survey, Vol. 7, No. 11, November 1967, pp. 791-806.

23. Chiu, Hungdah, "Peiping's Role in Communist Inter-Governmental Organizations," Issues and Studies (Taipei), Vol. 3, No. 9, June 1967, pp. 33-35.

24. _____, and R. R. Edwards, "Communist China's Attitude Toward the United Nations: A Legal Analysis," American Journal of International Law, Vol. 62, No. 1, January 1968, pp. 20-50.

25. Clubb, O. Edmund, "Formosa and the Offshore Islands in American Policy, 1950-55," Political Science Quarterly, Vol. 74, December 1959, pp. 517-31.

26. _____, "Sino-American Relations and the Future of Formosa," Political Science Quarterly, Vol. 80, No. 1, March 1965, pp. 1-21.

27. Cohen, Jerome Alan, "Chinese Attitudes Toward International Law--and Our Own," American Society of International Law, Proceedings, 1967, pp. 108-16.

28. Collins, Frederic W., "Washington Impasse: Red China," United Nations World, Vol. 7, Nos. 9-10, September-October 1953, pp. 16-17, 51.

29. Corea, Sir Claude, "A United Nations Seat for China," Ceylon Today, Vol. 9, No. 11, 1960, pp. 23-25, 28.

30. Cranmer-Byng, J. L., "The Chinese Attitude Towards External Relations," International Journal (Canada), Vol. 11, No. 1, Winter 1965-66, pp. 55-77.

31. Cruickshank, Earl F., "The Question of Representation of China in the United Nations," United Nations Report No. 32, Chamber of Commerce of the U.S., February 16, 1959.

32. Dai, Poeliu, "Canada and the Two-China Formula at the United Nations," Canadian Yearbook of International Law, Vol. 5, 1967, pp. 217-28.

33. Dai, Shen-yu, "What It's Like to Negotiate with the Chinese," New York Times Magazine, October 30, 1966, pp. 44 ff.

34. "Debate on the Chinese Delegation's Status: ECOSOC, February 7, 1950," United Nations Bulletin, Vol. 8, Feb. 15, 1950, pp. 159-60.

35. Edwards, R. Randle, "The Attitude of the People's Republic of China Toward International Law and the United Nations," Papers on China (Harvard University, East Asian Research Center), Vol. 17, 1963, pp. 235-71.

36. _____, "Formosa through China's Eyes," The New Republic, Vol. 139, October 13, 1958.

37. Fairbank, John K., "China's World Order: the Tradition of Chinese Foreign Relations," Encounter, Vol. 27, December 1966, pp. 14-20.

38. Fitzgerald, C. P., "The Chinese View of Foreign Relations," The World Today, Vol. 19, January 1963, pp. 9-17.

39. Fitzmaurice, G. G., "Chinese Representation in the United Nations," Yearbook of World Affairs, 1952, pp. 36-55.

40. Fletcher, Arthur, "Two Chinas in the United Nations?" Far Eastern Economic Review, Vol. 43, January 30, 1964, pp. 199-200.

41. _____, "Communist China is Still Knocking at the United Nations' Door," The Reporter, Vol. 15, No. 7, November 1, 1956.

42. Frye, William R., "18-17-16-and We Lost the Game," The Reporter, Vol. 14, No. 2, January 26, 1956.

43. Gardner, John D., "Where U.S. Opposes Self-Determination," Independent Formosa (Tokyo), Vol. 8, No. 1, Spring 1969, p. 10.

44. "The General Assembly's Decision to Seek Release of Prisoners in China," United Nations Review, February 1955, pp. 8-11.

45. Gitting, John, "The Great Power Triangle and Chinese Foreign Policy," China Quarterly, No. 39, July-September 1969, pp. 41-54.

46. Gross, Ernest A., "Some Illusions of Our Asian Policy," Far Eastern Survey, Vol. 26, December 1957.

47. Gurtov, Melvin, "The Foreign Ministry and Foreign Affairs during the Cultural Revolution," China Quarterly, No. 40, October-December 1969, pp. 65-102.

48. Gull, E. M., "Formosa and the United Nations," Contemporary Review, Vol. 194, November 1958, pp. 267-70.

49. Halpern, A. M., "Communist China and Peaceful Coexistence," China Quarterly, No. 3, July-September 1960, pp. 16-31.

50. _____, "The Foreign Policy Uses of the Chinese Revolutionary Model," China Quarterly, No. 7, July-September 1961, pp. 1-16.

51. Harrigan, A., "Our War with Red China in the United Nations," National Review, Vol. 18, March 8, 1966, pp. 207-08.

52. Healey, Denis, "Time for a Change: A British Labor M.P. Argues that Admission of Communist China to the United Nations is Essential to any Far East Settlement," The New Leader, Vol. 41, September 22, 1958, pp. 7-8.

53. "Helping Hands: Editorials, Reports, Letters Supporting the Admission of Communist China to the United Nations in the New York Times," National Review, Vol. 18, April 5, 1966, pp. 302-4.

54. Hornbeck, Stanley K., "Which Chinese?" Foreign Affairs, Vol. 34, No. 1, October 1955, pp. 24-39.

55. Houn, Franklin W., "The Principles and Operational Code of Communist China's International Conduct," Journal of Asian Studies, Vol. 27, No. 1, November 1967, pp. 21-40.

56. Hudson, G. F., "The Two Chinas," Current History, Vol. 31, July 1956.

57. Illsley, Walter, "Should Peiping be Admitted to the United Nations?" Foreign Policy Bulletin, July 15, 1953, pp. 4-6.

58. "The Independence of China? Question Referred to the Interim Committee by the United Nations General Assembly," United Nations Bulletin, Vol. 8, January 1, 1950, pp. 40-46.

59. Issacs, Harold R., "Old Myths and New Realities," Diplomat Magazine, Vol. 17, No. 196, September 1966, pp. 41-47.

60. Jain, J. P., "The Legal Status of Formosa: A Study of British, Chinese and Indian Views," American Journal of International Law, Vol. 57, No. 1, January 1963, pp. 25-45.

61. Johnson, D. E., "Red China and Russia: Their Position in the United Nations," Vital Speeches, Vol. 31, No. 5, December 15, 1964, pp. 141-43.

62. Khan, Mohammed Samin, "Legal Aspects of the Problem of China's Representation in the United Nations," Pakistan Horizon, Vol. 10, No. 3, Sept., 1957, pp. 138-44.

63. Klein, Donald W., "The 'Next Generation' of Chinese Communist Leaders," China Quarterly, No. 12, October-December 1962, pp. 57-74.

64. _____, "Peking's Evolving Ministry of Foreign Affairs," China Quarterly, No. 4, October-December 1960, pp. 28-39.

65. _____, "Peking's Leaders: A Study in Isolation," China Quarterly, No. 7, July-September 1961, pp. 35-43.

66. Knowland, William F., "United States Should Not Recognize Red China," Journal of International Affairs, Vol. 11, No. 2, 1957, pp. 160-70.

67. Lim, Keh-hiok, "Taiwan's Status in International Law," Taiwan Chinglien (Taiwan Youth) (Tokyo), No. 74, January 25, 1967, pp. 29-31; and No. 76, March 25, 1967, pp, 24-30.

68. McDougal, Myres S., and Richard M. Goodman, "Chinese Participation in the United Nations," American Journal of International Law, Vol. 60, No. 4, October 1966, pp. 671-727.

69. McLane, Charles B., "Chinese Words and Chinese Actions," International Journal (Canada), Vol. 18, No. 3, Summer 1963, pp. 310-26.

70. Mears, Helen, "The Case for Admitting Red China to the United Nations," The Progressive, October 1954, pp. 8-11.

71. "Membership in the United Nations: The Secretary-General's Recommendations," United Nations Monthly Chronicles, Vol. 1, November 1964, pp. 14-16.

72. Mitra, Rasanit, "Sino-Indian Crisis and the United Nations: Whether India Should Not Press for Collective Measures Against the Chinese Aggressor Through the United Nations," Economic Weekly (India), Vol 14, November 17, 1962, pp. 1767-68.

73. Narain, K. V., "Peking's Game at the United Nations," Atlas, Vol. 8, No. 4, November 1964, pp. 239-40.

74. Niebuhr, Reinhold, "China and the United Nations," Journal of International Affairs, Vol. 11, No. 2, 1957, pp. 187-89.

75. Ogley, Roderick C., "Decision-Making in the United Nations-- The Case of the Representation of China," International Relations (London), Vol. 2, No. 9, April 1964, pp. 588-608.

76. Ohira, Zengo, "'Two Chinas' Is No Myth," Journal of Social And Political Ideas in Japan (Tokyo), Vol. 4, No. 1, April 1966, pp. 69-72.

77. Parking, Ben, "China and the United Nations," United Asia (Bombay), Vol. 8, October-November 1956, pp. 333-37.

78. Peng, Ming-min, Hsieh Ts'ung-min, and Wei T'ing-ch'ao, "The Independence Declaration of Formosa," Independent Formosa (Tokyo), Vol. 5, Nos. 1-2, April 1966, pp. 2-9.

79. Pilkington, B., "Chinese Puzzle in the United Nations," Christian Century, Vol. 82, January 13, 1965, pp. 50-51.

80. Popovic, K., "Admission of the People's Republic of China to the United Nations," Yugoslav Review (London), Vol. 6, October-November 1956, pp. 19 ff.

81. Potter, Pitman B., "Communist China: Recognition and Admission to the United Nations," American Journal of International Law, Vol. 50, 1956, pp. 417-18.

82. _____. "Membership and Representation in the United Nations," American Journal of International Law, Vol. 49, No. 2, April 1955, pp. 234-35.

83. Ra'anan, Uri, "Foreign Policy Debate in Peking," Chicago Today, Vol. 4, No. 2, Spring 1967, pp. 27-30.

84. "Representation of China: Assembly Rejects the Proposal," United Nations Review, Vol. 10, December 1963, pp. 11-14.

85. Schick, F. B., "The Question of China in the United Nations," The International And Comparative Law Quarterly, Vol. 12, October 1963, pp. 1232-50.

86. Schoenbrun, David, "The Empty Chair at the United Nations," Diplomat Magazine, Vol. 17, No. 196, September 1966, pp. 119-21.

87. Schwartz, Benjamin I., "The Maoist Image of World Order," Journal of International Affairs, Vol. 21, 1967, pp. 92-102.

88. "The Secretary-General's Mission to Peking," United Nations Review, February 1955, pp. 2-8.

89. Sheerin, John B., "Persuading Red China to Join the United Nations," Catholic World, Vol. 204, February 1967, pp. 261-63.

90. Snow, Edgar, "Interview with Mao," The New Republic, Vol. 152, No. 9, February 27, 1965, pp. 19-23.

91. Sullivan, Walter, "The International Geophysical Year," International Conciliation, No. 521, January 1959.

92. Taylor, G. E., "United Nations Association Panel Report: A Comment," International Organization, Vol. 21, Spring 1967, pp. 238-53.

93. Thant, U, "A Burmese View of World Tensions," Annals of the American Academy of Political and Social Science, No. 318, July 1958, pp. 34-42.

94. Tsou, Tang, and Morton H. Halperin, "Mao Tse-tung's Revolutionary Strategy and Peking's International Behavior," American Political Science Review, Vol. 59, No. 1, March 1965, pp. 80-99.

95. Weiss, Thomas J., "Taiwan and United States Policy," Orbis, Vol. 12, No. 4, Winter 1969, pp. 1165-87.

96. Werner, Levi, "China and the United Nations," Current History, Vol. 47, No. 277, September 1964, pp. 149-55, 180.

97. Whelan, Joseph G., "The United States and Diplomatic Recognition: The Contrasting Cases of Russia and Communist China," China Quarterly, No. 5, January-March 1961, pp. 62-89.

98. Whitaker, Urban, "The United Nations and the Future of Formosa," Ilha Formosa, Vol. 1, No. 1, January 1963, pp. 5-8.

99. Wright, Quincy, "Chinese Recognition Problem," American Journal of International Law, Vol. 49, July 1955, pp. 320-38.

100. Yahuda, Michael B., "Chinese Foreign Policy After 1963: The Maoist Phases," China Quarterly, No. 36, October-December 1968 pp. 93-113.

101. Yu, Chung-lieh, "Chinese Ideology and Chinese Foreign Policy," Chan Wang (Look Fortnightly) (Hong Kong), No. 158, September 1, 1968, pp. 17-19.

102. Zhukov, G., "The Chinese People's Republic and Its Lawful Rights in the United Nations," International Affairs (Moscow), September 1959, pp. 18-22.

Indonesia, 100, 102, 132-135, 137, 139, 152, 156
International Agencies, 55, 57, 78, 84, 91, 139
International Bank for Reconstruction and Development (IBRD), 55, 91
International Civil Aviation Organization (ICAO), 55
International Court of Justice, 122
International Development Association (IDA), 55
International Finance Corporation (IFC), 55
International Geophysical Year (IGY), 117
International Monetary Fund (IMF), 57
International Olympic Games, 117
International Red Cross Conference, 117
International Women's Conference, 26
Inter-Parliamentary Union, 26
Iraq, 200
Ireland, 110
Israel, 97, 218
Italy, 28, 156, 173, 193
Ivory Coast, 137

Japan, 31, 50, 53, 56, 57, 75, 79, 80, 82, 131, 133, 155, 177, 221, 224
  Communist Party, 156
  Komeito, 179
  Peace Treaty, 190
  Sato Government, 173
  Shimonoseki Treaty, 78-79, 190, 192
Jenmin Jihpao, 97, 98, 111, 113, 124, 130, 132, 134, 139, 147-150, 153-155, 157, 160, 263, 199, 218, 220, 222
"Jen-sheng Kuan," 15
Johnson, Lyndon B., 100, 132
Johnson, U. Alexis, 99, 117
Joint Institute for Nuclear Research (JINR), 113
Jordan, 110

Kahin, George McT., 97

K'ang, Sheng, 171
Kaplan, Morton A., 4
Karol, K.S., 121
Kelsen, Hans, 203
Kennedy, Edward M., 175
Kennedy, John F., 123, 124, 129
Kenya, 137, 156
Khrushchev, Nikita S., 33, 61, 110, 113, 114, 121, 129, 131, 144, 145, 149, 152
Kissinger, Henry, 175, 178
Klein, Donald W., 28, 35
Knowland, William F., 100
Korea, 26, 31, 50, 78, 79, 83, 84, 85, 86, 90, 93-94, 98-99, 102, 114, 150, 156, 198, 208-209, 217-218
  North, 52, 85-86, 140, 141, 173, 178
  South, 32, 141, 173
Korean War, 32, 57, 78, 80, 81, 83, 85, 85-87, 89, 90, 91, 93-94, 95, 99, 102, 110, 124, 182, 192, 208, 209
Kosygin, Alexsei, 161, 162
Kuangming Jihpao, 111, 112
Kuangtung, 161
Kung, P'eng, 26
Kung P'u-sheng, 26
Kungtso T'unghsun, 128
Kuo, Mo-jo, 113
Kuomintang (KMT), 14, 31, 34, 74, 80, 82, 83, 106, 107, 129, 144, 192, 198, 221
  (See also China, Rupblic of)
Kuwait, 173, 193

Laos, 26, 121, 128, 209, 217
Lash, Joseph P., 34, 101
Latin America, 31, 42, 61, 63, 110, 128, 131, 141, 147, 162, 223
League of Nations, 4, 73, 74
Lebanon, 110, 123
Li, Hsien-nien, 35, 161, 171
Liao, Ho-shu, 162, 175
Libya, 193
Lie, Trygve, 76, 83, 85, 87, 202

Yao, Teng-shan, 152, 171
Yao, Wen-yuan, 146, 171
Yeh, Chien-ying, 171
Yeh, George K.C., 82
Yemen, 128
Yenan, 30-31, 33, 37, 79, 80, 213, 221

Yikiangshan Island, 104
Young, Kenneth, 122
"Yu-chou Kuan," 15
Yugoslavia, 145, 172-173, 215

Zambia, 156, 173

BYRON S. J. WENG is Assistant Professor of Political Science, Wright State University, Dayton, Ohio. Previous to his position at Wright State Dr. Weng taught at the University of Wisconsin and Miami University of Ohio.

Dr. Weng received his LL.B. from National Taiwan University and his M.S. and Ph.D. in political science from The University of Wisconsin.